Michael Moncur

SAMS
Teach Yourself

DHTML

in 24 Hours

SAMS

201 West 103rd St., Indianapolis, Indiana, 46290 USA

Sams Teach Yourself DHTML in 24 Hours

Copyright © 2002 by Sams Publishing

International Standard Book Number: 0-672-32302-8

Library of Congress Catalog Card Number: 2001096687

Printed in the United States of America

First Printing: December 2001

04   03   02   01   4   3   2   1

Trademarks

Warning and Disclaimer

ACQUISITIONS EDITOR
Scott D. Meyers

DEVELOPMENT EDITOR
Damon Jordan

MANAGING EDITOR
Charlotte Clapp

INDEXERS
Sandy Henselmeier
Ken Johnson

PROOFREADER
Plan-It Publishing

TECHNICAL EDITOR
Jason Byars

TEAM COORDINATOR
Amy Patton

INTERIOR DESIGNER
Gary Adair

COVER DESIGNER
Aren Howell

Contents at a Glance

270531

Table of Contents

PART V Learning Advanced Techniques   229

Hour 17 Dealing with Browser Differences   231

About the Author

Michael Moncur is the owner of Starling Technologies, a network consulting firm, and an independent Web developer. He has written a number of books, including *Sams Teach Yourself JavaScript in 24 Hours* and several other best-selling books on networks and MCSE training.

Dedication

To my family and friends, who tend to be neglected when I'm nearing a deadline, and especially to my wife, Laura.

Acknowledgments

I'd like to thank everyone at Sams for their help with this book, and for the opportunity to write it. In particular, Scott Meyers managed the project and kept things moving along, and Amy Patton was very helpful with some of the details. The editor, Damon Jordan, helped me write with clarity, and the tech reviewer, Jason Byars, saved me from glaring technical errors. Charlotte Clapp handled the final production process.

I'd also like to thank David Rogelberg, Vicki Harding, and the rest of the team at Studio B for their help throughout this project.

Finally, personal thanks go to my wife, Laura; my parents, Gary and Susan Moncur; the rest of the family (not to forget Matt, Melanie, Ian, and Kristen); and my friends, particularly Chuck Perkins, Matt Strebe, Cory Storm, Robert Parsons, Dylan Winslow, Scott Durbin, Ray Jones, James Chellis, Richard Easlick, Curt Siffert, and Henry J. Tillman. I couldn't have done it without your support.

Tell Us What You Think!

As the reader of this book, *you* are our most important critic and commentator. We value your opinion and want to know what we're doing right, what we could do better, what areas you'd like to see us publish in, and any other words of wisdom you're willing to pass our way.

You can e-mail or write me directly to let me know what you did or didn't like about this book—as well as what we can do to make our books stronger.

Please note that I cannot help you with technical problems related to the topic of this book, and that due to the high volume of mail I receive, I might not be able to reply to every message.

When you write, please be sure to include this book's title and author, as well as your name and phone or fax number. I will carefully review your comments and share them with the author and editors who worked on the book.

E-mail: webdev@samspublishing.com
Mail: Mark Taber
         Associate Publisher
         Sams Publishing
         201 West 103rd Street
         Indianapolis, IN 46290 USA

Introduction

The World Wide Web started out as a novelty used by engineers, programmers, and other nerds, and has evolved into the most talked-about communication medium of the new millennium. As the Web evolves, so do the technologies behind it.

DHTML (Dynamic HTML) is a combination of technologies that work together to give Web developers unprecedented control over their pages. Pages can be laid out in precise fashion, and content within the page can be reformatted, added, or changed in real time.

The components of DHTML include the HTML language that formed the foundation of the Web, the JavaScript scripting language, the CSS standard for style sheets, and the newly standardized W3C DOM (document object model).

CSS (Cascading Style Sheets) are an important aspect of DHTML and account for four chapters of this book. CSS gives developers control over fonts, colors, layout, and positioning, using a standard syntax.

While you can do some incredibly sophisticated things with DHTML, you can also do simple things. If you've created Web pages with HTML and tried a bit of scripting in JavaScript, DHTML will be easy to add to your library of skills.

DHTML allows you to do some truly exciting things, and I've had lots of fun while writing this book. I hope you find your DHTML experience equally enjoyable as well as practical.

While you can have all sorts of fun adding DHTML to your Web pages just by copying the scripts in this book, I hope you'll take the time to learn the techniques behind them. The Web has only scratched the surface of DHTML, and before long you'll be developing innovative new features for your site.

How to Use This Book

This book is divided into 24 lessons. Each covers a single DHTML topic, and should take about an hour to complete. The lessons start with the basics of DHTML and CSS, and continue with more advanced topics. You can study an hour a day, or whatever pace suits you.

Q&A, Quiz, and Exercises

At the end of each hour's lesson, you'll find three final sections. Q&A answers a few of the most common questions about the hour's topic. The Quiz includes three questions to test your knowledge, and the Exercises offer ways for you to gain more experience with the techniques the hour covers.

A Note About Browsers

The Web is in flux, and many different browsers are in use—most of them versions of Microsoft Internet Explorer and Netscape. DHTML made its debut in the 4.0 versions of these browsers, but has vastly changed in the latest versions.

The new W3C DOM makes cross-browser DHTML possible, and this book's emphasis is on the cross-browser features of the DOM. This means that most of the examples in this book will require one of the following browsers:

- Internet Explorer 5.0 or later
- Netscape 6.0 or later

Some listings will also work in the 4.0 browsers or can be easily adapted to them, and these are pointed out as they appear.

While there are differences between the latest versions of Internet Explorer and Netscape, and compatibility issues are described in connection with some of the examples, there are no single-browser examples in this book. The emphasis is on standard code for standards-compliant browsers.

This Book's Web Site

Since DHTML and other Web technologies are constantly changing and books are static, you should keep an eye on the latest developments after reading this book. This book's Web site, maintained by author Michael Moncur, includes the latest updates for this book and the latest DHTML news.

The site also includes downloadable versions of the listings and graphics for the examples in this book, answers to the exercises in this book, and a message board where you can discuss DHTML with other users. Here's the URL:

`http://www.starlingtech.com/dhtml/`

If you have questions or comments about this book, have noticed an error, or have trouble getting one of the scripts to work, you can also reach the author by e-mail at `dhtml@starlingtech.com`. (Please check the Web site first to see if your question has been answered.)

PART I
Getting Started

Hour

HOUR 1

Understanding DHTML

While it started with some confusion between Netscape and IE versions, DHTML has been one of the hottest browser technologies introduced in the past few years. It adds life to otherwise boring Web documents and allows Webmasters to go beyond basic tools such as HTML and JavaScript.

To begin your 24-hour tour of DHTML, this hour presents an overview of DHTML—what it is, where it comes from, and how it can make your life easier and your Web pages more exciting.

Hour 1 covers the following topics:

- What DHTML is and what it can do
- The components that make up DHTML
- The history of DHTML
- What the DOM is and how its versions differ
- Which browsers support DHTML

What Is Dynamic HTML?

Dynamic HTML (DHTML) is a combination of technologies that allow Web designers to control the appearance and behavior of Web pages in new ways. While there is no official definition of DHTML, it is generally considered to be a combination of four key technologies:

- HTML (Hypertext Markup Language), the standard language for defining Web pages
- CSS (Cascading Style Sheets), a standard method of specifying the appearance of Web pages
- JavaScript, the most popular client-side scripting language for Web pages
- The DOM (Document Object Model), a set of objects that can be used to control every aspect of Web pages from JavaScript or other languages

Both Microsoft and Netscape introduced DHTML with their 4.0 browsers, but the specifications had little in common besides their name. Fortunately, thanks chiefly to the W3C's standard for the DOM, cross-browser DHTML is becoming easier to manage.

 The name DHTML might give you the idea that DHTML is a version of HTML. It isn't. Rather, it's a way of using various technologies (including HTML) to create more dynamic pages than HTML by itself is capable of.

Static and Dynamic Pages

If you're reading this book, chances are you've used HTML before. HTML (Hypertext Markup Language) is the foundation of the Web. HTML tags are used to define every part of a Web page, from its title to the fine print at the bottom. Basic HTML documents are *static*; the display on your browser generally doesn't change unless you follow a link to a new page.

JavaScript, a scripting language first introduced in Netscape 2.0 in 1995, revolutionized Web pages by making them *dynamic*. JavaScript has brought us forms that update dynamically and warn you when you enter incorrect data, graphics that change when you move the mouse over them, and those annoying scrolling status-line messages.

While JavaScript adds life to static HTML, it doesn't make an entire Web page dynamic: Scripts can change graphics, the status line, or forms in real time, but there is no way to change the heading on the top of a page or an arbitrary bit of text within the page.

DHTML removes these limitations. Using the DOM, your script can modify any portion of the page: any word, any link, or even the entire page. You can use the same JavaScript language to achieve this, using the new objects made available by the DOM.

Dynamic HTML Menus

As an example of the power of DHTML, think about the mouseovers, or graphics that change when you move the mouse pointer over them, that are prevalent on today's Web. These are accomplished by using JavaScript to replace one image with another.

Using DHTML, you can bring this same ability to text menus. The words in your menu can change color, style, or font dynamically. You can even use DHTML to create a menu system similar to the one your computer uses.

As an example, Figure 1.1 shows the main page of Microsoft's Web site. Notice that the options at the top expand into submenus of further options. The MSN menu is currently selected.

FIGURE 1.1

Microsoft's Web site uses DHTML menus.

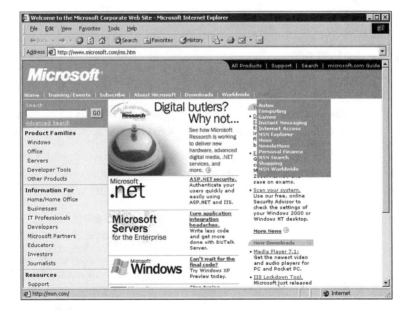

At this writing, Microsoft's site uses DHTML specific to Internet Explorer, and the menus won't work in Netscape. If you follow the guidelines in this book, your own menus will work in any browser that supports the W3C DOM.

Positioning and Animation

While normal HTML does not allow you to specify the exact position of an object in the browser window, you can do this with CSS and DHTML. Furthermore, you can dynamically change the position of the object, allowing for animation.

DHTML animation is useful for games and special effects, but it can also be used in standard pages—menus can slide on to the screen when activated, or text can move across the screen for emphasis.

While DHTML animation ranks right up there with blinking text and scrolling messages on the list of Things You Should Think Twice About Before Doing, when used conservatively and appropriately it can be a striking effect.

> You'll learn more about DHTML animation and create some examples in Hour 16, "Using DHTML for Animation," and Hour 22, "Creating Complex Animations."

Layers

When DHTML first appeared in the 4.0 browsers, it was centered around the concept of *layers*: blocks within a Web page that can be hidden, shown, or moved dynamically. While Netscape and Internet Explorer supported vastly different methods of using layers, they were still a popular element of dynamic sites.

While the new DOM allows you to control just about anything on the page dynamically in a cross-browser fashion, layers are still a useful way of handling blocks within a page, such as sidebars or menus. You'll learn how to work with layers in Hour 6, "Creating Positionable Elements (Layers)."

> Another reason to use layers is that you can create a version of your script that works in Netscape 4.0 or IE 4.0. You will learn how to do this in Hour 17, "Dealing with Browser Differences."

Text Effects

CSS (Cascading Style Sheets) revolutionizes the use of text on the Web. Now there's a standard and precise way to control the font, size, color, and position of text within your Web pages.

While you can control the presentation of text to some extent with regular HTML, it produces complex HTML that doesn't meet standards and can even crash some browsers. Using CSS, you can control your page's appearance in a standard way, and older browsers will still be able to view your document without the benefit of the style sheet.

> You'll learn the details of CSS in Part III, "Working with Style Sheets."

You can also use DHTML to make text dynamic. You can make text fade in or out, move across the screen, or change size, color, or font on command. You'll learn how to create various text effects in Hour 15, "Creating DHTML Text Effects."

The Components of DHTML

As mentioned earlier in this hour, DHTML is actually the combination of several different technologies that add dynamic features to HTML. In the following sections, you'll learn more about how these components interact to form a dynamic page.

HTML

HTML, the language still used for most Web documents, is a standard defined by the W3C (World Wide Web Consortium). DHTML is not a version of HTML—rather, it's a way to add dynamic features to HTML Web pages.

A Dynamic HTML document begins with basic HTML. You will still use the same tags to define headings, paragraphs, and links as always. The newest HTML standard also includes some tags, such as `<div>` to define a section of text, that are very useful with DHTML.

> As you begin to work with DHTML, it is more important than ever to be sure you are using HTML syntax correctly. You'll review what you need to know about HTML in Hour 2, "Reviewing HTML."

CSS (Cascading Style Sheets)

HTML was always meant to define the *content* of documents—titles, paragraphs, headings, links, and so on. Nevertheless, over the years Web designers and browser makers have coerced it into defining *presentation*—fonts, sizes, colors, and layout.

CSS (Cascading Style Sheets) is an effort by the W3C (World Wide Web Consortium) to create a separate standard to define presentation. This can be used alongside HTML and provides even more control, while still allowing for older browsers and for viewers who prefer to keep their own styles.

Since CSS is an important part of DHTML, you'll spend four hours learning more about it in Part III, "Working with Style Sheets."

The Document Object Model (DOM)

The most important part of DHTML is the Document Object Model, or DOM. The DOM is a hierarchy of *objects* that represent the various parts of a Web page. For example, there is an object for the body of the page, defined by the <body> tag, and objects under this object for all of the paragraphs, links, and other elements within the page.

JavaScript

While the DOM defines objects for each part of a Web page, the objects are still static until you use a *scripting language* to change them dynamically. JavaScript is the Web's most popular scripting language, and has existed in some form since the release of Netscape 2.0 in 1995.

Scripting languages use short sets of commands, or *scripts*, to perform various functions. Since JavaScript is a fundamental part of DHTML, you will review the language in Hour 3, "Understanding JavaScript."

While JavaScript is the most popular scripting language and will be used throughout this book, you can also use other scripting languages, such as Microsoft's VBScript, to work with the DOM and Dynamic HTML. Other Web languages, such as Java, can also work with the DOM.

Along with its popularity, JavaScript is also the most universal Web scripting language. VBScript, Microsoft's alternative language, is supported only on Windows platforms.

History of DHTML and the DOM

1

DHTML has had a short but stormy history. It began with the brief selection of features introduced with JavaScript, and was expanded in two different directions by Netscape and Microsoft with the release of the 4.0 browsers. With the newest browsers and the W3C DOM standards, DHTML has been revolutionized once again.

Since the DOM is at the foundation of DHTML, the following sections take a brief look at the different DOM versions.

DOM Level 0

When Netscape first released JavaScript, it included a hierarchy of objects referred to as the DOM, and more objects were added in Netscape 3.0. While these were not standardized, they were largely supported by Microsoft as they developed the subsequent versions of Internet Explorer.

If you have ever used JavaScript to manipulate the status line, a window, forms, or images, you've used this simple DOM. These objects are informally referred to as DOM Level 0, although they are not a W3C standard. Figure 1.2 shows the basic hierarchy of objects in the Level 0 DOM.

You can find more information about the Level 0 DOM in JavaScript books, such as *Sams Teach Yourself JavaScript in 24 Hours* by Michael Moncur. Some Web references for the Level 0 DOM are listed in Appendix A, "Other JavaScript and DHTML Resources." Appendix D, "DOM Quick Reference," summarizes the Level 0 DOM objects.

FIGURE 1.2

DOM Level 0 uses a simple hierarchy of objects.

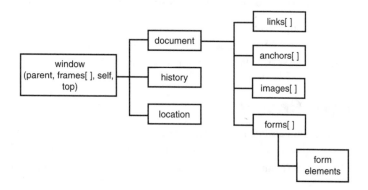

Browser-Specific DOMs

As browsers became more sophisticated, so did their object models. With the release of the 4.0 browsers, both Microsoft and Netscape proudly announced that they had invented Dynamic HTML. Both had also vastly expanded the selection of DOM objects supported.

The new DOM features allowed dynamic features such as layers. Unfortunately, the two browsers used two different object models for the new objects. They had very little in common, and the hardest part of using DHTML was detecting which browser was in use and arranging separate script commands for each one.

DOM Level 1

Fortunately, the W3C stepped in and created a standard hierarchy of DOM objects, known as DOM Level 1. This W3C recommendation includes the basic Level 0 objects that were generally already supported by both popular browsers.

Level 1 also includes objects that allow the manipulation of any part of a Web page. These allow the same features as the browser-specific extensions, but in a standard way.

After much protest from Web designers who had endured their share of headaches dealing with multiple DOMs, both Netscape and Microsoft pledged to support the W3C DOM standard. Netscape 6.0 and Internet Explorer 5.0 were the first versions to support the standard DOM.

DOM Level 2

The W3C continued to work on the DOM specification and has now released DOM Level 2 as a recommendation. Level 2 adds a number of features, including the ability to change styles (those defined by CSS style sheets) dynamically in a standard way.

At this writing, the W3C is currently working on DOM Level 3, which focuses mainly on supporting XML (extensible markup language). For details on the DOM specifications, see the W3C's Web page at `http://www.w3.org/DOM/`.

DHTML Browsers

As mentioned earlier in this hour, Netscape 6.0 and Internet Explorer 5.0 were the first two browsers to support the new style of DHTML using the W3C DOM. Unfortunately, neither of these supports it perfectly and there are still differences between the browsers.

Browser differences will be mentioned throughout this book in the appropriate places. Hour 17 provides details on the differences between browsers, including older browsers.

1

Unless otherwise noted, all of the examples in this book were tested and will run on Netscape 6.0 or later and Internet Explorer 5.0 or later. You should have one of these browsers to follow along with the examples in the remaining hours of the book. Many of the examples can also be adapted to work in the version 4.0 browsers using the techniques described in Hour 17.

Summary

In this hour, you've learned the basis of DHTML. You've learned about HTML, JavaScript, CSS, and the DOM and how they work together to create dynamic pages. You've also learned the history of DHTML and the DOM, and how the current browsers support DHTML.

In the next hour, you'll take a step back and review the HTML language. You'll learn the important parts of HTML syntax that can make or break a DHTML document, and the special objects that are important for DHTML.

Q&A

Q. DHTML sounds difficult. Do I need to take programming classes to understand it?

A. Absolutely not! If you can understand HTML and some basic JavaScript, you can easily add DHTML features to your pages. In fact, CSS and DHTML sometimes offer an easier way to accomplish something than traditional HTML and JavaScript.

Q. Why should I support Netscape? Everyone uses Internet Explorer anyway.

A. This attitude is surprisingly common. Actually, for most sites, between 10 and 25% of users still use Netscape browsers. More importantly, if you follow the W3C standards, you can be sure your dynamic pages will work with future browsers from Microsoft, Netscape, or anyone else.

Q. Can I use Java, ActiveX, or other Web programming languages with the DOM?

A. Yes, the DOM is language-independent. However, you should check whether browsers support these features.

Quiz

Test your knowledge of the material covered in this hour by answering the following questions.

Questions

1. Which of the following is a collection of objects that represent parts of a Web page?

   a. CSS

   b. DOM

   c. DHTML

2. Which of the following is a good description of DHTML?

   a. A new version of HTML with dynamic features

   b. A catchy marketing abbreviation that doesn't really mean anything

   c. A combination of technologies that add dynamic features to HTML documents

3. Who developed the new, standard DOM?

   a. Microsoft

   b. Netscape

   c. The W3C

Answers

1. b. The DOM (Document Object Model) is a collection of objects that represents parts of a Web page.

2. c. DHTML (Dynamic HTML) is a combination of technologies that allows you to add dynamic features to HTML documents. (If you chose answer B, you're partially correct. You must have suffered through the browser wars long enough to become a cynic.)

3. c. The DOM is a standard developed by the W3C (World Wide Web Consortium).

Exercises

If you'd like to get a better idea of what DHTML can do for Web pages, perform these exercises:

- Prepare yourself for the rest of this book by making sure you have Internet Explorer 5.0 or later or Netscape 6.0 or later installed on your computer.

- Open this book's Web site, `http://www.starlingtech.com/dhtml/`. There you'll find links to a variety of DHTML examples you can try in your browser.

1

Hour 2

Reviewing HTML

The Web has revolutionized the world of information, and the HTML language is a key part of Web technology. Although it adds powerful features, DHTML still uses HTML at its core.

Before you delve deeper into DHTML, you should have a grasp on the fundamentals of HTML. This hour reviews the basics of HTML—its syntax, ways of defining document sections, text styles, and forms.

Hour 2 covers the following topics:

- The syntax of basic HTML documents
- How to define document header, body, and other sections
- How HTML achieves basic text styling
- Creating forms in HTML
- Creating a basic HTML Web page

Basic HTML Syntax

If you've ever created a Web page, you've worked with HTML (Hypertext Markup Language). HTML is the fundamental language of the Web, and all of the parts of a page—headings, paragraphs, lists, and links—are represented by HTML.

When you create Dynamic HTML pages, you will use the same HTML tags. However, for dynamic features to function properly, you should be sure you are creating valid HTML. The following sections review the basics of HTML syntax.

> If you're an HTML expert, you can skim this hour. But be sure that you review the information on the <div> and <span> tags, and be sure you understand the example in the Workshop section.

Tags

Tags are the fundamental unit of HTML syntax. An HTML document is essentially a text document, with tags surrounding portions of the text. Tags use the less-than and greater-than symbols (< and >) around each keyword.

Most tags have a beginning tag and an ending tag. The ending tag uses a slash (/) to indicate the end of that block. As an example, here is a simple section of HTML that uses the <p> and </p> tags to define a paragraph:

```
<p>This is a paragraph.</p>
```

Some tags don't require closing tags. For example, the <br> tag defines a line break, as shown in this example:

```
<p>This is a paragraph.<br>
It's split into two lines.</p>
```

> The rest of this hour presents some of the most useful HTML tags. However, this is by no means a complete reference. See Appendix A, "Other JavaScript and DHTML Resources," for a list of Web sites with HTML information.

Attributes

Many HTML tags use one or more *attributes*, or parameters that define options for the tag. For example, the following tag defines an image:

```
<img src="eggplant.gif">
```

This `<img>` tag uses the `src` attribute to assign the filename and location for the image to be displayed (`eggplant.gif`).

> A number of attributes can be present for any type of tag. These include the `style` and `class` attributes for CSS styles, and the ID attribute for styles and DHTML. You'll learn more about these later in this book.

2

The HTML Standard

The HTML standard is maintained by the W3C (World Wide Web Consortium). This organization is responsible for keeping the official documentation of HTML syntax, which you can find on their Web site: `http://www.w3c.org/`.

The current version of HTML is HTML 4.01. With each version, the W3C adds new standard tags. Some older tags might be *deprecated*, meaning they might still be supported but should be avoided. For example, the `<center>` tag, which centers text, is deprecated in HTML 4.0.

> While deprecated tags, like `<center>` and `<font>`, still work in today's browsers, it's likely they'll be unsupported at some point in the future. Tags are usually deprecated because alternative methods, such as CSS styles, exist for the same purpose.

Defining Parts of a Document

The HTML tags you use most often will define the structure of the Web page, dividing it into large sections such as the header and body, and smaller sections such as individual paragraphs. The following sections review some of the most important HTML tags for document structure.

The `<html>`, `<head>`, and `<body>` Tags

There are some tags you'll never create an HTML document without:

- The `<html>` and `</html>` tags are the first and last tags in any document. Anything between the opening and closing `<html>` tags is expected to be in the HTML language.
- The opening and closing `<head>` tags define a header for the document.

- The <title> tag is used in the header of the document to assign it a title. This is typically displayed in the browser's title bar.
- The opening and closing <body> tags define the actual body of the document. All tags that define the page's content will reside between the <body> tags.

Listing 2.1 shows the skeleton of a typical HTML document using all of these tags.

LISTING 2.1   The Structure of a Typical HTML Document

```
<html>
<head>
<title>This is the title</title>
</head>
<body>
The body text goes here.
</body>
</html>
```

In this example, notice two fundamental rules of HTML structure: First of all, each tag has an opening and closing tag. Second, when tags are nested (contained) within other tags, the inner tag ends before the outer one: For example, the </body> tag comes before the </html> tag.

> Today's browsers are pretty forgiving, and will often display a document even if you omit a closing tag or use the wrong order for nested tags. However, DHTML relies on good HTML syntax, so following these rules will prevent some difficult debugging as you add dynamic features.

Paragraphs

As we've already mentioned, you can use the <p> and </p> tags to delimit paragraphs within your document, and the <br> tag for line breaks. Here's another quick example:

```
<p>This is the first paragraph.</p>
<p>This is another paragraph.<br>
It's split into two lines.</p>
```

In earlier versions of HTML, the <p> tag could be used by itself between paragraphs, without the closing </p> tag, and this still works in most browsers. However, to ensure your documents will work with DHTML and CSS style sheets, you should always use both opening and closing tags as in the example above.

Headings

You can use the <h1> through <h6> tags to define headings within your document. <h1> headers are displayed with the largest font, and lower-level headers are displayed in smaller fonts. Ideally, you will use <h1> to label the largest sections of your document, and other headings to label smaller sections within those sections.

> In today's popular browsers, <h1> headings are quite large and imposing, and <h6> headings are actually smaller than body text. In Part III, "Working with Style Sheets," you'll learn how to solve these problems using CSS.

Each heading tag can have an align attribute with the value of left, center, or right to determine its location horizontally on the page. Here is an example of two headings, one centered and one aligned to the left by default:

```
<h1 align="center">Top-level heading</h1>
<h2>Next-level heading</h2>
```

Ordered and Unordered Lists

HTML also allows you to define lists of items with two tags:

- <ul> defines an *unordered list*, usually displayed as a bulleted list
- <ol> defines an *ordered list*, usually displayed as a numbered list

Within the opening and closing tags for a list, the <li> tag defines each item in the list. Here is a quick example of an unordered list:

```
<ul>
<li>First item</li>
<li>Second item</li>
<li>Third item</li>
</ul>
```

> HTML includes other, less commonly used types of lists, including dictionary lists and directory lists. Consult one of the HTML references in Appendix A for more information.

Images

The `<img>` tag allows you to insert an image into your document, typically in the GIF, JPEG, or PNG format. As mentioned earlier in this hour, you use the `src` attribute to specify the image's filename.

You can also use other attributes, including `width` and `height` to specify the image's size and `align` to specify how it should line up with text. Here is an example of an `<img>` tag with these attributes:

```
<img src="persimmon.gif" align="center" width="100" height="200">
```

> The `width` and `height` attributes are normally optional. One reason to include them is that they speed up the display of a page. However, when you are using DHTML to dynamically change a document, you should always include these tags to avoid potential browser errors.

Links and Anchors

You can use the `<a>` tag to define an *anchor* within the page. Anchors are most commonly used to link to another Web page, whether on the same site or anywhere else on the Web. The `href` attribute specifies the URL for the destination of the link, and the text between the opening and closing `<a>` tags is highlighted and clickable in the browser. Here are two examples of links:

```
<a href="page2.html">Next Page</a>
<a href="http://www.Microsoft.com/">Visit Microsoft</a>
```

You can also name an anchor, whether linked or unlinked, with the `<a>` tag's `name` attribute. This allows you to link to a fragment of a large document. The following is an example defining an anchor called `glossary`:

```
<a name="glossary"> </a>
```

To link to an anchor within a page, you use the pound sign (#) followed by the anchor name. The following is a link to the anchor defined in the previous example:

```
<a href="#glossary">Go to the glossary</a>
```

Divisions and Spans

Last but not least, the `<div>` and `<span>` tags allow you to define arbitrary parts of a document:

- Sections defined by `<div>` are displayed with a line break before and after them, but with no other explicit formatting. You can use the `align` attribute to specify the text's horizontal position: `left`, `center`, or `right`.

- Sections defined by `<span>` aren't formatted in any particular way at all.

While these might seem like the most useless tags in the language, they're actually very important for CSS and DHTML, and you'll use them constantly throughout this book.

You can use the `ID`, `style`, and `class` attributes with either of these tags to uniquely identify a section of text. You can then manipulate that text's style with CSS, or even pick up the text and move it across the screen using DHTML. Here's a quick example with an `ID` attribute:

```
<div ID="article">This is the text within the tags.</div>
```

You can also use these attributes on other HTML tags, such as headings or paragraphs. `<div>` and `<span>` are just good ways to assign styles or dynamic properties without causing the browser to format the text in any particular way.

> The `<div>` tag has another purpose: `<div align="center">` is currently the best way to display centered text, rather than using the deprecated `<center>` tag.

Styling Text

HTML also includes a number of tags that can be used to change the appearance or layout of text. The following sections review some of the most common tags for styling text.

Bold and Italics

The `<b>` and `<i>` tags define bold and italic sections of text. The following example shows both in action:

```
<p>This is normal text. <b>This sentence is bold.</b>
<i>This one is italic. <b>This is both bold and italic.</b></i></p>
```

You can also use the `<u>` tag to define underlined text. However, this is not commonly used because most browsers use underlining to indicate links, and has been deprecated in the HTML 4.0 standard. In most cases, underlining can be denoted by the use of italics. You can also underline text in a standard way using CSS styles.

Fonts

You can use the `<font>` tag to define a particular font for a section of a document. For example, the following displays some text in a sans-serif font, two sizes larger than normal and red in color:

```
<font face="sans-serif" size="+2" color="red">Hello!</font>
```

You won't be seeing the `<font>` tag again in this book. Why? Because it's deprecated in HTML 4.0, and style sheets are a much better way to assign fonts, sizes, and colors to text.

> CSS style sheets can do everything the `<font>` tag can do and much more. You'll learn more about them in Part III.

Indenting

You can use the `<blockquote>` tag to enclose text that is quoted from another source. This is typically displayed with an indentation. If you need a more versatile method of indenting text, this is available using style sheets.

Using Tables for Layout

Tables allow you to lay the content of a document out in columns and rows. The `<table>` tag is used to define the start and end of the table, `<tr>` tags enclose table rows, and `<td>` tags enclose each cell of the table. `<th>` tags define cells that are headings for the table.

The following is an example of a simple table:

```
<table>
 <tr>
   <th>Fruits</th><th>Vegetables</th>
 </tr>
 <tr>
   <td>Apples</td><td>Peas</td>
 </tr>
 <tr>
   <td>Oranges</td><td>Carrots</td>
 </tr>
</table>
```

Creating Forms

Forms are an important part of interactive Web pages. They can be used with server-side languages such as CGI to gather information, and can also be used with JavaScript and DHTML to add interactivity to pages.

> Using DHTML, you can change forms dynamically based on information the user enters. This is explained in Hour 18, "Using DHTML with Forms."

The `<form>` Tag

Forms begin and end with the `<form>` and `</form>` tags. Here is a simple example using these tags:

```
<form name="form1">
form elements go here
</form>
```

The following sections will review some of the elements you can use within a form. Figure 2.1 shows an example of these form elements in use.

FIGURE 2.1
Forms can include a variety of elements.

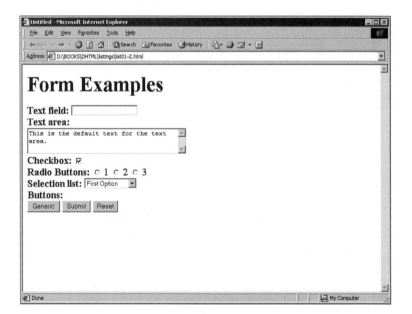

Text Input

You can use the `<input type="text">` tag to define a text input within a form. For example, this tag defines a text input 10 characters wide with the default value of "your name here":

```
<input type="text" name="thename" value="your name here" size="10">
```

The `value` attribute specifies the default value. The `name` attribute gives the field a name—this will be useful if you are using JavaScript or DHTML to work with this form element.

You can also define a larger area for text input with the `<textarea>` tag. This allows you to define an area with a number of rows and columns for text. The text between the opening and closing `<textarea>` tags is the default contents. Here's an example:

```
<textarea name="text1" rows="5" cols="70">
This is the default text for the text area.
</textarea>
```

Checkboxes and Radio Buttons

Checkboxes are handy for a simple on/off value or yes/no choice. You can define them using the `<input type="checkbox">` tag. Here is an example:

```
<input type="checkbox" name="check1" value="yes" checked>
```

You can include the `checked` attribute, as in this example, to indicate that the checkbox will be checked by default. If the `checked` attribute is omitted, the checkbox will be unchecked by default.

Radio buttons are similar to checkboxes, but you can only choose one option within each group of buttons. You define radio buttons with the `<input type="radio">` tag. Here is an example with three choices:

```
<input type="radio" name="group" value="opt1" checked> 1
<input type="radio" name="group" value="opt2"> 2
<input type="radio" name="group" value="opt3"> 3
```

To include the radio buttons in a group, you give them the same value for the `name` attribute. You can have several groups of radio buttons within a form with different group names. You can specify the `checked` attribute for one of the buttons in a group to make it the default selection.

Drop-Down Selections

Another way to give the user a choice of options is a drop-down list, or *selection list*. To define a list, you use the `<select>` and `</select>` tags, with two or more `<option>` tags in between. Here is an example with two options:

```
<select name="choice">
<option value="1" selected>First Option</option>
<option value="2">Second option</option>
</select>
```

The text between the `<option>` and `</option>` tags is displayed in the drop-down list when that option is selected. You can use the `selected` attribute to indicate a default choice.

Buttons

Last but not least, you can use one or more buttons within a form. Buttons are commonly used to submit a form's contents, but you can also use buttons to interact with JavaScript and DHTML.

You define buttons with the `<input>` tag. There are three types of buttons:

- `<input type="submit">` creates a submit button. This submits the data in the current form to the server.
- `<input type="reset">` creates a reset button. This simply clears all of the fields within the current form.
- `<input type="button">` creates a generic button. It doesn't do anything unless you use JavaScript to perform an action.

As an example, here is the HTML that was used to create the three buttons in Figure 2.1:

```
<input type="button" name="generic" value="Generic">
<input type="submit" name="submit" value="Submit">
<input type="reset" name="reset" value="Reset">
```

Workshop: Creating a Web Page with HTML

To complete this hour's tour of HTML, you will now create a simple HTML document. This document will be the home page of Figby Industries, an imaginary company with imaginary products. Your HTML document will include the following:

- `<html>`, `<head>`, and `<body>` tags to define the basic structure
- A heading using `<h1>` tags

- An image displaying the company logo

- A paragraph of introductory text

- Several links to other pages within the site

- A table to lay out the links in a row

Listing 2.2 shows the complete HTML document.

LISTING 2.2   The Example HTML Document

```html
<html>
<head>
   <title>Figby Industries, Inc.</title>
</head>
<body>
<img align="center" src="logo.gif"
width="486" height="180" border="0" alt=""><br>
<h1>Welcome to Figby Industries!</h1>
<p>Welcome! This is the home page of Figby Industries,
your source for all sorts of imaginary products. Follow the links
below to learn more about our company and our products.
</p>
<table border="1" align="center">
  <tr>
    <td width="20%"><a href="products.html"><b>Products</b></a></td>
    <td width="20%"><a href="sales.html"><b>Sales</b></a></td>
    <td width="20%"><a href="service.html"><b>Service</b></a></td>
    <td width="20%"><a href="staff.html"><b>Staff</b></a></td>
    <td width="20%"><a href="jobs.html"><b>Employment</b></a></td>
  </tr>
</table>
<p>Any truly legitimate company would have much more text in this
part of the page than we have.</p>
</body>
</html>
```

This example will work in Netscape 2.0 or later or Internet Explorer 3.0 or later. However, you should have a copy of Netscape 6 or Internet Explorer 5 or later for future examples.

To try this example, type the HTML into a text editor. You can use a word processor, but be sure to save the file as an ASCII text file. Save the file, giving it a name with the .htm or .html extension.

To display this document properly, you'll need the image, `logo.gif`, referenced in the `<img>` tag. You can download this image from this book's Web site: `http://www.starlingtech.com/dhtml/`. You can also download the HTML document to avoid typing it yourself.

After you've saved the file, you can load it into a browser. Figure 2.2 shows how Netscape 6 displays this example.

FIGURE 2.2

Netscape displays the completed HTML document.

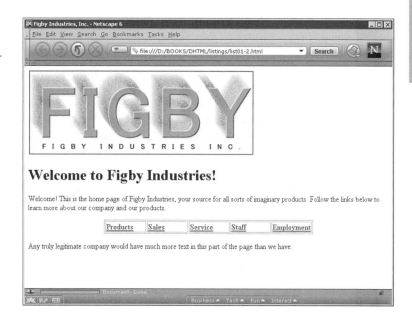

2

The example HTML document you have created isn't much yet, but we will enhance it in the upcoming hours with JavaScript and DHTML.

Summary

In this hour, you've reviewed the basics of HTML. You've learned about some of the most useful HTML tags and attributes, including those for forms and some tags that will be useful for DHTML. Finally, you created a simple HTML document.

In the next hour, you'll review the JavaScript language, another essential part of DHTML. You'll also use JavaScript to add features to the HTML document you created in this hour.

Q&A

Q. What happens if I make a mistake in my HTML coding? Will the browser display an error message?

A. It depends. Some errors will cause an error message to be displayed. However, more likely, the browser will do its best to display the page despite the errors, with somewhat unpredictable results.

Q. Can I test whether my HTML is valid?

A. Yes. Several HTML validation programs are available. See Appendix A for links to some of them.

Q. I've heard about XHTML. How does this relate to HTML?

A. XHTML is a version of HTML based on the XML (extensible markup language) standards. It is similar to HTML 4.01, but with stricter syntax. The HTML examples in this book follow the HTML 4.01 standard.

Quiz

Test your knowledge of the material covered in this hour by answering the following questions.

Questions

1. `<input type="text">` is an example of which of the following?

    a. An HTML attribute

    b. An HTML tag

    c. A DHTML tag

2. Which of the following will display a title in large text within the body of a Web page?

    a. `<p size="large">This is the Title.</p>`

    b. `<title>This is the Title.</title>`

    c. `<h1>This is the Title.</h1>`

3. Which of the following tags will not affect the display of the document at all unless you use style sheets or DHTML?

    a. `<center>`

    b. `<div>`

    c. `<span>`

Answers

1. b. `<input type="text">` is an example of an HTML tag.

2. c. You can use the `<h1>` tag to display a title in the body of the page in large text. The `<title>` tag (choice b) sets a title for the document, but it is only displayed in the browser's title bar.

3. c. The `<span>` tag does not affect the document's display at all by default. `<div>` (choice b) is close, but it does display with line breaks and can be used to align text.

Exercises

If you'd like to get a little bit more practice with HTML before you move on to bigger and more dynamic things, try the following exercises:

- Add a second row of links to the HTML example in the Workshop section.

- Visit a few of your favorite Web sites, use your browser's View Source option, and notice just how complicated HTML can get.

HOUR 3

Understanding JavaScript

DHTML isn't a new Web language—it's just a set of objects that allows you to use a scripting language (such as JavaScript) to manipulate the page you set up in standard HTML.

In this hour, you'll review the essentials of the JavaScript language. If you're already a JavaScript expert, feel free to skim this chapter, but you should have a solid grasp of JavaScript to understand the DHTML examples in the rest of this book.

The following topics will be covered in this hour:

- The basics of JavaScript syntax
- How to avoid problems with older browsers
- How variables, strings, and arrays work in JavaScript
- Using JavaScript objects to store data and functions
- Using Conditional statements in JavaScript
- Using loops to repeat JavaScript statements
- Creating and using functions in JavaScript

JavaScript Basics

JavaScript was the first of the client-side Web scripting languages. It first appeared in 1995 in Netscape 2.0. You can use JavaScript directly within a Web page without using any special tools to create or compile scripts, and it works on most of today's browsers.

Despite the name, JavaScript has little to do with the Java language. Some of the commands are similar, but it's a different language with a different purpose.

 This hour will only give you a quick review of the essentials of JavaScript. See Appendix A, "Other JavaScript and DHTML Resources," for a list of Web sites and books with further information.

Beginning and Ending Scripts

You can place JavaScript commands anywhere in an HTML document. To begin and end the script, you use the <script> tag. This tells the browser to interpret the commands between the tags as JavaScript rather than HTML.

The <script> tag specifies the language to be used. Here is a simple example of a JavaScript command with beginning and ending <script> tags:

```
<script language="JavaScript">
document.write("Hello World");
</script>
```

Supporting Older Browsers

There are actually several versions of JavaScript, and you can specify a version number in your <script> tag to avoid confusing older browsers. The following tag specifies JavaScript 1.1:

```
<script language="JavaScript1.1">
```

The current version of JavaScript is 1.5. However, you should not specify a version number at all unless you are using features unique to that version. Throughout this book, we will use <script> tags that do not specify a version unless they require a feature of a later version.

Hiding JavaScript Code

Some older browsers, such as Netscape 1.0 and Internet Explorer 1.0, don't support JavaScript at all. There are two important ways to accommodate these browsers when you use JavaScript.

The `<noscript>` Tag

The `<noscript>` tag is used to display a message to non-JavaScript browsers. This includes older browsers as well as current browsers with JavaScript turned off. To use it, simply place text between the opening and closing `<noscript>` tags:

```
<noscript>Your browser doesn't support JavaScript.</noscript>
```

Browsers that do support JavaScript ignore the text between the `<noscript>` tags. Older browsers ignore the `<noscript>` tags and display the text.

> Unfortunately, the `<noscript>` tag isn't perfect. Netscape 2.0 doesn't recognize this tag, even though it supports basic JavaScript.

Using HTML Comments

One problem with older browsers is that they might ignore the `<script>` tags and display your JavaScript code in the body of the page. To avoid this, you can enclose your JavaScript code within HTML comments:

```
<script language="JavaScript">
  <!--
  document.write("Your browser supports JavaScript.");
  // -->
</script>
```

The `<!--` and `-->` tags begin and end the HTML comment. This will prevent older browsers from displaying the script, while allowing the script to work on browsers that support it. The `//` in the last line is a JavaScript comment—this prevents the HTML comment tag from being detected as a JavaScript error.

> This technique for hiding scripts is not perfect. Certain characters, such as the > (greater-than) symbol, might end the comment prematurely if they appear in your script.

JavaScript Statements

Within the `<script>` tags, you can use one or more JavaScript *statements*, or commands, to create a script. Each statement should end with a semicolon (;). Here's a simple example that displays an alert message:

```
<script language="JavaScript">
alert("Hello!");
</script>
```

Most browsers treat the semicolons as optional, but if you include them it will make debugging easier.

Creating Event Handlers

Often, you won't even need to use the <script> tag to include JavaScript in a document. Instead, you can use *event handlers*. These are special HTML 4.0 attributes for HTML tags, and can be used to respond to *events*: things that happen in the browser.

For example, the onMouseOver event for an HTML tag occurs when the user moves the mouse pointer over that portion of the page. The following HTML defines a link with an onMouseOver event handler:

```
<a href="next.html" onMouseOver="alert('hello!');">
```

Within the quotation marks for the event handler, you can use one or more JavaScript statements, separated by semicolons. You will use an event handler like this in the Workshop section of this chapter.

There are actually many events available. Since these are a key part of DHTML, Hour 8, "Responding to Events," discusses all of the events in detail.

Understanding Variables

JavaScript *variables* are virtual containers you can use to store data: a number, a string of text, or something else. For example, the following statement assigns the variable score a value of 10:

```
score = 10;
```

JavaScript variable names (and most commands) are case-sensitive. Once you name a variable, be sure you use the same name consistently.

Declaring Variables

JavaScript includes a command, var, that you can use to declare variables. This is a way of announcing that a variable will be used and, optionally, assigning it a value. Here's an example:

```
var b=5;
```

This statement creates a variable, b, and assigns it an initial value of 5. Most of the time, you can omit the var keyword and simply use a variable. Whether you need to use this keyword depends on the variable's *scope*:

- *Local variables* are defined within a function, and can be used only within that function.
- *Global variables* are defined outside any function, and can be used anywhere.

The var keyword is only truly required when you declare a local variable within a function that has the same name as a global variable. Using var will insure that a local variable is created rather than assigning a new value to the global one.

> Functions are groups of commands that you can treat as a unit. They are explained in detail later in this hour.

If you're unsure whether or not to use var , you can simply always use it the first time you assign a value to a variable. This makes it easy to avoid errors and will never cause a problem.

Using Arrays

When you need to store a number of similar values, you can use an *array*. Arrays are groups of numbered variables. Each variable within the array has a unique *index*, and is called an *element* of the array.

Unlike variables, arrays must be declared. You declare an array using the new keyword. For example, the following statement declares an array called subtotals with 10 elements:

```
subtotals = new Array(10);
```

After the array is set up, you can refer to any element just like a variable. For example, this statement assigns the value 5 to the first element of the array:

```
subtotals[0] = 5;
```

Array indices begin with zero. Thus, the ten elements in the `subtotals` array in the example would have the indices 0 through 9.

Using Strings

So far, you've seen variables used to store numbers. Variables can also store strings of text. For example, the following statement stores the phrase "No time to lose" in a string variable called `phrase`:

```
phrase="No time to lose";
```

Many built-in JavaScript functions use strings. For example, the `document.write` function displays text as part of the current Web page:

```
document.write("This text came from JavaScript.");
```

Using Conditions and Loops

You can accomplish quite a bit using simple JavaScript commands, but for more complex applications you need ways of controlling how your script executes. The following sections will introduce you to conditions and loops, two important ways of controlling your scripts.

Using the `if` Keyword

The `if` statement allows you to test conditions. For example, your script can display an alert if a variable has a certain value:

```
if (score == 0) alert("You lose!");
```

An `if` statement has two parts: a condition (`score==0` in the example) and an action (the `alert` statement in the example.) If the action is a single statement like this, nothing else is required. If you need more than one statement in the action, you enclose them in braces (`{}`):

```
if (score==10) {
    alert("You win!");
    score=0;
} else {
    alert("You lose!");
}
```

This example checks the `score` variable. If it is equal to 10, it displays an alert and resets `score` to zero. It also includes the `else` clause. This clause allows you to specify what should happen if the condition of the `if` statement was *not* true.

Conditional Operators

In the previous example, you might have noticed the double-equals sign (==). This is the *equality operator*, and detects whether two values are equal. JavaScript includes a number of other conditional operators:

- == (is equal to)
- != (is not equal to)
- < (is less than)
- <= (is less than or equal to)
- > (is greater than)
- >= (is greater than or equal to)

A common JavaScript error is to confuse the equality operator (==) with the assignment operator (=). Always use = to assign a value to a variable, and == to test conditions.

Using for Loops

One of the nice things about programming languages is that you can let the computer handle repetitive tasks. You can use the for keyword in JavaScript to execute a block of statements a number of times. Here is a simple example:

```
for (i=1; i<10; i++) {
  //statements to repeat go here
}
```

The for statement includes three elements within the parentheses, separated by semi-colons. These include the following:

- An initial value for a variable (i=1 in the example)
- A condition that must remain true for the loop to continue (i<10 in the example)
- An *increment expression* to change the value of the variable (i++ in the example)

The i++ in the example adds one to the value of i. ++ is called the *increment operator*. You can also use the *decrement operator*, - -, to subtract one from a variable's value.

The `for` statement is followed by a block of statements enclosed in braces. The statements are executed repeatedly as the variable changes, until the condition is no longer met. As an example, the following `for` loop displays the numbers 1 through 10:

```
for (i=1; i<=10; i++) {
    document.write(i + " ");
}
```

Using `while` Loops

Sometimes, rather than executing statements a certain number of times, you'll want them to continue to execute until something happens. You can use the `while` keyword to create this type of loop. Here's an example:

```
while (score < 10) {
   //statements to repeat go here
}
```

This statement would execute the block of code in braces over and over until the variable `score`'s value reached 10 or more. The loop itself doesn't change the variable's value.

> In the example above, if none of the statements within the `while` loop change the value of the `score` variable, the loop will never exit. This is called an *infinite loop*, and should be avoided. This type of loop can even crash some browsers.

Using Functions

Functions are groups of JavaScript statements that have been combined under a single name. You've already used built-in functions, such as `document.write`. You can also define your own functions. This allows you to create modular programs, and to repeat the same statements with different values.

Defining a Function

To define a function, you use the `function` keyword. The following statements define a short function:

```
function Linebreak() {
    document.write("<br>");
}
```

This function outputs a single HTML line break (using the <br> tag). While this uses a single statement, the true power of functions is to execute several statements at once.

Calling Functions

Once you've defined a function, you can *call* the function from any script on the same page. To call a function, simply use its name followed by parentheses. This statement calls the `Linebreak` function you created earlier:

```
Linebreak();
```

Using Arguments

Functions can have one or more *arguments*, or variables passed to the function. To define a function with arguments, you include one or more variable names within the parentheses. If you are using more than one argument, separate them with commas.

For example, the following is the definition for a function to display an HTML paragraph:

```
function Para(text) {
    document.write("<p>" + text + "</p>");
}
```

This function displays the string you send it in the `text` variable, with paragraph tags on either side. To call this function, simply specify the value of `text` in the parentheses:

```
Para("Welcome to my paragraph.");
```

> Variables you use for function arguments are always local variables, and can't be used outside the function.

Returning Values

Functions can also return a value to the script that called the function. This allows you to create functions that answer questions. For example, here is the definition for a function that returns the average of three numbers:

```
function Average(a,b,c) {
  total = a + b + c;
  return total / 3;
}
```

This function accepts three arguments, a, b, and c. It uses the variable `total` to add the numbers, then divides the total by three to get the average. The `return` keyword returns a value. Here is an example of a script to call the `Average` function and display the result:

```
z = Average(2,4,6);
document.write("The average is " + z);
```

To use a function, it must be defined in the same HTML document with which you are working. The best place to define functions is in the <head> section of the document, since the definitions themselves don't create any output.

Understanding Objects

JavaScript also includes *objects*, a special type of variable that can store multiple data items and even functions to work with those items. In fact, strings and arrays in JavaScript are just special types of objects.

Object Properties and Methods

JavaScript supports a number of built-in objects, including those in the DOM. Objects can have *properties*, or variables associated with the object. Object and property names are separated by periods.

For example, the `location.href` property contains the current document's URL. You can change this property to force the browser to go to another Web page:

```
location.href="http://www.mcp.com/";
```

Objects can also have *methods*, or functions associated with the object. You've already used one of these: The `document.write` function is actually the `write` method of the `document` object.

Appendix D includes a summary of the objects, such as document, in the Level 0 DOM. You'll begin to learn about the objects in the W3C DOM, their properties and methods in Hour 5, "Understanding the DOM."

Workshop: Adding a Script to a Web Page

You should now have a basic understanding of JavaScript. To bring together what you've learned, you will now create a simple script and get it working on a Web page.

In the previous hour's Workshop section, you created a simple HTML document for the Figby Industries Web page. You can now use JavaScript to add a feature: descriptions that appear in the status line when the user moves the mouse pointer over the links in the page.

This hour has presented a quick introduction to JavaScript, but there's much more to learn. See Appendix A for a list of Web sites and books with further information.

Adding Event Handlers

To add descriptions to the links, you can use two event handlers:

- onMouseOver—occurs when the mouse pointer moves over an object
- onMouseOut—occurs when the mouse pointer leaves an object

The listing below shows one of the links from the Figby Industries page with both of these event handlers added.

```
<a href="products.html"
  onMouseOver="window.status='Learn about our products';return true;"
  onMouseOut="window.status='';return true;">
  <b>Products</b></a>
```

The onMouseOver event handler assigns a value to the window.status property, which displays the message in the status line. The return true statement tells the browser to keep this message in the status line rather than rewriting it with the link's URL.

The window.status property is part of the Level 0 DOM. See Appendix D for a summary of Level 0 DOM objects, properties and methods.

The onMouseOut event handler assigns a null string to window.status to clear the status line.

Putting It All Together

By adding event handlers to the links in the original Figby Industries page, you can make the status line display helpful descriptions. Listing 3.1 shows the complete example with all of the event handlers.

LISTING 3.1 The Complete JavaScript Example

```
<html>
<head>
  <title>Figby Industries, Inc.</title>
</head>
```

LISTING 3.1   continued

```
<body>
<img align="center" src="logo.gif"
width="486" height="180" border="0" alt=""><br>
<h1>Welcome to Figby Industries!</h1>
<p>Welcome! This is the home page of Figby Industries,
your source for all sorts of imaginary products. Follow the links
below to learn more about our company and our products.
</p>
<table border="1" align="center">
<tr>
  <td width="20%"><a href="products.html"
  onMouseOver="window.status='Learn about our products';return true;"
  onMouseOut="window.status='';return true;">
  <b>Products</b></a></td>
  <td width="20%"><a href="sales.html"
  onMouseOver="window.status='Contact our sales department';return true;"
  onMouseOut="window.status='';return true;">
  <b>Sales</b></a></td>
  <td width="20%"><a href="service.html"
  onMouseOver="window.status='Service and Support';return true;"
  onMouseOut="window.status='';return true;">
  <b>Service</b></a></td>
  <td width="20%"><a href="staff.html"
  onMouseOver="window.status='Meet our staff';return true;"
  onMouseOut="window.status='';return true;">
  <b>Staff</b></a></td>
  <td width="20%"><a href="jobs.html"
  onMouseOver="window.status='Employment opportunities';return true;"
  onMouseOut="window.status='';return true;">
  <b>Employment</b></a></td>
</tr>
</table>
<p>Any truly legitimate company would have much more text in this
part of the page than we have.</p>
</body>
</html>
```

In this document, the links within the table include onMouseOver and onMouseOut event handlers. Since all of the functions are performed within event handlers, there's no need for the <script> tag at all.

 This example requires an image, logo.gif. As with the other examples in this book, you can download this image and the HTML document itself from this book's Web site, http://www.starlingtech.com/dhtml/.

To try this example, save it as an HTML document and load it into a browser. Figure 3.1 shows Internet Explorer's display of this example. In the figure, the mouse pointer is over the "Service" link.

FIGURE 3.1

*Internet Explorer
shows the complete
JavaScript example.*

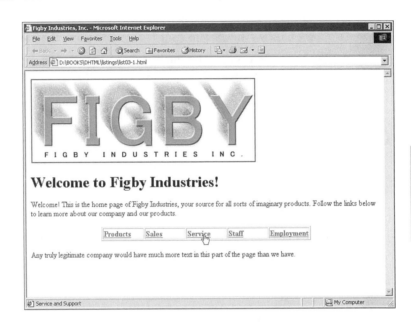

3

Summary

In this hour, you've reviewed the basics of JavaScript: its syntax, and how to use variables, loops, functions, and conditional statements. You've also completed a simple JavaScript example.

In the next hour, you'll get down to business by creating a DHTML example.

Q&A

Q. Can JavaScript display text on a Web page after it's already loaded?

A. No, but Dynamic HTML can do this and much more. You'll use DHTML to change text within a page in the next hour.

Q. I already know Microsoft's VBScript language. Can I use it with DHTML?

A. Yes, VBScript includes access to the DOM. However, your applications will only work in Internet Explorer.

Q. What's the difference between JavaScript and JScript?

A. JScript is Microsoft's implementation of JavaScript. For most purposes, it is compatible with JavaScript. All of the JavaScript examples in this book will work in Internet Explorer or Netscape.

Q. Can I hide my JavaScript code from users using the View Source option?

A. No. While there are a few complicated methods that obscure your code, a determined user can always view the source of your HTML document and its associated JavaScript code.

Quiz

Test your knowledge of the material covered in this hour by answering the following questions.

Questions

1. Which JavaScript keyword would be the best choice if you need to create a loop that executes exactly five times?

   a. `while`

   b. `for`

   c. `wherefore`

2. Which of the following `if` statements correctly checks the variable a for the value of 20?

   a. `if a==20`

   b. `if (a=20)`

   c. `if (a==20)`

3. Which type of JavaScript variable is ideal for storing a series of numbers?

   a. array

   b. string

   c. numeric variable

Answers

1. b. A `for` loop would be the best way to execute a loop exactly five times.

2. c. The correct statement is `if (a==20)`. Notice that the equality operator (`==`) must be used, and the parentheses around the condition are required.

3. a. A JavaScript array is ideal for storing a series of numbers.

Exercises

If you'd like to practice using JavaScript before you continue, try the following exercises:

- Modify Listing 3.1 to use a function to handle the status line instead of assigning `window.status` directly. You can use the text for the status line as an argument to the function.

- Try including the `average` function described earlier in this hour to the `<head>` section of an HTML document. Add a `<script>` section within the body of the document to display the average of the numbers 7, 12, and 20.

3

HOUR 4

Creating a Simple DHTML Example

In the last three hours, you've learned the basics of what DHTML can do, and you've reviewed the HTML and JavaScript you need to know. Now you're ready to delve into the details of DHTML in Part II. Before you do, this hour will give you an idea of what's in store by guiding you through a simple example.

The following topics will be covered in this hour:

- Starting with a simple HTML document
- Identifying DOM objects
- Detecting DHTML-compatible browsers
- Using event handlers with DHTML
- Creating a working DHTML example

Starting with an HTML Document

Back in Hour 2, "Reviewing HTML," you used HTML to create the Figby Industries
Web page. In Hour 3, "Understanding JavaScript," you added JavaScript statements to
display link descriptions in the status line. While this is a useful feature, the status line is
not the most obvious place for descriptions, and browsers normally use it to display
URLs.

In this hour, you will start with the same HTML document. This time you will use
DHTML to add link descriptions in a much more visible place within the body of the
page. This allows the descriptions to fit into the design of the site, and allows the status
line to display URLs and browser status as it was intended.

Listing 4.1 shows the original HTML document, and Figure 4.1 shows how it appears in
a browser.

LISTING 4.1   The HTML Document Before Adding Dynamic Features

```
<html>
<head>
   <title>Figby Industries, Inc.</title>
</head>
<body>
<img align="center" src="logo.gif"
width="486" height="180" border="0" alt=""><br>
<h1>Welcome to Figby Industries!</h1>
<p>Welcome! This is the home page of Figby Industries,
your source for all sorts of imaginary products. Follow the links
below to learn more about our company and our products.
</p>
<table border="1" align="center">
  <tr>
    <td width="20%"><a href="products.html"><b>Products</b></a></td>
    <td width="20%"><a href="sales.html"><b>Sales</b></a></td>
    <td width="20%"><a href="service.html"><b>Service</b></a></td>
    <td width="20%"><a href="staff.html"><b>Staff</b></a></td>
    <td width="20%"><a href="jobs.html"><b>Employment</b></a></td>
  </tr>
</table>
<p>Any truly legitimate company would have much more text in this
part of the page than we have.</p>
</body>
</html>
```

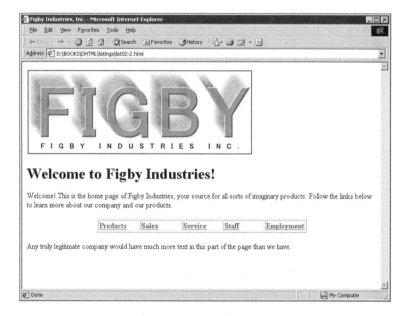

Finding Objects

Using DHTML, you can display your link descriptions anywhere you choose on the
page. One convenient place is directly below the row of links. You can use the following
line of HTML to add a row to the table that holds the links:

```
<tr><td ID="desc" align='center' colspan="5">...</td></tr>
```

The <tr> tag defines a new table row. This row contains a single table cell. The cell's
<td> tag uses the colspan attribute to extend the cell across the entire row, and the
align attribute to center the cell's contents.

When it is initially displayed, the added table cell will display three periods. Your
DHTML script will later change this to the appropriate link description.

Notice the ID="desc" attribute in the <td> tag. This assigns an identifier (desc) to the
table cell. While this doesn't affect the way the page is displayed, it will make it easy to
add dynamic features.

Using a DHTML Function

You are now ready to start using DHTML. You can change the contents of the new table
cell you created by finding its object within the DOM hierarchy. Fortunately, this is easy

to do when you have assigned an identifier to the object. The following line of JavaScript returns the DOM object for your new table cell:

```
box=document.getElementById("desc");
```

This assigns the variable box to the appropriate object for the table cell with the identifier desc. The getElementById function is one of the new methods supported by DOM-compliant browsers. You'll learn more about these methods starting in Hour 5, "Understanding the DOM."

Note the confusing spelling of the getElementById function: You might expect the initial g or the final d to be uppercase. It will only work if you type it exactly as shown here.

Detecting Browser Support

As you learned earlier in this book, the new W3C DOM was first supported in Internet Explorer 5.0 and Netscape 6.0. Since many older browsers are still around, your script should make sure it is dealing with a new browser before attempting to use the DHTML features of the W3C DOM.

While you could use JavaScript to find out exactly which browser is in use, this isn't always the best way. If you detect specific browsers, you'll have to update your code when new browsers are released, or your dynamic features will stop working. Additionally, there might be browsers besides the "big two" that support the W3C DOM, and there's no sense in leaving them out.

You can avoid these issues by simply detecting browsers that support the DOM functions you will be using. You can do this in JavaScript with an if statement like this:

```
if (document.getElementById) {
```

This checks for the presence of the getElementByID function, without actually calling the function. In older browsers, this will simply return a false value without causing an error. You can also use the ! (not) operator to test the same value:

```
if (!document.getElementById) return;
```

This statement uses the return command to exit from the current function if the getElementById method is not supported. You will use this method in your script to prevent errors on older browsers.

You'll learn more about ways to detect browsers and the differences between them in Hour 17, "Dealing with Browser Differences."

Creating the Script

You should now know what you need to complete the DHTML example. The following sections will guide you through the process of adding DHTML to the Figby Industries Web page.

Adding Event Handlers

In the previous hour, you used the onMouseOver and onMouseOut events to execute a JavaScript function. You can use a similar function to add DHTML features. Here is the section of the HTML doc￼ ￼roducts link, with event handlers added:

```
<td ￼                    onMouseOut="Describe('...');"
                 ￼ our exciting products');">
```

￼ send it in the table cell below the links
￼nt calls Describe with a description for the
￼with a default value.

4

￼n

￼on, which will use DHTML to display
￼ibe function:

￼text variable. It then uses the
￼t whether the current browser sup-
￼not exist, the return statement

￼ById function to find the object
￼he value passed as a parameter is

This is where the page becomes dynamic. The `innerHTML` property represents the contents of an object, in this case the table cell. When you assign new text to `box.innerHTML`, the text is displayed in the table cell in place of its original contents.

Workshop: Putting It All Together

Now that you have written the `Describe` function and determined how to call it using event handlers, you can combine these with the original HTML document for the Figby Industries Web page to create a complete, dynamic version of the page. Listing 4.2 shows the complete DHTML example.

> This listing is a bit long. To save some typing, you can download this and all of the book's other examples at this book's Web site, `http://www.starlingtech.com/dhtml/`. The graphic, `logo.gif`, required by this example is also available there.

LISTING 4.2   The Complete DHTML Example

```
<html>
<head>
   <title>Figby Industries, Inc.</title>
<script language="JavaScript">
function Describe(text) {
   if (!document.getElementById) return;
   box=document.getElementById("desc");
   box.innerHTML=text;
}
</script>
</head>
<body>
<img align="center" src="logo.gif" width="486" height="180" border="0"><br>
<h1>Welcome to Figby Industries!</h1>
<p>Welcome! This is the home page of Figby Industries,
your source for all sorts of imaginary products. Follow the links
below to learn more about our company and our products.
</p>
<table border="1" align="center">
<tr>
   <td width="20%"><a href="products.html" onMouseOut="Describe('...');"
   onMouseOver="Describe('Information about our exciting products');">
   <b>Products</b></a></td>
```

LISTING 4.2 continued

```
        <td width="20%"><a href="sales.html" onMouseOut="Describe('...');"
          onMouseOver="Describe('Contact our Sales Department');">
        <b>Sales</b></a></td>
        <td width="20%"><a href="service.html" onMouseOut="Describe('...');"
          onMouseOver="Describe('Find service and support information');">
        <b>Service</b></a></td>
        <td width="20%"><a href="staff.html" onMouseOut="Describe('...');"
          onMouseOver="Describe('Learn about or contact our staff');">
        <b>Staff</b></a></td>
        <td width="20%"><a href="jobs.html" onMouseOut="Describe('...');"
          onMouseOver="Describe('Employment opportunities available');">
        <b>Employment</b></a></td>
</tr>
<tr><td ID="desc" align='center' colspan="5">...</td></tr>
</table>
<p>Any truly legitimate company would have much more text in this
part of the page than we have.</p>
</body>
</html>
```

In this listing, three changes have been made to the original HTML document:

- The <script> section in the header of the document defines the Describe function.

- In the table, onMouseOut and onMouseOver event handlers have been added to each link to call the Describe function.

- A new row has been added at the end of the table, including the cell identified as desc that will display the item description.

To try this example, type it in using a text editor, save it, and load it into a browser. When you move the mouse pointer over one of the links, you should see a description in the lower row of the table.

Figure 4.2 shows the completed DHTML example as displayed by Netscape 6. In the figure, the description for the Service link is being displayed.

> You must use Netscape 6.0 or later or Internet Explorer 5.0 or later to test this example and most of the DHTML examples in the rest of this book. This example will work equally well with either of these browsers.

4

FIGURE **4.2**

Netscape shows the completed DHTML example.

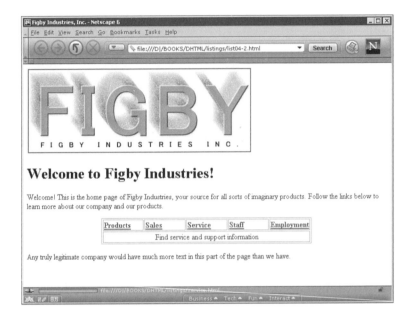

Summary

In this hour, you've learned how to use a JavaScript function and DOM functions and properties to add a simple dynamic feature to an HTML document. You've also learned how to ensure that your script won't cause errors in older browsers.

Congratulations—you've reached the end of Part I! In Part II, you will learn more of the technical details of DHTML and the DOM, and use them to create several examples.

Q&A

Q. Are there actually any browsers besides Netscape and Internet Explorer that support DHTML?

A. Yes. The Opera browser (http://www.opera.com/) has limited support for the Level 2 DOM, and the developers plan to add more support.

Q. Can I change the text in an object other than a table cell?

A. Absolutely. If you assign the ID attribute to a different object, such as a paragraph or heading, you can change its contents instead.

Q. Is a dynamic page like this one possible in the version 4.0 browsers?

A. Yes. While you can't change the contents of a table cell in these browsers using the W3C DOM, you could use a layer to display a description. See Hour 17 for details on supporting older browsers.

Quiz

Test your knowledge of the material covered in this hour by answering the following questions.

Questions

1. Which of the following is the correct function to obtain the object for the HTML element with the identifier `thirdline`?

   a. `obj=document.getElementById("thirdline");`

   b. `obj=GetElementById("thirdline");`

   c. `obj=document.getElementByID("thirdline");`

2. `obj.innerHTML="test";` is a statement in which language?

   a. HTML

   b. JavaScript

   c. DHTML

3. `onMouseOver` is an example of what?

   a. HTML property

   b. HTML function

   c. An event handler

Answers

1. a. The correct command is `obj=document.getElementById("thirdline");`. Notice the lower-case g and d in `getElementById`.

2. b. While this statement uses a DHTML property, the language is still JavaScript.

3. c. `onMouseOver` is an example of an event handler.

Exercises

If you'd like to explore this hour's DHTML example a bit further before you move on, try the following exercises:

- Try modifying Listing 4.2 by removing the ID="desc" attribute from the table cell, and adding it instead to a different HTML tag, such as the <h1> tag at the top or the paragraph at the bottom. Notice that the descriptions will now be displayed in the area you specified instead of in the table cell.

- Currently, if the Describe function in Listing 4.2 detects a browser that doesn't support the DOM, it doesn't do anything. Try adding an else clause that displays the messages in the status line for older browsers, similar to what you did in Hour 3's Workshop section.

PART II
Learning DHTML Basics

Hour

HOUR 5

Understanding the DOM

Welcome to Part II! In the next four hours, you'll learn more about DHTML. In particular, you'll learn quite a bit more about the W3C DOM that enables cross-browser DHTML in the latest browsers.

To begin with, this hour will introduce you to the DOM's basic structure. You'll learn how the W3C DOM fits in with the older Level 0 DOM, and some of the properties and methods you can use with DOM objects.

Hour 5 covers the following topics:

- The structure of the Level 0 and Level 1 DOM
- How the hierarchy of DOM objects represents a Web page
- Relationships between DOM objects
- Using DOM properties and methods
- Hiding and showing objects using DHTML

Learning DOM Structure

In the previous hour, you used a DOM object to create a dynamic page. While you can do this without knowing how the DOM organizes objects, the structure of DOM objects is something you'll need to know as you pursue more advanced features.

The Level 0 DOM

As you learned earlier in this book, the Level 0 DOM is the informal label for the DOM objects that Netscape introduced with the JavaScript language, and Internet Explorer also supports. This DOM includes objects for working with windows, frames, documents, images, and forms.

Figure 5.1 shows how the basic objects of the Level 0 DOM are organized. Notice that the document object is at the top of the hierarchy for the document. This is where the W3C DOM connects with the Level 0 DOM.

FIGURE 5.1

The Level 0 DOM's object hierarchy.

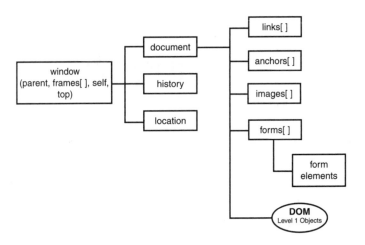

Since this is a book about DHTML, when we refer to the DOM, we are usually talking about the Level 1 DOM. Keep in mind, however, that the Level 0 DOM and Level 1 DOM are part of the same hierarchy.

The Level 1 DOM

The Level 1 DOM is what makes cross-browser DHTML truly dynamic. While the Level 0 DOM only includes objects for certain parts of a document, such as windows and images, the Level 0 DOM allows you to access—and modify—any object on a page.

To give you an idea of how the DOM organizes the objects within a Web page, Listing 5.1 shows a simple HTML document that includes a title, a heading, and a single paragraph.

LISTING 5.1   A Simple HTML Document

```
<html>
<head>
<title>A simple HTML Document</title>
</head>
<body>
<h1>This is a Heading</h1>
<p>This is a paragraph</p>
</body>
</html>
```

The DOM stores an object for each tag in the document in a hierarchy, starting with the HTML element at the top. Figure 5.2 shows how this document would be represented in the DOM.

FIGURE 5.2
How the DOM represents an HTML document.

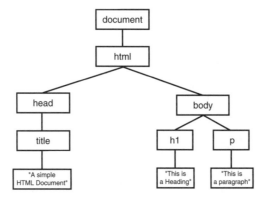

Although this book focuses on the W3C DOM, keep in mind that the Level 0 DOM is not obsolete—on the contrary, it's included in the Level 1 DOM specification. You can still use the objects in the Level 0 DOM to work with windows, frames, and images, and to obtain information about the current document.

Appendix D, "DOM Quick Reference," includes a summary of Level 0 DOM objects.

Nodes

Each container or element in a document is called a *node* in the DOM hierarchy. In Figure 5.2, each of the boxes is a node, and the lines form relationships between the nodes.

A document's DOM hierarchy includes a node for each HTML tag within the document. For container tags, such as <p>, there is a further node that defines the text within the container. This node is called a *text node*.

You've already worked with individual nodes using the ID attribute, and that's usually the easiest way. However, you can also access any node based on its relationships with other nodes.

Parents and Children

Each object in the DOM can have a *parent*—the node above it in the hierarchy—and one or more *children*—the nodes below it in the hierarchy.

In Figure 5.2, the document object is the parent of all of the objects below it. The <h1> and <p> containers are children of the body object, and the text within those containers forms a child node for each one.

Siblings

DOM objects can also be referred to as *siblings*. As you might have guessed if you have siblings of your own, these are nodes that share the same parent object. In Figure 5.2, the <h1> and <p> nodes are siblings under the <body> node.

Using DOM Objects

You should now have a basic understanding of how the DOM organizes objects. You can now start to learn how to deal with these objects in your scripts.

DOM Object Properties

Each object in the DOM has a number of *properties*, or attributes. The actual list of properties depends on the HTML tag the object represents. Each object has properties that correspond to the HTML tag's attributes. There are also several general properties that apply to every node:

- nodeName is the name of the node (not the ID). Possible node names include the tag name for HTML tag nodes, #document for the document node, and #text for text nodes.

- nodeType is a number describing the node's type: 1 for HTML tags, 3 for text nodes, and 9 for the document.
- id is the value of the ID attribute for the node.
- classname is the value of the class attribute for the node. This attribute is typically used to assign the same style to a number of elements—you'll learn more about it in Hour 9, "Introducing Style Sheets."
- nodeValue is the value for a node. HTML tag nodes have a null value, while the value of a text node is the text contained within it.
- innerHTML is the HTML contents of a container node. You used this property in the previous hour to change the text within a node.

The nodeValue and innerHTML properties are explained in more detail in Hour 7, "Working with DOM Properties and Methods."

Node Relationship Properties

In addition to the basic properties, each node has a number of properties that describe its relationship with other nodes in the DOM hierarchy. These properties include the following:

- firstChild is the first child node for the current node.
- lastChild is the last child node for the current node.
- childNodes is a list of all of the child nodes under a node, which you can access as an array in JavaScript.
- previousSibling is the sibling before the current node
- nextSibling is the sibling after the current node.
- parentNode is the object that contains the current node.

Style Properties

Each node in the DOM hierarchy has a style property. This is a child object whose properties describe how the object appears on the page: its position, color, and whether it's hidden or visible. Each style property corresponds to an attribute that can be used in a CSS style sheet.

You can use the style properties for any visible object on the page. This means headings, paragraphs, images, and other visible objects, but not the document, body, or other

5

objects that don't represent a visible part of the page. Here are some of the most useful properties:

- visibility controls whether the object is visible on the page. You can set this property to visible (default) or hidden to show or hide the object. A third value, inherit, means that the object will be visible if its parent object is visible. This property only affects the object, and does not affect the page's layout.

- display also controls the object's visibility. A value of block, inline, or list-item shows the object, and the value of none hides it. Unlike visibility, if you hide an object with display, it changes the page's layout—objects below it on the page will move up into the empty space. See Hour 6, "Creating Positionable Elements (Layers)," for information about the various display values.

- left is the horizontal position of the object. It can be a numeric offset from the main browser window, a percentage, auto to allow the browser to determine the position, or inherit to inherit the position of the parent object.

- top controls the vertical position of the object. It supports the same values as left. The top and left properties have no effect unless the position property has been changed to a value other than static.

- right and bottom provide an alternate way of setting the horizontal and vertical position of an object.

 You'll learn more of the available style properties and practice using the left and top properties in Hour 6, "Creating Positionable Elements (Layers)," and in Part III, "Working with Style Sheets."

Document Object Methods

The DOM also includes a number of *methods*, or functions, for working with objects. Several of the most important of these are methods of the document object:

- document.getElementById(*ID*) returns the element with the specified identifier. You used this function in the previous hour to manipulate objects on a page.

- document.getElementsByTagName(*tag*) returns an array of the elements with a specified tag name. You can use the asterisk (*) as a wildcard to return a collection of all of the nodes in the document, which you can access as an array.

- document.createElement(*tag*) creates a new element with the specified tag name. You can use this method to add content to a document, as you'll learn in Hour 7, "Working with DOM Properties and Methods."

- document.createTextNode(*text*) creates a new text node containing the specified text.

Internet Explorer 4's DHTML model used a document.all array containing all of the objects in a document. If you are used to this style of DHTML, you can use document.getElementsByTagName(*) to return a similar array in IE 5 or Netscape 6.

Node Object Methods

Node objects in the DOM also have their own set of methods. You can use these to add or remove elements within a page. These include the following:

- appendChild(newnode) adds a new child node to the node after all of its existing children.

- insertBefore(newnode,oldnode) inserts a new child node before the specified existing child node.

- replaceChild(newnode,oldnode) replaces the specified old child node with a new child node.

- removeChild(oldnode) removes an existing child node.

- hasChildNodes() returns a Boolean value of true if the node has one or more children, or false if it has none.

To use these methods, you separate the node name and the method name with a period. For example, this code finds an element with the ID attribute "lastone" and removes its first child node:

```
obj=document.getElementById("lastone");
obj.removeChild(obj.firstChild);
```

Hour 7 describes these methods in detail, and the Workshop section of Hour 7 uses them to add and remove text within a Web page.

JavaScript and the DOM

What do all of these properties and methods mean for practical scripting? Well, if you want to manipulate just one child node you can continue to use the `getElementById` method to obtain an object for that node.

The `getElementsByTagName` method is also useful if you want to work with more than one object—for example, all of the paragraphs on the page or all of the headings.

The relationship properties and methods become useful if you want to create a script that works with more than one node on the page, or even with all of the nodes. You'll use some of these methods to add and remove text within an existing Web page in Hour 7.

Workshop: Hiding and Showing Objects

Now that you've learned the basics of DOM properties and methods, you can create a simple example that uses DHTML to hide and show objects on a page. While this example will hide or show headings, you can just as easily use any other object.

You can accomplish this easily by doing three things:

- Assign an `ID` attribute to the elements you want to show or hide.
- Use the `getElementById` method to find the objects for the elements.
- Use the `style.visibility` property of each object to control its visibility.

In this example, you'll use these techniques to show or hide two headings. Two check-boxes in a form are used to control the visibility.

Creating the JavaScript Function

The `ShowHide` function will handle the actual showing or hiding of the objects on the page. Here is the JavaScript code for this function:

```
function ShowHide() {
 if (!document.getElementById) return;
    var head1 = document.getElementById("head1");
    var head2 = document.getElementById("head2");
    var showhead1 = document.form1.head1.checked;
    var showhead2 = document.form1.head2.checked;
    head1.style.visibility=(showhead1) ? "visible" : "hidden";
    head2.style.visibility=(showhead2) ? "visible" : "hidden";
}
```

This function first checks for the existence of the `getElementById` method, to verify that the browser supports the needed DOM functions. Next, it finds the objects for the two headings and stores them in the `head1` and `head2` variables.

Next, it reads the checkboxes in the form and stores their values in the showhead1 and showhead2 variables. Finally, it uses these values to assign either the visible or hidden values to the style.visibility property of the headings.

Creating the HTML Document

Listing 5.2 shows a complete HTML and JavaScript document for showing or hiding headings.

LISTING 5.2 Hiding and Showing Objects

```
<html>
<head>
<title>Dynamic Text in JavaScript</title>
<script language="Javascript">
function ShowHide() {
 if (!document.getElementById) return;
    var head1 = document.getElementById("head1");
    var head2 = document.getElementById("head2");
    var showhead1 = document.form1.head1.checked;
    var showhead2 = document.form1.head2.checked;
    head1.style.visibility=(showhead1) ? "visible" : "hidden";
    head2.style.visibility=(showhead2) ? "visible" : "hidden";
}
</script>
</head>
<body>
<h1 ID="head1">Now You See It</h1>
<h1 ID="head2">Now You Don't</h1>
<p>The W3C DOM and DHTML allow you to
hide or show the two headings on this page.</p>
<form name="form1">
<input type="checkbox" name="head1"
    checked onClick="ShowHide();">
<b>Show first heading</b><br>
<input type="checkbox" name="head2"
    checked onClick="ShowHide();">
<b>Show second heading</b><br>
</form>
</body>
</html>
```

This HTML document includes the ShowHide function in its <script> section. The two <h1> headers are assigned the ID attributes head1 and head2 so that they can be manipulated by the script.

The onClick event handlers on lines 24 and 27 ensures that the ShowHide function is called each time one of the checkboxes is clicked.

5

To try this example, type it into a text editor and save it as an HTML document. Load the document into Netscape 6.0 or later or Internet Explorer 5.0 or later. Figure 5.3 shows this example in action with both of the headings displayed.

FIGURE 5.3

The example in action, with both headings currently visible.

Summary

In this hour, you've begun to delve into more of the details of DHTML. You learned some of the properties and methods of the W3C Level 1 DOM, and you've learned how it fits in with the old Level 0 DOM. Finally, you applied your knowledge to create an example that hides and shows objects, a technique you will use many times in later hours of this book.

In the next hour, you will learn how to use layers in DHTML. You'll learn more about the positioning properties of objects, and how to move objects on the screen.

Q&A

Q. Can I use node properties to change the font, size, or color for text within a document?

A. Yes, and much more. You will learn the complete list of style properties in Part III.

Q. Is there a way to get the entire HTML source code for the current page?

A. Yes, it's the value of the `document.documentElement.innerHTML` property. This is explained in detail in Hour 7.

Q. Is there a way to show or hide objects in the version 4.0 browsers?

A. Not exactly. You can't hide arbitrary objects like our example does with headings. However, you can create layers containing HTML tags, and show or hide the layers, for much the same effect. You'll learn how to use layers in 4.0 browsers in Hour 17, "Dealing with Browser Differences."

Quiz

Test your knowledge of the material covered in this hour by answering the following questions.

Questions

1. Which of the following functions is the easiest way of adding dynamic features to a single object on a page?
   a. `getElementById`
   b. `getElementsByTagName`
   c. `hasChildNodes`

2. Which of the following properties can hide or show an object, without affecting the layout of the remaining objects on the page?
   a. `style.display`
   b. `style.hide`
   c. `style.visibility`

3. If you define a simple paragraph of text in HTML, which of the following is a child object of the <p> tag's node?
   a. The </p> tag
   b. A text node with the paragraph's contents
   c. The object has no children

5

Answers

1. a. Using getElementById is the easiest way to work with a single object on a page.

2. c. The style.visibility property can be used to hide or show an object without affecting the page's layout.

3. b. In a simple HTML paragraph, the paragraph object has a single child object, a text node containing the text within the paragraph.

Exercises

If you'd like some more practice working with the DHTML techniques you learned in this hour before you move on, try the following exercises:

- Modify Listing 5.2 to allow showing and hiding of the text paragraph on the page as well as the headings. You'll need to add an ID attribute for the paragraph, add a checkbox to the form, and modify the ShowHide function to support the additional object.

- Modify Listing 5.2 to use the display property instead of the visibility property to show or hide the headings. Notice that the page collapses when you hide them, moving the paragraph of text up.

HOUR **6**

Creating Positionable Elements (Layers)

One of the most useful features of DHTML is the ability to move objects around on the screen. You can create layers, or groups of movable objects, and position them using JavaScript. You can also use DOM properties to move any object within a Web page.

In this hour, you'll learn how to define layers using the CSS standard, the properties you can use, and how to work with layers and other positionable objects using JavaScript.

Hour 6 covers the following topics:

- Why layers are useful
- Defining layers in HTML
- Positioning properties for layers and other objects
- Creating a simple layered document
- Using JavaScript to make layers dynamic

Why Layers?

When Netscape and Microsoft released their version 4.0 browsers, they both included a feature called *layers*. Layers are areas of a Web page that can be moved, hidden, or shown, can overlap in whatever way you specify, and can be manipulated using JavaScript.

Layers were the first DHTML feature available to the world. Unfortunately, these two browsers supported entirely different ways of defining and using layers. Webmasters who wanted to use this feature had to either settle on a single browser to support, or develop cross-browser code using both techniques.

Fortunately, the W3C stepped in with a standard for layers, now known as *positionable elements*. You can define layers with CSS style sheets and attributes. This type of layer is supported by the 4.0 browsers, but the methods for working with layers in JavaScript differ.

When you combine the CSS layer standard with the new W3C DOM supported by Internet Explorer 5 and Netscape 6, you can now easily create layers and manipulate them using cross-browser code.

Actually, with the new W3C DOM, you can position, show or hide anything in a Web page—for example, in the previous hour, you used DHTML to hide and show headings on a page.

Layers are still a useful concept when you want to define an area that contains content over which you want control, and you will continue to use them later in this book. You'll also learn the properties for positioning objects in DHTML in this hour, which apply equally to layers and other objects.

> Another good reason to use layers is that you can create a script that works with the 4.0 browsers as well as newer browsers. You will create such an example in Hour 17, "Dealing with Browser Differences."

HTML Tags for Layers

Typically, you create a layer using the `<div>` tag in HTML. In order for a division to act as a layer, you need to specify certain positioning properties. The following is a simple layer definition:

```
<div ID="layer1" STYLE="position:absolute; left:100; top:50">
<p>This text is contained in the layer.</p>
</div>
```

The position:absolute in the layer definition specifies that the layer will be positioned relative to the browser window, and left and top define its initial position. These properties are further explained in the next section.

You can also use the <span> tag to define layers. Additionally, with the W3C DOM, you can assign a position attribute to any HTML tag that displays an object on the screen. If you also assign an ID attribute, you can change the object's position using JavaScript.

The style attribute in the layer definition sets up CSS style information, which includes positioning as well as font, size, and other style parameters. You'll learn more about style sheets in Part III, "Working with Style Sheets."

Positioning Objects

To define a layer, or any positionable object, you can define one or more positioning properties in the object's style definition. The most important of these is the position property. The position property can have one of four values:

- static (default) defines items that are laid out along with the rest of the HTML document, and cannot be moved.
- absolute allows you to position the item by specifying left and top coordinates.
- relative defines an item that is offset a certain amount from the static position, where it was laid out by the browser.
- fixed defines an item that can be moved like the absolute value, but doesn't scroll with the page contents. This property is not supported by current browsers.

All of the properties described here are style properties. This means you refer to them using the style object, as in obj.style.position. These can also be set in a style sheet.

6

Along with position, a number of other properties are available. You can set these in the style sheet definition for a layer, or set them later using JavaScript.

Setting Coordinates

Layers and other positionable objects can be positioned anywhere within the browser window. You can use the following properties to set an object's location:

- `left` is the horizontal position of the item. For absolute positioning, coordinates start at the left side of the browser window; for relative positioning, they start at the object's original position.
- `top` is the vertical position of the object. This is relative to the top of the browser window for absolute positioning, and relative to the original position for relative positioning.
- `right` and `bottom` are alternate ways to set the horizontal and vertical position. You can use these when you need to align the object's right or bottom edge on the page.
- `width` and `height` specify the object's width and height. For objects containing text, the text will wrap at the specified width.
- `z-index` specifies how the object overlaps with other objects. Indexes are assigned in order, so layers defined later in the HTML document are "on top" of previous layers. You can change this value to bring an object to the top.

Using Units

The `left`, `top`, `right`, and `bottom` properties can be set to `auto` to let the browser position the object, `inherit` to inherit the position of the parent object, or a number. Numbers for all of these properties can be specified in several different units:

- `px`: Pixels (for example, `15px`)
- `pt`: Points (for example, `10pt`)
- `ex`: Approximate height of the letter x in the current font (for example, `1.2ex`)
- `em`: Approximate width of the letter m in the current font (for example, `1.5em`)
- `%`: Percentage of the containing object's value (for example, `150%`)

If you assign a numeric value to a property without specifying a unit, pixels are typically assumed.

 Since these units are used for style sheets, they are explained in more detail in Hour 9, "Introducing Style Sheets."

Showing and Hiding Objects

As you learned in the previous hour, there are two properties that allow you to control whether an element appears on the Web page: `visibility` and `display`.

The visibility property controls the item's visibility, without affecting the page layout. It can be set to visible (default), hidden, or inherit. A value of inherit uses the visibility setting of a parent object.

The display property specifies whether the object is visible in the page. The page layout shifts to account for changes to this property. The possible values for display include the following:

- block displays the object as a block-level element, meaning that it is preceded and followed by line breaks.
- inline displays the object as an inline element, with no line breaks.
- list-item displays the object as a list item, formatted as a member of the current list defined by an <ol> or <ul> tag.
- none removes the object from the page's display, and adjusts the page layout to fill in the empty space.

Background Properties

The following properties are used to specify the background of a layer. See Hour 10, "Using Style Sheet Properties," for more background-related properties.

- background-color specifies the background color for the layer. This can be a named color, such as blue, a specific RGB color, such as #FF3355, or the keyword transparent, meaning that any object below the layer will show through the background.
- background-image specifies a background image for the layer.

Since these attributes include a hyphen, they are specified as backgroundColor and backgroundImage in JavaScript.

Handling Overflow

Sometimes, the content inside a layer will be larger than the size assigned to the layer can display. In this case, the overflow property tells the browser what to do with the extra content:

- visible will make the content visible even if it's outside the layer's box.
- hidden hides the content outside the box.
- scroll hides the content outside the box and provides scroll bars to allow the user to see the entire content.

6

- `auto` lets the browser make its own decision about the overflow, usually displaying scroll bars.

- `inherit` inherits the overflow value from a parent object.

> You'll use the `overflow` property to create a scrolling window in Hour 24, "DHTML Tips and Tricks."

Border Properties

Sometimes you'll want to place a visible border around your layer. You can do this by assigning the following properties:

- `border-width` sets the width of the border for all four sides. This can be a numeric value or the keywords `thin`, `medium`, or `thick`.

- `border-style` sets the style of border. Values include `none` (default), `dotted`, `dashed`, `solid`, `double`, `groove`, `ridge`, `inset`, or `outset`.

- border-color sets the color of the border.

> There are actually a variety of more specific border properties. These are described in Hour 10.

Creating a Layered Document

You can create a layered document using `<div>` tags and positioning properties. Listing 6.1 shows a simple example that creates two layers and specifies their positions.

LISTING 6.1   A Simple Document with Layers

```
<html>
<head><title>Layers Example</title></head>
<body>
<h1>Example Layered Document</h1>
<div ID="layer1"
 STYLE="position: absolute; left: 280; top: 100; width:250; height:150;
  background-color:yellow">
<h1>First Layer</h1>
```

LISTING 6.1   continued

```
This is the first layer. It appears on the right side of the page,
although it was defined first.
</div>
<div ID="layer2"
 STYLE="position: absolute; left: 20; top: 100; width:250; height:150;
  background-color:Aqua">
<h1>Second Layer</h1>
This is the second layer. It appears on the left side, although it
was defined second.
</div>
</body>
</html>
```

In this listing, the two <div> tags define the layers. This example uses the left and top properties to position the layers, width and height to set each layer's size, and background-color to assign different colors to each one.

Figure 6.1 shows how this example appears in Internet Explorer.

FIGURE 6.1

The simple layered document as displayed in Internet Explorer.

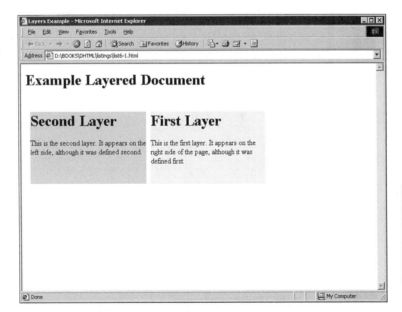

6

Workshop: Manipulating Layers with JavaScript

You can set the properties of a layer or other object dynamically using JavaScript. You used this technique in the previous hour to hide and show objects on a page. For example, the following JavaScript moves an object with the ID attribute layer to a new position:

```
obj=document.getElementById("layer");
obj.style.left=100;
obj.style.top=200;
```

Using this example, you can expand your layered document and add the ability to move the various layers around the page.

Creating the Control Panel

To move the objects on the page, you can create a control panel in its own layer. The control panel will use a form, and will include two basic sections:

- A set of radio buttons to allow you to choose which object to move
- Four buttons to move the chosen object left, right, up, or down
- Two buttons to increase or decrease the z-index property

The following is the HTML <form> section for the control panel:

```
<form name="form1">
Use these controls to move the layers and other elements on the page.
<br>
<input type="radio" name="what" value="layer1" checked> Layer 1
<input type="radio" name="what" value="layer2"> Layer 2
<input type="radio" name="what" value="heading"> Heading
<input type="radio" name="what" value="control">This Panel<br>
<table align="center">
<tr><td colspan="2" align="center">
<input type="button" name="up" value="Up" onClick="move(0,-30,0);">
</td></tr>
<tr><td align="left">
<input type="button" name="left" value=" Left " onClick="move(-30,0,0);">
</td>
<td align="right">
<input type="button" name="right" value="Right" onClick="move(30,0,0);">
</td>
</tr>
<tr><td colspan="2" align="center">
<input type="button" name="down" value="Down" onClick="move(0,30,0);">
<br>
<input type="button" name="zminus" value="Z minus" onClick="move(0,0,-1);">
```

```
<input type="button" name="zplus" value="Z plus" onClick="move(0,0,1);">
</td></tr>
</table>
</form>
```

The `<form>` tag starts a form with the name `form1`. The name will be needed later to read the form's contents. The document then defines four radio buttons with the name `what` and different values. You will be able to choose to move Layer 1, Layer 2, the control panel layer itself, or a heading on the page.

The `<table>` tag is used to lay out the Up, Down, Left, Right, Z-plus, and Z-minus buttons in a user-friendly shape. The buttons in the control panel include an `onClick` event handler. Each one calls a function, `move`, with three parameters: the amount to move the left position, the top position, and the Z index.

> Since browser coordinates start with zero at the top-left corner, the `move` function will use positive numbers (addition) to move the object down or to the right, and negative numbers (subtraction) to move the object up or to the left.

Creating the `move` Function

Next, you need to create the `move` function itself. This function will read the form to determine the object to move, and move it the appropriate amounts. Here's the JavaScript code for the `move` function:

```
function move(x,y,z) {
  if (!document.getElementById) return;
  for(i=0;i<4;i++) {
      if (document.form1.what[i].checked)
        tomove=document.form1.what[i].value;
  }
  obj=document.getElementById(tomove);
  obj.style.left = parseInt(obj.style.left) + x;
  obj.style.top = parseInt(obj.style.top) + y;
  obj.style.zIndex=parseInt(obj.style.zIndex) + z;
}
```

6

Here's a breakdown of how the `move` function works:

- The `function` keyword lists the three arguments, x, y, and z.

- The `for` loop finds out which of the radio buttons is checked, and the `if` statement sets the variable `tomove` to the name of the object that should be moved.

- Finally, the function reads the current value of the `left`, `top`, and `z-index` properties and adds the numbers in the x, y, and z variables to them.

This example reads the object's current position from the `obj.style.left` and `obj.style.top` properties. With current browsers, this technique will only work if you have already set the object's position in a style definition or using JavaScript. If the object was laid out by the browser, you can't read its position.

Putting It All Together

Finally, you can combine the layered document, the control panel, and the move function into a single HTML document to create the complete example. Listing 6.2 shows the complete dynamic layers example.

LISTING 6.2   The Complete Dynamic Layers Example

```
<html>
<head><title>Layers in DHTML</title>
<script language="JavaScript">
function move(x,y,z) {
  if (!document.getElementById) return;
  for(i=0;i<4;i++) {
     if (document.form1.what[i].checked)
       tomove=document.form1.what[i].value;
  }
  obj=document.getElementById(tomove);
  obj.style.left = parseInt(obj.style.left) + x;
  obj.style.top = parseInt(obj.style.top) + y;
  obj.style.zIndex=parseInt(obj.style.zIndex) + z;
}
</script>
</head>
<body>
<h1 ID="heading" style="position: absolute; left: 20; top: 5">
Controlling Layers with DHTML</h1>
<div ID="layer1"
 STYLE="position: absolute; left: 20; top: 50; width:250; height:150;
  background-color:yellow">
<h1>First Layer</h1>
This is the first layer. It started out on the left side of the page.
</div>
<div ID="layer2"
 STYLE="position: absolute; left: 280; top: 50; width:250; height:150;
  background-color:Aqua">
<h1>Second Layer</h1>
This is the second layer. It started out on the right side of the page.
</div>
<div ID="control"
```

LISTING 6.2   continued

```
STYLE="position: absolute; left: 20; top: 210; width:350; height:255;
  background-color:lightblue">
<h1>Control Panel</h1>
<form name="form1">
Use these controls to move the layers and other elements on the page.
<br>
<input type="radio" name="what" value="layer1" checked> Layer 1
<input type="radio" name="what" value="layer2"> Layer 2
<input type="radio" name="what" value="heading"> Heading
<input type="radio" name="what" value="control">This Panel<br>
<table align="center">
<tr><td colspan="2" align="center">
<input type="button" name="up" value="Up" onClick="move(0,-30,0);">
</td></tr>
<tr><td align="left">
<input type="button" name="left" value=" Left " onClick="move(-30,0,0);">
</td>
<td align="right">
<input type="button" name="right" value="Right" onClick="move(30,0,0);">
</td>
</tr>
<tr><td colspan="2" align="center">
<input type="button" name="down" value="Down" onClick="move(0,30,0);">
<br>
<input type="button" name="zminus" value="Z minus" onClick="move(0,0,-1);">
<input type="button" name="zplus" value="Z plus" onClick="move(0,0,1);">
</td></tr>
</table>
</form>
</div>
</body>
</html>
```

In this listing, the <script> section sets up the move function. The <h1> tag defines the heading, giving it an ID attribute and a position so that it can be moved later.

The first <div> section defines the layer1 layer, and the second defines the layer2 layer. Finally, the third <div> section sets up the control panel in a layer called control.

To try this example, save it as an HTML document and load it into a browser. Figure 6.2 shows the initial display of the document in Netscape 6.

After you have loaded the document, try moving different parts of the page using the control panel. Figure 6.3 shows Internet Explorer's display of the example after all of the objects have been rearranged in this way.

6

FIGURE 6.2

The dynamic layer example before any layers are moved.

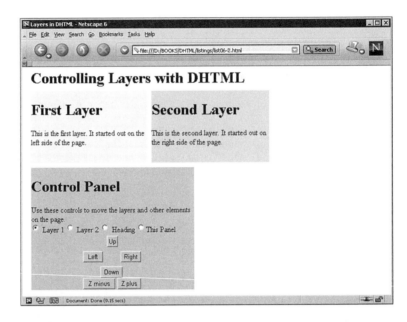

FIGURE 6.3

The dynamic layer example after objects have been moved.

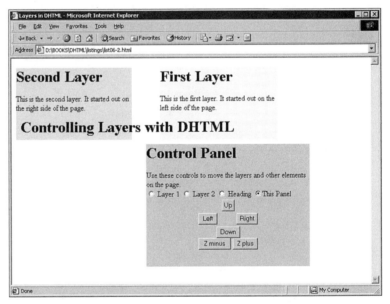

Summary

In this hour, you've learned how to use DHTML to position objects on a page. You've learned about layers, groups of objects that can be dynamically positioned, and learned the positioning properties you can use for layers and for other objects. Finally, you created an example that allows you to move layers and other objects using JavaScript.

In the next hour, you'll learn more about the structure of the DOM for a Web page. You'll learn how to manipulate the nodes in the DOM to add new text or other objects to a page, or remove existing objects.

Q&A

Q. I've seen the `<layer>` tag used before. Doesn't this have something to do with layers?

A. Yes. `<layer>` was the tag used to define layers in Netscape when they were first introduced. This technique still works in Netscape 4.0, but not in Netscape 6 or Internet Explorer.

Q. Can I move a layer or object that was defined using relative positioning?

A. Yes. With these objects, a position of `left:0` and `top:0` refers to the original position. If you want to read the position, be sure to assign an initial offset (zero is fine) when you define the layer.

Q. Can I make the example in Listing 6.4 work in Netscape 4.0 or Internet Explorer 4.0?

A. Yes. You can use the same layer definitions, but you will need to replace the code that uses the `getElementById` method in the `move` function with the appropriate object for the browser.

Quiz

6

Test your knowledge of the material covered in this hour by answering the following questions.

Questions

1. Which of the following tags is a good way to create a layer?

    a. `<body>`

    b. `<div>`

    c. `<layer>`

2. Which value should you use for the `position` attribute in a layer if you want to position it at a specific coordinate?

   a. `absolute`

   b. `static`

   c. `relative`

3. If you already have the object for a layer stored in the `obj` variable, what's the correct JavaScript statement to set a new horizontal position for the layer?

   a. `document.obj.left=100;`

   b. `obj.style.left=100;`

   c. `obj.left=100;`

Answers

1. b. `<div>` is a good tag to use to create a layer, since it has little effect on the document's formatting.

2. a. The `absolute` value for the `position` attribute allows you to set its coordinates.

3. b. The correct syntax is `obj.style.left=100;`.

Exercises

If you'd like to practice using layers and positioning before you move on to the next hour, try the following exercises:

- Add a "start over" button to Listing 6.4. When the button is clicked, an event handler should call a new function, `startover`, that resets all of the objects to their original positions.

- Try positioning one or more of the layers in Listing 6.4 using relative positioning.

HOUR 7

Working with DOM Properties and Methods

You have now learned the basics of the DOM objects that allow DHTML to work, and how layers can make dynamic pages. However, layers limit you to working with overlapping, rectangular areas of a page. The new W3C DOM overcomes this limitation—you can virtually rewrite the HTML of a page dynamically, change anything, and watch the browser's display update instantly.

In this hour, you'll explore more of the properties and functions you can use to take full advantage of the new DOM in your dynamic pages. You'll learn how to dynamically add items to a page, remove them, and modify the attributes of any part of a page.

This hour covers the following topics:

- Working with DOM node properties
- Using methods and properties of the document object
- Creating new elements and adding them to a page

- Changing attributes of HTML tags dynamically
- Adding and removing HTML elements

Understanding Node Properties

As you have learned earlier in this book, each element on a Web page is called a *node*. For example, consider the following fragment of HTML:

```
<body>
<h1 ID="head1">This is a heading</h1>
<p>This is a paragraph</p>
</body>
```

This HTML defines the body of a page with a body node containing the remaining nodes, an h1 node defining a heading, and a p node defining a paragraph. In addition, there are two *text nodes* defining the text within the <h1> and <p> tags.

You can work with any of the nodes that make up a Web page by examining or modifying the node's properties. To access these properties, you refer to the node's object. The easiest way to do this is using the getElementById method, as you learned earlier.

In the HTML example above, notice that the <h1> tag included an ID attribute assigning the identifier head1 to the heading. The following example displays the tagName property of the heading:

```
h=document.getElementById("head1");
alert("tag name is " + h.tagName);
```

> You might be tempted to simply refer to head1.tagName after assigning the ID attribute, but this won't work—you need to work with the *object*, not the identifier. You should always obtain the correct object using the getElementById method, or by referring to its relationship with other objects.

In Hour 5, "Understanding the DOM," you learned a few of the most useful properties of DOM objects. In the following sections, you'll take an in-depth look at more of the available properties.

The `nodeValue` Property

Each node has properties that define any text, or HTML, contained within the node. The first of these is the `nodeValue` property, which contains the actual text for a text node. For example, the following HTML defines a paragraph:

```
<p ID="para">This is a simple paragraph.</p>
```

To change the text within this paragraph, you can change the `nodeValue` attribute for the text node:

```
obj=document.getElementById("para");
obj.firstChild.nodeValue="New Text";
```

Notice that the paragraph itself doesn't have a `nodeValue` property; instead you need to refer to the text node contained by the paragraph, `obj.firstChild` in the example.

The `InnerHTML` Property

The `innerHTML` property is similar to `nodeValue`, but it works for any node and can include HTML, not just text. For example, here is an alternate way to change the text of a paragraph:

```
obj=document.getElementById("para");
obj.innerHTML="This is the <b>new</b> text.";
```

With `innerHTML`, there is no need to refer to a text node. You can change the contents of the paragraph directly. This creates a new text node, including a bold section defined by the `<b>` tag.

This is one of the most powerful DOM properties available. By adding HTML tags to the `innerHTML` property, you can drastically change the document—in fact, you can rewrite it completely. When using this property to add HTML elements, be sure to include all opening and closing tags and follow proper HTML syntax, so you don't create a browser error.

 In Hour 4, "Creating a Simple DHTML Example," you used the `innerHTML` property to change text within a page.

Offset Properties

Although you can set any style property for an object using JavaScript, you often can't read the values of these properties. For example, unless an object is positioned absolutely, you can't read its position with the `style.left` and `style.top` properties.

7

While not part of the W3C DOM standard, both Internet Explorer and Netscape support a number of properties that allow you to overcome this limitation:

- `offsetLeft` is the horizontal position of the object.
- `offsetTop` is the vertical position of the object.
- `offsetWidth` is the width of the object.
- `offsetHeight` is the height of the object.

Unfortunately, the way these properties are supported is not consistent. In Internet Explorer, when an object is laid out within another object, such as a table, the offset properties are relative to the containing object.

In Netscape, the offset values are always measured from the edges of the browser window, although they don't include the page margins.

> The offset properties are not style properties, and are accessed directly under an object rather than under its `style` property.

Using Document Methods and Properties

The DOM also includes a number of useful methods that you can access from the document object. You have already learned about two of these:

- `document.getElementById` gets the object for an element.
- `document.getElementsByTagName` gets a collection of objects with the specified tag name, which you can access as a JavaScript array.

The following sections will introduce you to some other useful things you can do with methods of the `document` object.

Creating Text Nodes

The `document.createTextNode` method allows you to create a new text node. For example, this statement creates a node containing a simple line of text:

```
n=document.createTextNode("This is the text.");
```

This creates a new text node and stores its object in the variable n. However, it does not display the text on the page—to do that, you will need to insert the node somewhere on the page, as described later in this hour.

Creating Elements

The `document.createElement` method creates a new HTML element. For example, the following statement creates a new node defining a paragraph and stores its object in the variable p:

```
p=document.createElement("P");
```

The parameter defines the type of node by specifying its HTML tag, without the angle brackets: simply P instead of <p>. As with the previous method, the new element is not placed on the Web page yet—you'll need to insert it.

> Notice that `document.createElement` doesn't include any content within the paragraph you created. You can add text to the paragraph using the `innerHTML` property or by adding a text node under the paragraph.

The `documentElement` object

Although the `document` object is at the root of the DOM hierarchy, you can't access its properties directly. For example, you can't look at the `nodeName` or `nodeType` properties for the document itself. Instead, you need to use the `documentElement` object. This object is a child of the `document` object. It also represents the root of the hierarchy and allows access to all properties.

For example, `document.documentElement.nodeName` is the name of the HTML tag that defines the document: HTML, referring to the <html> tag. `document.documentElement.firstChild` is the HEAD object, and `document.documentElement.lastChild` is the BODY object.

> The `documentElement` object includes some powerful features. For example, you can use `document.documentElement.innerHTML` to access the entire HTML document for the current Web page.

Using Node Methods

Along with the document methods, the DOM provides a number of methods that work directly on individual nodes. The following sections describe some of the most useful node methods.

7

Cloning a Node

You have already learned how to create new nodes using document methods. If you want to create a node similar to one that already exists, you can also use the `cloneNode` method. For example, this statement creates a copy of the `obj` object:

```
newobj=obj.cloneNode(true);
```

The parameter for `cloneNode` is a Boolean value. If its value is `true`, any child objects of the node are also copied to the clone; if the value is `false`, the child objects are not cloned.

As with the other methods that create nodes, the new node is simply stored in a variable (`newobj` in the example) that you can later use to insert the node.

Appending a New Node

The `appendChild` method adds a new child object for a node, effectively adding a node to the document. This is one way to add a node you have created with `cloneNode`, `createElement`, or `createTextNode` to the document.

For example, suppose you have a span defined within an HTML document, like this:

```
<span ID="addhere"></span>
```

The following JavaScript statements would add the `newobj` node, which you have previously created, as a child of the span:

```
span=document.getElementById("addhere");
span.appendChild(newobj);
```

> You can also use `appendChild` with a node that is already on the page. In this case, the object the node represents will move to the new position.

Inserting a New Node

The `insertBefore` method provides another way to insert a new child node. It works similarly to `appendChild`, except that you also specify an existing child node. The new node is inserted before the node you specify.

To use `insertBefore`, you specify the new node as the first parameter, and the existing child node as the second parameter. For example, the following statements use appendChild to add a child object to a span, and then use insertBefore to add another object before the one already inserted:

```
span=getElementById("addhere");
span.appendChild(obj);
span.insertBefore(newobj,obj);
```

Replacing Nodes

The replaceChild method is another way to add an object to a document. In this case, the new object replaces an existing child object. The replaceChild method has two parameters: the new object and the one it should replace. For example, suppose you have defined a span like this:

```
<span ID="changeme"><p ID="para">This is a paragraph</p></span>
```

The following statements would replace the paragraph with a heading:

```
span=document.getElementById("changeme");
p=document.getElementById("para");
newobj=document.createElement("H1");
newobj.innerHTML="This is a heading.";
span.replaceChild(newobj,p);
```

These statements get objects for the span and the paragraph, and create a new object for the heading. Since the heading is created without any text, you can add it using the innerHTML property. Finally, the replaceChild method swaps the objects.

Alternately, the replaceNode method can also replace a node. In this case, it works directly on a node rather than a child object. This statement could be used in place of the replaceChild method in the example:

```
p.replaceNode(newobj);
```

> The replaceNode method is not part of the W3C DOM standard, and at this writing, is supported only by Internet Explorer for Windows. I recommend using replaceChild instead to avoid browser issues.

Removing Nodes

You have now learned how to add elements to a page in various ways. You can also remove part of a page using the removeChild method. For example, suppose you defined a span containing a paragraph like the previous example:

```
<span ID="changeme"><p ID="para">This is a paragraph</p></span>
```

7

The following statements remove the paragraph from the span, leaving it empty:

```
span=document.getElementById("changeme");
span.removeChild(span.firstChild);
```

Notice the shortcut here: Rather than get the object for the paragraph, you can simply refer to it as `span.firstChild` since you know it is the only child object of the span.

The `removeNode` method works similarly, but works directly on a node. The parameter for `removeNode` is a flag: If it is `true`, any child objects of the node are also removed. If it is `false`, the child objects remain. For example, these statements would delete the span in the previous example, paragraph and all:

```
span=document.getElementById("changeme");
span.removeNode(true);
```

 The `removeNode` method is not part of the W3C DOM standard, and is currently supported only by Internet Explorer for Windows. I recommend you avoid using it until it is better supported by browsers.

Working with Attributes

Along with the nodes that represent HTML tags, you can also work with *attributes* in DHTML. These are parameters specified in the HTML tag. For example, this image tag has `align` and `src` attributes:

```
<img align="center" src="line.gif">
```

The DOM includes several methods you can use on nodes to manipulate their attributes. These include the following:

- `getAttribute(attribute_name)` gets the value of the attribute you specify and stores it in a variable.
- `setAttribute(attribute_name, value)` sets the value of an attribute.
- `removeAttribute(attribute_name)` removes the attribute you specify.
- `hasAttributes()` simply returns `true` if the node has attributes, and `false` if it has none.

 Currently, the `hasAttributes` method only works in Netscape 6. The other methods discussed here work in Netscape 6.0 or later and Internet Explorer 5.0 or later.

As a simple example of using attributes, you can create a script that allows the user to change the align attribute of a heading. Listing 7.1 shows the HTML and JavaScript document for this example.

LISTING 7.1 Changing Attributes of HTML Tags

```
<html>
<head>
<title>Modifying Attributes with DHTML</title>
<script language="JavaScript">
function AlignMe(a) {
   if (!document.getElementById) return;
   h=document.getElementById("head1");
   h.setAttribute("align",a);
}
</script>
</head>
<body>
<h1 ID="head1" align="left">Modifying Attributes</h1>
<p>This is a demonstration of changing HTML attributes
using DHTML. You can change the alignment of the heading
above to <a href="javascript:AlignMe('left');">left</a>,
<a href="javascript:AlignMe('right');">right</a>,
or <a href="javascript:AlignMe('center');">centered</a>
using the links in this paragraph.
</p>
</body>
</html>
```

In this listing, the AlignMe function changes the heading's alignment. This accepts a parameter, and sets the align attribute for the heading with the ID head1 to the value specified. The <h1> tag defines the heading itself, and the links within the body text call the AlignMe function to change the attribute.

Notice that the links in lines 16–18 begin with javascript:. This is an easy way to make a link call a JavaScript statement or function without using an event handler.

> You might recognize the first line in the AlignMe function: if
> (!document.getElementById) return;. This is an easy way to prevent errors
> on browsers that do not support DHTML, and we will use it throughout this
> book.

7

Figure 7.1 shows Netscape's display of this example after the heading's alignment has been moved to the right side.

FIGURE 7.1

Netscape shows the attribute changing example in action.

Workshop: Adding and Removing Text on a Page

As a way to demonstrate some of the methods you learned in this hour, you can create an HTML document that can modify itself—using a form, you will be able to add paragraphs, headings, or horizontal lines to the page or delete items from the page.

Setting Up the HTML Document

To begin creating this example, you can start with the HTML you will need. In particular, you will need a place to insert the new nodes on the page. The <span> tag is an ideal way to set aside a space for the new nodes:

```
<span ID="addhere">
</span>
```

Next, you will need the HTML form that allows the user to add and remove nodes. This is simply a text field, and buttons for the Add Paragraph, Add Heading, Add Line, and Delete a Node functions:

```
<form name="form1" ID="form1">
<input type="text" name="newtext" size="70"><br>
<input type="button" value="Add Paragraph"
   onClick="AddNode('P');">
<input type="button" value="Add Heading"
   onClick="AddNode('H3');">
<input type="button" value="Add Line"
   onClick="AddNode('HR');">
<input type="button" value="Delete a Node"
   onClick="DeleteNode();">
</form>
```

The AddNode Function

When the buttons in the form are clicked, they will call a JavaScript function using the onClick event handler. All of the buttons that add an element use the same function. Here is the JavaScript code to define the AddNode function:

```
function AddNode(tag) {
   if (!document.getElementById) return;
   element = document.createElement(tag);
   if (tag != "HR") {
      txt = document.form1.newtext.value;
      element.innerHTML=txt;
   }
   s=document.getElementById("addhere");
   s.appendChild(element);
}
```

This function creates a new element using the tag name specified as a parameter. If the tag is not an <hr> tag, it also creates text for the element based on the form's text field. Finally, the appendChild method adds the new element to the page.

The DeleteNode Function

The Delete a Node button will simply delete the last node that has been added. The DeleteNode function finds the object for the span and removes its last child node:

```
function DeleteNode() {
   if (!document.getElementById) return;
   s=document.getElementById("addhere");
   s.removeChild(s.lastChild);
}
```

Putting It All Together

7

You can now combine the functions and HTML you have created into a single HTML document to create the complete example. Listing 7.2 shows the complete HTML document.

LISTING 7.2   The Complete Example to Add and Remove Nodes

```
<html>
<head>
<title>Adding and Removing Nodes</title>
<script language="JavaScript">
function AddNode(tag) {
   if (!document.getElementById) return;
   element = document.createElement(tag);
   if (tag != "HR") {
      txt = document.form1.newtext.value;
      element.innerHTML=txt;
   }
   s=document.getElementById("addhere");
   s.appendChild(element);
}
function DeleteNode() {
   if (!document.getElementById) return;
   s=document.getElementById("addhere");
   s.removeChild(s.lastChild);
}
</script>
</head>
<body>
<h1>Adding and Removing Nodes</h1>
<p>Enter some text and use the buttons below to add
or remove nodes from this page's DOM hierarchy.</p>
<span ID="addhere">
</span>
<form name="form1" ID="form1">
<input type="text" name="newtext" size="70"><br>
<input type="button" value="Add Paragraph"
   onClick="AddNode('P');">
<input type="button" value="Add Heading"
   onClick="AddNode('H3');">
<input type="button" value="Add Line"
   onClick="AddNode('HR');">
<input type="button" value="Delete a Node"
   onClick="DeleteNode();">
</form>
</body>
</html>
```

In this listing, the `<script>` section defines the `AddNode` and `DeleteNode` function. The `<span>` tag provides a place for the added content, and the `<form>` section creates the form that allows you to change the document.

Once you load this document into a browser, you can add or remove nodes using the form. Figure 7.2 shows Internet Explorer's display of the example after several nodes have been added.

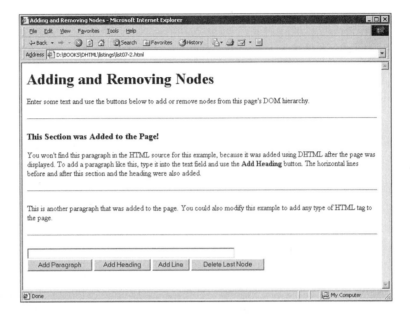

FIGURE 7.2

The document with several added nodes.

Summary

In this hour, you've started to learn some of the truly powerful things you can do with DHTML: adding elements to a page, replacing them, moving, or removing them. This allows you to create dynamic pages that can change in any way you choose.

In the next hour, you'll learn more about event handlers and how they can be used with DHTML.

Q&A

Q. Which attributes of HTML tags can I change using DHTML?

A. In theory, any of them. However, browsers might not support all attributes, so you should test with several browsers.

Q. Do I have to use a span to create an area to add or remove nodes?

A. No, not at all. You can use any object on the page that can have child objects, including the body of the page itself.

Q. Is there a way to add and delete nodes that will work with version 4.0 browsers?

A. No. You can sometimes do similar things using layers, but the flexible DHTML features of the W3C DOM aren't available in older browsers.

7

Quiz

Test your knowledge of the material covered in this hour by answering the following questions.

Questions

1. Which method should you use to create a new paragraph?
   a. `document.createTextNode`
   b. `document.createElement`
   c. `document.createNew`

2. Which method adds a new node as the last child of an existing node?
   a. `appendChild`
   b. `appendNode`
   c. `insertBefore`

3. Which of the following is the correct command to get the SRC attribute of an image stored in the object image1?
   a. `x = image1.SRC`
   b. `x = image1.getAttribute("src");`
   c. `x = getAttribute("src",image1);`

Answers

1. b. To create a new paragraph, use `document.createElement`.
2. a. The `appendChild` method adds a new node as the last child of an existing node.
3. b. The correct command is `image1.getAttribute("src");`

Exercises

If you'd like more practice using the DHTML techniques you learned in this hour, try the following exercises:

- In Listing 7.2, try modifying the Delete Node button to delete the first added node instead of the last one.

- Add a new button labeled Add Line Break to the form in Listing 7.2, and make it add a <br> tag to the page.

HOUR **8**

Responding to Events

You've nearly reached the end of Part II. In the last seven hours, you've learned much of what you need to know to get started with DHTML. As a final subject before you move on to other topics, this hour deals with events.

In this hour, you'll review the available event handlers and how they can be useful in your dynamic pages. You'll also create an example that uses DHTML to log events as they happen.

This hour covers the following topics:

- The basics of event handlers
- Using the event object to find out about an event
- Using Dynamic event handlers
- Using Mouse events
- Using Keyboard events
- Using the onLoad event
- Using events with forms

Understanding Event Handlers

You've already used event handlers in many of the scripts in this book. An event handler is used to detect when an event (such as the user clicking the mouse) occurs for an object (such as a link or image.) Here is the basic HTML for an event handler:

```
<body onLoad="StartHere();">
```

This example is an HTML <body> tag, with an onLoad event defined with an event handler. This particular event occurs when the document first loads. When the event is detected, the browser calls the StartHere function. While functions are useful for event handlers, you can also include one or more JavaScript statements directly in the event handler, separated by semicolons.

> Because the event handler attribute is enclosed in double quotation marks, you can't use double quotation marks (") in your JavaScript statements here. However, you can use single quotation marks (').

Using the event Object

When an event occurs, you might need to know more about the event—for example, for a keyboard event, you need to know which key was pressed. JavaScript includes an event object that provides this information.

To use the event object, you can pass it on to your event handler function. For example, this statement defines an onKeyPress event that passes the event object to a function:

```
<body onKeyPress="getkey(event);">
```

You can then define your function to accept the event as a parameter:

```
function getkey(e) {
...
}
```

Unfortunately, while both Internet Explorer and Netscape support the event object, they support different properties. One property that is the same in both browsers is event.type, the type of event. This is simply the name of the event, such as mouseover for an onMouseOver event, and keypress for an onKeyPress event. The following sections list some additional useful properties for each browser.

8

The workshop section of this hour demonstrates how to deal with browser differences when using these properties. The W3C DOM Level 2 standard defines a browser-independent way of detecting events, but it is not yet well-supported.

Internet Explorer event Properties

The following are some of the commonly-used properties of the event object for Internet Explorer 4.0 and later:

- event.button: The mouse button that was pressed. This value is 1 for the left button and usually 2 for the right button.
- event.clientX: The x-coordinate (column, in pixels) where the event occurred.
- event.clientY: The y-coordinate (row, in pixels) where the event occurred.
- event.altkey: A flag that indicates whether the ALT key was pressed during the event.
- event.ctrlkey: Indicates whether the CTRL key was pressed.
- event.shiftkey: Indicates whether the SHIFT key was pressed.
- event.keyCode: The key code (in Unicode) for the key that was pressed.
- event.srcElement: The object where the element occurred.

Netscape event Properties

The following are some of the commonly-used properties of the event object for Netscape 4.0 and later:

- event.modifiers: Indicates which modifier keys (SHIFT, CTRL, ALT, etc.) were held down during the event. This value is an integer that combines binary values representing the different keys.
- event.pageX: The x-coordinate of the event within the Web page.
- event.pageY: The y-coordinate of the event within the Web page.
- event.which: The keycode for keyboard events (in Unicode), or the button that was pressed for mouse events (1 for the left button, 3 for the right).
- event.target: The object where the element occurred.

The `event.pageX` and `event.pageY` properties are based on the top-left corner of the element where the event occurred, not always the exact position of the mouse pointer.

Dynamic Event Handlers

Event handlers are stored as objects in the DOM, corresponding with the objects for which they handle events. Rather than specifying an event handler as an HTML attribute, you can assign the event handler dynamically using JavaScript.

This technique is useful if you wish to change an event handler, or activate or deactivate one. To change an event handler, you specify the property for the object with the same name as the event handler. For example, this statement makes the function `HandleKeys` the event handler for `onKeyPress` events within the document:

```
document.onkeypress = HandleKeys;
```

For this to work, you must separately define the `HandleKeys` function using the `function` keyword.

Using Mouse Events

A number of the available events deal with the mouse. Your scripts can detect when the mouse pointer moves, and when a mouse button is clicked or released.

Remember that different browsers support events differently, and some events aren't detected in all browsers. Be sure to test any event handler you create in the latest browsers.

Using `onMouseOver` and `onMouseOut` Events

One of the common mouse event handlers used is `onMouseOver`. This event is triggered when the mouse pointer moves over an object within the browser window.

Traditionally, `onMouseOver` worked only with links and images. However, in the new DOM-based browsers, this event can be detected for any object in the HTML document: paragraphs, headings, list items, and so on.

The opposite handler, `onMouseOut`, is triggered when the mouse pointer moves out of range of an object it previously entered. This is useful for undoing whatever action you performed on the `onMouseOver` event.

You used the onMouseOver and onMouseOut event handlers in Hour 4, "Creating a Simple DHTML Example." You will use them again later in this book, beginning in Part IV, "Dynamic HTML in Action."

Using the onMouseMove Event

The onMouseMove event occurs any time the mouse pointer moves. As you might imagine, this happens quite often—the event can trigger hundreds of times as the mouse pointer moves across a page.

Because of the large number of generated events, browsers don't support the onMouseMove event by default. To enable it for a page, you need to use *event capturing*. This is similar to the dynamic events technique you learned earlier in this hour, but requires an extra step for Netscape browsers.

The basic syntax to support this event, for both browsers, is to set a function as the onMouseMove handler for the document, or another object. For example, this statement sets the onMouseMove handler for the document to a function called MoveHere, which must be defined in the same page:

```
document.onMouseMove=MoveHere;
```

Additionally, Netscape requires that you specifically enable the event using the document.captureEvents method:

```
document.captureEvents(Event.MOUSEMOVE);
```

In Hour 22, "Creating Complex Animations," you'll create an example that captures the onMouseMove event in both Netscape and Internet Explorer.

Detecting Mouse Clicks

Your scripts can also detect clicks of the mouse on a particular object. The basic handler for this is onClick. In earlier browsers, this event handler only worked with clickable items—links, buttons, and images—but in the DOM-compliant browsers, it works on any object.

A mouse click really consists of two actions: the button going down, and then coming back up. You can detect these two events separately using the onMouseDown and onMouseUp event handlers. You can also detect double-clicks using the onDblClick event handler.

When a mouse button event occurs, you can use the properties of the event object to determine which button was clicked. As mentioned earlier in this hour, this depends on the browser in use:

- For Netscape, the event.which property indicates the button clicked, 1 for the left button and 3 for the right.

- For Internet Explorer, the event.button property indicates the button clicked, 1 for the left button and 2 for the right. This only works on the onMouseDown and onMouseUp events, not on onClick.

> Internet Explorer displays a context menu when the right button is clicked, and thus the onClick event only occurs when the left button is clicked. Internet Explorer 4 doesn't generate any events for the right button, while Internet Explorer 5 and later generate onMouseDown and onMouseUp events.

To support both browsers, you'll need to use the if statement when checking buttons. Rather than checking for a particular browser, it's better to detect the event properties directly. For example, here is the shell of an if statement to handle buttons:

```
if (event.button) button=event.button;
   else button=event.which;
```

This checks for the existence of the event.button property, indicating that the browser follows Internet Explorer's model. If this property doesn't exist, it uses the Netscape model's event.which instead.

> The example in the Workshop section of this hour uses this technique to detect mouse buttons browser-independently.

Using Keyboard Events

You can also detect keys being pressed using event handlers. The basic event handler for this is onKeyPress. You can attach this handler to the <body> tag to detect any keypress, or to form elements, such as text fields, to detect keys pressed within a field.

As with mouse clicks, a keypress really consists of two events: the key coming down, and going back up. You can detect these separately using the onKeyDown and onKeyUp event handlers.

You can use the properties of the event object to determine the key that was pressed. As with mouse events, how you do this depends on the browser:

- For Netscape, the event.which property stores the key code for the key pressed.
- For Internet Explorer, the event.keyCode property stores the key code for the key pressed.

In both cases, the key code is a numeric value representing the key. You can convert this to a character using the String.fromCharCode method. For example, this code detects a key, determines the key code browser-independently, and displays the character for the key:

```
if (event.keyCode) key=event.keyCode;
  else key=event.which;
alert("Key pressed: " + String.fromCharCode(key));
```

 The key codes used in JavaScript are in the Unicode format. This is similar to the old ASCII code, but supports 32-bit codes to handle international characters.

The onLoad Event

The onLoad event handler is one you will use often. If you specify an onLoad event handler for the <body> tag of a document, the script you specify is called as soon as the HTML document is fully loaded by the browser. This is useful for initializing variables in a script or starting an animation.

You can also specify an onLoad event for an <img> tag. In this case, the event handler will be called when the image finishes loading.

Form Events

Last but not least, there are a few events that are only used on form elements—text fields, buttons, and so on. These include the following:

- onFocus occurs when an element gets focus (when it is clicked on, typically moving the cursor there). This can be used on the Window object as well as form elements.
- onBlur occurs when an element loses focus.
- onChange occurs when a text field or <select> drop-down value is changed.

- onSubmit occurs when a submit button for the form is pressed. This handler is attached to the <form> tag itself. If the event handler returns false, the form is not submitted.

- onReset occurs when a reset button for the form is pressed. This handler is attached to the <form> tag itself. If the event handler returns false, the form fields are not reset.

Workshop: Displaying an Event Log

Using the event handlers you learned this hour and a bit of DHTML, you can create a page that demonstrates events by displaying event names as they happen. Listing 8.1 shows the complete HTML document for this example.

 You can download the HTML file for this example from this book's Web site: http://www.starlingtech.com/dhtml/.

LISTING 8.1   The Event Logging Example

```
<html>
<head>
<title>Event Handlers Example</title>
<script language="JavaScript">
function DisplayEvent(e) {
   span=document.getElementById("addhere");
   logentry= e.type;
   if (e.type=="keypress") {
      if (e.keyCode) keycode=e.keyCode;
       else keycode=e.which;
      key=String.fromCharCode(keycode);
      logentry += " key=" + key;
   }
   if (e.type=="mousedown"||e.type=="mouseup"||e.type=="click") {
      if (e.button) button=e.button;
        else button=e.which;
      logentry += " button=" + button;
   }
   txt=document.createTextNode(logentry);
   span.appendChild(txt);
   span.appendChild(document.createElement("BR"));
}
</script>
</head>
<body onKeyPress="DisplayEvent(event);">
```

LISTING 8.1   continued

```
<h1>Event Handlers Example</h1>
<p>Move the mouse in and out of the heading below,
or click on it. The events that occur will be listed below.</p>
<h1 style="color:blue" align="center"
 onMouseOver="DisplayEvent(event);"
 onMouseOut="DisplayEvent(event);"
 onClick="DisplayEvent(event);"
 onMouseUp="DisplayEvent(event);"
 onMouseDown="DisplayEvent(event);"
>
Generate Events Here
</h1>
<b>Event Log:</b><hr>
<span ID="addhere"></span>
</body>
</html>
```

Here is a breakdown of how this example works:

- The DisplayEvent function displays each event. It displays the event type, and uses the techniques you learned earlier in this chapter to determine the key or mouse button that was pressed. DHTML is used to insert the log entries into the document.

- The <body> tag assigns the onKeyPress event handler for the entire document to the DisplayEvent function.

- The body begins with a <h1> header with a large number of defined event handlers, all set to call the DisplayEvent function when events occur.

- The body ends with an empty <span> tag with the ID attribute addhere. This is where the log entries will be added.

To test the example, load it into a browser and try generating events by moving the mouse over the blue text, clicking on it, and pressing keys. Figure 8.1 shows Netscape's display of this example after a few events have occurred.

Notice that the event detection isn't perfect in current browsers—for example, in Internet Explorer, the button for onClick events is undefined, but the onMouseDown and onMouseUp events correctly specify the button.

FIGURE 8.1

Netscape 6 displays the event logging example.

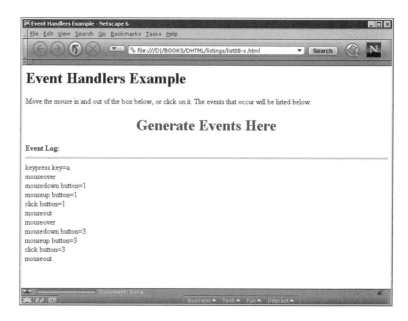

Summary

In this hour, you've reviewed the events that are available to your DHTML scripts. You've learned how to obtain information about events, and used DHTML to create an event log.

Congratulations—you've reached the end of Part II! In Part III, you'll learn about style sheets: how to create and use them effectively, and how to control them dynamically. You'll begin in the next hour by learning the fundamentals of style sheets.

Q&A

Q. Doesn't the W3C DOM do something about the differences between Internet Explorer and Netscape event handlers?

A. Yes, DOM Level 2 defines a standard way of capturing and referring to events. This is currently supported by Netscape 6.

Q. If I can specify an `onMouseOver` event handler for any object, are some objects better choices than others?

A. Yes. If you can use a link as the target for the event handler, you have the best chance of supporting older browsers.

Q. When I use an onSubmit event handler, why is the form no longer submitted?

A. You need to make sure you include `return true` as the last statement in the event handler. Otherwise the submission is cancelled.

Quiz

Test your knowledge of the material covered in this hour by answering the following questions.

Questions

1. Which event handler is triggered when you move the mouse into the area an image uses?

    a. `onMouseMove`

    b. `onMouseOver`

    c. `onMouseEnter`

2. Which of the following indicates which mouse button was clicked in Internet Explorer?

    a. `event.which`

    b. `event.onClick`

    c. `event.button`

3. Which is the correct statement to display the key that was pressed as a character, presuming you have stored the keycode in the `key` variable?

    a. `alert(String.fromCharCode(key));`

    b. `alert(key.fromCharCode());`

    c. `alert(toCharCode(key));`

Answers

1. b. The `onMouseOver` event occurs when the mouse pointer moves into the area used by an image (or any other object).

2. c. The `event.button` property indicates the mouse button used in Internet Explorer. The `event.which` property performs the same function in Netscape.

3. a. The correct statement is `alert(String.fromCharCode(key));`.

Exercises

If you'd like to practice using event handlers further before you move on, try the following exercises:

- Modify Listing 8.1 to display the mouse button pressed as "left" or "right" rather than a number. Keep in mind that different browsers might use different values for the right button.

- Add onKeyDown and onKeyUp event handlers to the <body> tag in Listing 8.1, and make any changes needed to the script to display these events in the log.

PART III

Working with Style Sheets

Hour

HOUR 9

Introducing Style Sheets

Welcome to Part III! For the next four hours, you will focus on style sheets. The CSS (Cascading Style Sheets) standard defines ways to control a document's style—colors, fonts, margins, and so on—while staying within the bounds of the HTML standard.

In this hour, you'll learn the basics of style sheets—the rules they use, the formats you can use to create style sheets, and some of the basic style properties you can use in your documents.

This hour covers the following topics:

- Why style sheets are useful
- How style sheets fit in with HTML documents
- Using external style sheets
- Basic properties for style sheets
- Creating a simple style sheet

Why Style Sheets?

If you've created a Web page or two, you've undoubtedly noticed that it isn't always easy to give your document the exact appearance you desire using HTML—in fact, even when you've created the perfect page, chances are it will display differently for users with certain browsers or computers.

Content versus Presentation

You can't precisely control the layout, the margins, fonts, colors, or spacing with HTML. There's a reason for this—HTML is a language meant to specify the *content* of a document, not the *presentation*.

If you look at the majority of HTML tags, you'll notice that they describe part of the content of a document—a paragraph, a list, a heading, or a link to another page. They don't specify exactly how to present these items.

When you specify an <h1> heading, you just know it will be displayed in large text, probably larger than that of an <h2> heading. You don't know the exact font or size that will be used.

This sounds like a deficiency of HTML, but it's actually a good thing. The fact that HTML doesn't focus on font sizes or colors means that a single HTML document can be displayed on vastly different browsers—ranging from high-end computers to TV-based systems to tiny screens on mobile phones.

There are even some highly specialized browsers—for example, browsers for the blind can read an HTML document using a speech synthesizer, typically using different voice styles to speak headings, paragraphs, and other components. The HTML language's emphasis on content makes this possible.

 HTML's structure also makes it easy for search engines to find headings and other important text in a document, without having to make judgments based on font sizes.

The Traditional Approach

While HTML's emphasis on content is noble, it's not very attractive to the graphic designers and marketing folks who have moved to the Web. It's hard to understand why you can easily create a flyer or magazine ad in the exact style you want, but your Web page has to resemble all of the others.

This has led to a variety of techniques for making HTML into a presentation language. Some, like the `<font>` tag, were introduced by browser makers. Designers focused on style have even gone overboard at times—for example, making the entire Web page one huge graphic image in order to use the fonts and layout they prefer.

Adding Style to Substance

Fortunately, before things like this got too far out of control, the W3C decided that there should be a standard way of adding style to HTML. Rather than change the HTML language, they created a way of defining styles that gives you full control over presentation without compromising HTML's ability to focus on content.

This effort resulted in the CSS (Cascading Style Sheets) standard. The version 4.0 browsers began to support style sheets, and the support in newer browsers is even more complete. Using CSS styles, you can create a stylish document that will work in any standards-compliant browser.

> Another important aspect of style sheets is that they are separate from HTML and optional. Users can configure their browsers to ignore your style sheet if they wish, and can even specify their own style sheet for all of the HTML documents they view.

Integrating Style Sheets with HTML

You can add style sheets to your HTML documents in several ways:

- Using *inline styles* within HTML tags
- Using the `<style>` tag within a document
- Creating an external style sheet

The following sections explain each of these options.

Inline Styles

One simple way to use CSS styles is to use the STYLE attribute in one or more individual HTML tags. For example, the following HTML defines a heading that is blue in color:

```
<h1 STYLE="color:blue;">This is a blue heading.</h1>
```

You've seen this method earlier in this book, and it's very easy to use. However, this method doesn't give you the full advantage of style sheets—using the same style for a number of different elements.

The `<style>` Tag

A more sophisticated way of using style sheets is by using the `<style>` tag within the `<head>` section of your HTML document. You can enclose a block of *rules* between the `<style>` and `</style>` tags, as in this example:

```
<style TYPE="text/css">
H1,H2 {color: blue; text-align: center}
P {color: red}
</style>
```

This style sheet includes two rules. The first sets headings using the `<h1>` and `<h2>` tags to be centered and blue in color, and the second sets paragraphs using the `<p>` tag to be red.

The `TYPE="text/css"` attribute in the `<style>` tag tells the browser to use the CSS standard for styles. Netscape 4.0 supported an alternate type known as JavaScript Style Sheets, but these were proprietary and are not supported in Netscape 6.

> To avoid errors in older browsers, you might wish to use HTML comment tags (`<!--` and `-->`) to enclose the contents of your `<style>` tags.

Creating Rules

Rules within a style sheet use a set syntax. Consider this simple rule from the earlier example:

```
P {color: red}
```

Each rule includes three components:

- A *selector* (`P` in the example) describing which HTML tags will be effected.
- One or more *property names* (`color` in the example).
- A *value* for each property name (`red` in the example).

Using Classes

Rather than specifying an HTML tag in a CSS rule, you can also create a *class* and specify rules for the class. This allows you to create styles that can apply to several different HTML tags, or only to certain tags.

For example, you might want all of the text within your page's menu to have a specific style. You can create a `.menu` class for this purpose in the style sheet:

```
.menu {color: blue}
```

The period at the beginning of .menu tells the browser that this is a class selector rather than a specific HTML tag. Anything with the specified class will be displayed as blue. To assign the class, include the CLASS attribute in one or more HTML tags:

```
<p CLASS="menu">
```

For more complex styles, you can also specify a rule for a class and a specific HTML tag:

```
h1.menu {color: black}
```

This rule sets the color to black for any <h1> tag that has been assigned the menu class.

Using IDs

You can also assign a style sheet rule to a specific ID. You've seen the ID tag already, used to assign a unique identifier to a particular HTML element. The following rule sets the style for a specific ID:

```
#head1 {color: red}
```

This sets the color to red for the HTML tag with the ID head1. This might be assigned to a heading tag like this:

```
<h1 ID="head1">No Time to Lose</h1>
```

> You should only assign each unique ID to one HTML tag. If you want to assign a style to two or more tags, use a class instead.

Using Units

Style sheet properties support a wide variety of units, or types of values you can specify. Most properties that accept a numeric value support the following types of units:

- px: Pixels (for example, 15px). Pixels are the smallest addressable units on a computer screen or other device. In some devices with non-typical resolutions (for example, handheld computers) the browser might rescale this value to fit the device.

- pt: Points (for example, 10pt). Points are a standard unit for font size. The size of text of a specified point size varies depending on the monitor resolution. Points are equal to 1/72 of an inch.

- ex: Approximate height of the letter x in the current font (for example, 1.2ex).

- em: Approximate width of the letter m in the current font (for example, 1.5em). This is usually equal to the font-size property for the current element.
- %: Percentage of the containing object's value (for example, 150%).

Which unit you choose to use is generally a matter of convenience. Point sizes are commonly used for fonts, pixel units for the size and position of layers or other objects, and so on.

> Whenever possible, use percentages, em, or ex sizes. This will make values relative to the current font, and will scale if the user has specified their own font.

Some style properties accept a URL as their value. This uses a special syntax. For example, this rule sets the URL for the background-image property:

```
body {background-image: url(path/background.gif);}
```

External Style Sheets

While a simple style sheet is easy to include within an HTML document using the <style> tag, you might find it useful to create an *external style sheet* instead. This allows you to separate all of the styles into their own file. More importantly, you can use the same external style sheet for several pages or even an entire site.

To use an external style sheet, type your list of style rules into a text file, without the opening and closing <style> tags. Save the document with the css extension, for example styles.css.

Once you have an external style sheet, you need to link it to one or more HTML documents. You can use the <link> tag within the <head> section of your document to do this:

```
<link rel="stylesheet" href="styles.css">
```

> You can link more than one external style sheet to a document, and the styles will be combined. You can also use inline styles or the <style> tag in the document to override styles in an external style sheet.

Cascading Styles

The "C" in CSS stands for *cascading*, and this is the method browsers use to combine styles you have specified. For example, suppose you use the following <body> tag to specify a style:

```
<body STYLE="color: red;">
```

The style you specify here is inherited by all of the children of the <body> tag—the entire document. But if you specify a style for one of these elements, it overrides the inherited style.

In a complex situation, the browser might need to combine styles from one or more external style sheets, styles in a <style> block, and inline styles, along with inherited styles. This is done using a set of rules for cascading styles.

You can ensure that a rule you specify comes out on top in the cascade process by specifying the !important attribute. This will ensure that the style overrides others that would control the style of the same elements. For example, the following is an important rule to set the color of paragraph text:

```
P {color: black !important}
```

Basic Style Properties

There are a wide variety of properties you can use in defining styles. Some, such as text colors, can be used for any tags, while others are specific to certain types of HTML tags. The following sections describe some of the most useful properties.

You'll learn more of the available style properties in Hour 10, "Using Style Sheet Properties."

Aligning Text

One of the most useful features of style sheets is the capability to change the spacing and alignment of text. Most of these features aren't available using standard HTML. The following properties are available:

- letter-spacing—Specifies the spacing between letters.
- vertical-align—Allows you to move the element up or down to align with other elements on the same line.

- `text-align`—Specifies the justification of text. This can be `left`, `right`, `center`, or `justify`.

- `text-indent`—Allows you to specify the amount of indentation for paragraphs and other elements.

- `line-height`—Allows you to specify the distance between the top of one line of text and the top of the next.

Defining Colors and Background Images

You can also use style sheets to gain more control over the colors and background images used on your Web page. CSS includes the following properties for this purpose:

- `color`—Specifies the text color of an element. This is useful for emphasizing text or for using a specific color scheme for the document.

- `background-color`—Specifies the background color of an element. By setting this value, you can make paragraphs, table cells, and other elements with unique background colors. The value can be a color or `transparent` for a see-through background.

- `background-image`—Specifies the URL of an image to be used as the background for the element, or `none` for no background image. If you specify a background image, you should also specify a matching background color in case the image can't be accessed.

- `background-repeat`—Specifies whether the background image is repeated (tiled). The image can be repeated horizontally, vertically, or both. The value can be `repeat`, `repeat-x` for horizontal tiling, `repeat-y` for vertical tiling, or `no-repeat`.

- `background-attachment`—Controls whether the background image scrolls when you scroll through the document. `fixed` means that the background image stays still while the document scrolls; `scroll` means the image scrolls with the document, as with background images on normal Web documents.

- `background-position`—Allows you to offset the position of the background image. You can specify horizontal and vertical values, separated by a space. The keywords `top`, `center`, and `bottom` for vertical positioning and `left`, `center`, and `right` for horizontal positioning are also supported.

- `background`—This provides a quick way to set all of the background elements in this list. You can specify all of the attributes in a single `background` rule.

You can specify color values using named colors, such as `red` and `blue`, or RGB combinations, such as `#12AA05`. These use three hexadecimal numbers to represent the decimal values 0-255 for red, green, and blue color levels.

Positioning Objects

In Hour 6, "Creating Positionable Elements (Layers)," you learned how to use positioning properties to control the position of layers. These same properties can be used in style sheets to specify the position of any object:

- `position` specifies how the element will be positioned. This property can have one of three values: `static` (default) defines items that are laid out along with the rest of the HTML document, and cannot be moved; `absolute` allows you to position the item by specifying coordinates; and `relative` defines an item that is offset a certain amount from the `static` position, where it was laid out by the browser.

- `left` is the horizontal position of the item. For absolute positioning, coordinates start at the left side of the browser window; for relative positioning, they start at the object's original position.

- `top` is the vertical position of the object. This is relative to the top of the browser window for absolute positioning, and relative to the original position for relative positioning.

- `right` and `bottom` allow you to position objects by lining up the right-hand or bottom edges rather than the left and top.

- `width` and `height` specify the item's width and height. For objects containing text, the text will wrap at the specified width.

- `z-index` specifies how the object overlaps with other objects. Indexes are assigned in order, so layers defined later in the HTML document are "on top" of previous layers. You can change this value to bring an object to the top.

- `display` specifies whether the item is visible in the browser. The page layout shifts to account for changes to this property. Values include `none` to hide the object, `block` for a block element, `inline` for an inline element, and `list-item` for a member of a list.

- `visibility` controls the item's visibility, without affecting the page layout. Values include `visible` (default), `hidden`, and `inherit`. A value of `inherit` uses the visibility setting of a parent object.

Review Hour 6 for more details about the `display` property, and an example of using some of these positioning properties in a script.

9

Workshop: Creating a Simple Style Sheet

Back in Hours 2–4, you created a simple Web document for a fictional company, Figby Industries. You can use style sheets to control the alignment, text styles, and colors of the document in a browser-independent way.

Listing 9.1 shows the HTML document with an included style sheet.

LISTING 9.1   A Simple Web Document with a Style Sheet

```
<html>
<head>
<title>Figby Industries, Inc.</title>
<style type="text/css">
BODY {color: yellow;}
P {color: black;}
H1 {color: black;
    text-align: center;}
 .menu {font-weight: bold;}
#bottomtext {font-style: italic;
             text-align: center;}
</style>
</head>
<body>
<div align="center">
<img src="logo.gif" width="486" height="180" border="0" alt="">
</div><br>
<h1>Welcome to Figby Industries!</h1>
<p>Welcome! This is the home page of Figby Industries,
your source for all sorts of imaginary products. Follow the links
below to learn more about our company and our products.
</p>
<table border="1" align="center">
<tr class="menu">
   <td width="20%"><a href="products.html">Products</a></td>
   <td width="20%"><a href="sales.html">Sales</a></td>
   <td width="20%"><a href="service.html">Service</a></td>
   <td width="20%"><a href="staff.html">Staff</a></td>
   <td width="20%"><a href="jobs.html">Employment</a></td>
</tr>
</table>
<p ID="bottomtext">Any truly legitimate company would have
 much more text in this part of the page than we have.</p>
</body>
</html>
```

This example requires a graphic, `logo.gif`, which you can download from this book's Web site: `http://www.starlingtech.com/dhtml/`. You can also download the HTML document there.

This document uses the following styles, defined in the `<style>` block:

- The `<body>` tag is set to have yellow text. However, notice that no yellow text appears on the page. This is because each item has its color set by another style.

- Paragraphs are set to be displayed in black.

- `<h1>` headings are set to be displayed in black and centered.

- A class, `.menu`, is set to have bold text. This is used in the `<tr>` tag of the table, and is inherited by all of the link text in the `<td>` tags.

- An ID, `#bottomtext`, is set to have italic, centered text. This ID is assigned to the final paragraph in the body of the page.

To test this example, load it into a browser. It should work in Netscape 4.0 or later and Internet Explorer 4.0 and later. Figure 9.1 shows Internet Explorer's display of the styled document.

FIGURE 9.1

The styled document as displayed by Internet Explorer.

Summary

In this hour, you've learned the basics of style sheets—why they're important, how to combine them with HTML documents, and some of the properties you can use in a style sheet. You've also created a simple style sheet within an HTML document.

In the next hour, you'll learn more of the specific properties you can use in style sheets. These will give you control of fonts, margins, borders, links, and other aspects of your Web pages.

Q&A

Q. I just want to set a few font sizes and colors. Can't I use the `<font>` tag rather than messing with style sheets?

A. Yes, but remember that the `<font>` tag is deprecated in HTML 4.0, and might not work with future browsers. There are also advantages to using style sheets now—for example, if you want to change the font or color for all of the headings in your site, you can change a single line in the style sheet rather than changing hundreds of `<font>` tags.

Q. How can I set my browser to ignore style sheets on the sites I visit, or format them using my own style sheet?

A. In Internet Explorer 5.0 and later, you can change these options by selecting Tools, Internet Options from the menu, then clicking the Accessibility button. In Netscape 6, select View, Use Stylesheet from the menu.

Q. Once I have set up a style sheet, can I change it later using JavaScript?

A. Yes—the DOM includes a full set of objects for working with dynamic styles. You'll learn about these in Hour 11, "Controlling Styles with JavaScript."

Quiz

Test your knowledge of the material covered in this hour by answering the following questions.

Questions

1. Which of the following is an example of an inline style?

   a. `<link rel="stylesheet" href="styles.css">`

   b. `<p STYLE="color: blue;">`

   c. `P {color: blue;}`

2. Which of the following HTML tags correctly specifies a class called code?

    a. `<p STYLE=".code">`

    b. `<p CLASS="code">`

    c. `<p STYLE="class: code;">`

3. Suppose you want to create a sidebar on the right-hand side of your Web page. This sidebar will contain paragraphs and links, and you want them all to use a certain font size. What would be the best place to assign styles?

    a. To each `<p>` and `<a>` tag in the sidebar section

    b. To each ID attribute used in the sidebar section

    c. To a class assigned to each tag in the sidebar section

Answers

1. b. `<p STYLE="color: blue;">` is an example of an inline style.

2. b. The correct statement is: `<p CLASS="code">`

3. c. The best way to assign styles would be to create a class, assign styles to the class, and assign the elements within the sidebar to that class.

Exercises

If you'd like to gain a bit of experience with style sheets before you move on, try the following exercises:

- Add a new paragraph at the end of Listing 9.1, and assign it the menu class. Before you display the document, try to figure out in what color and style the new paragraph will be displayed.

- If you add a bulleted list using the `<ul>` and `<li>` tags to Listing 9.1, in what color will it be displayed? Add a list to the document and display it in a browser to see if you are correct.

HOUR **10**

Using Style Sheet Properties

You have now learned the basics of how style sheets work, and how you can use them to control colors, text formatting, and other aspects of your Web pages.

In this hour, you'll delve deeper into the list of available properties and values you can use in style sheets. In particular, you'll learn how to set text alignment, fonts, margins, and borders.

This hour covers the following topics:

- Creating styled text
- Using fonts in CSS
- Setting margin and border properties
- Using CSS for centering
- Setting link, mouse pointer, and list styles
- Creating and using an external style sheet

Creating Styled Text

One of the benefits of style sheets is that you can apply some of the same techniques used in desktop publishing to the Web—aligned text, precise spacing and height, and other effects. These text effects are widely supported by the most recent browsers.

Alignment

The CSS specification includes two properties for alignment of text:

- `text-align` —specifies the horizontal alignment of text. Values include `left`, `right`, `center`, and `justify` for right-justified text. The `justify` value is not supported completely by the version 4.0 browsers, but is supported by Netscape 6 and Internet Explorer 5.

- `vertical-align` —specifies the vertical alignment of text relative to other text. Values include `baseline`, `sub` for subscript, `super` for superscript, `top`, `text-top`, `middle`, `text-bottom`, and `bottom`.

Spacing

CSS includes a number of properties that set the spacing and indentation of text:

- `word-spacing`—sets the spacing between words. Values include `normal` (default) or a length, typically in pixels, `em` or `ex` units.

- `letter-spacing`—specifies the spacing between letters. The value can be `normal` (default) or a length in pixels, `em`, or `ex` units. This value is also referred to as *kerning*.

- `text-indent`—specifies the amount of indentation for a block of text. This value can be specified as an exact number in pixels or other units, or a percentage. You can use this property to indent the first line of a paragraph.

- `white-space`—normally, if you include two or more blank spaces, the browser displays only one space. Set this property to `pre` to display the spaces exactly as you have included them, or `nowrap` to prevent word wrap. The default value is `normal`. Currently, Internet Explorer 5.5 does not support the `pre` value, but Netscape 6 does.

- `line-height`—Specifies the height of text lines. Values include `normal` (default), a specified number of pixels, `em`, or `ex` units, or a percentage. This is known as the *leading* value.

Capitalization

The text-transform property allows you to force text to be uppercase or lowercase. Values include none (default), capitalize (first letter is uppercase), uppercase, and lowercase. This property is supported by Netscape and Internet Explorer starting with the 4.0 versions.

Decorating Text

The text-decoration property allows you to set underlining and other effects. Values include none (default), underline, overline, line-through, and blink. Like the <blink> tag, the blink value is supported only by Netscape 4.0.

Working with Fonts

10

The <font> tag first appeared in Netscape 2.0, and allows you to specify a font for text. While a welcome addition, it's deprecated in HTML 4.0—more importantly, it's inconvenient to include separate <font> tags each time you wish to change fonts.

CSS allows you to specify fonts in a similar way, but you can set fonts for certain tags or for the entire document without multiple rules. Several different properties allow you to choose a font, set its size, and add attributes such as bold and italics.

Choosing a Font

The font-family property allows you to choose a font. You can specify exact font names, but they will only work if the user has the exact font installed. Alternatively, you can specify a generic name, supported by all CSS browsers.

> Hour 12, "Creating Consistent Styles," includes lists of commonly-available fonts for various computer platforms.

To combine the best of both of these options, you can also specify a list of fonts—the browser will use the first one on the list that it can support. If you list a generic font last, the browser will use it if none of your specific choices are available. For example, the following rule sets the font for paragraphs:

```
P {font-family: "Times New Roman", times, serif;}
```

This tag lists a Windows-specific font (Times New Roman), a Macintosh font (Times), and a generic font (serif). The generic fonts available include serif, sans-serif, cursive, fantasy, and monospace. Notice that you should enclose font names that include spaces within quotation marks.

Different browsers might use different fonts to represent the generic fonts. In Netscape 6, in fact, you can choose your own fonts for each of the generic types.

The ultimate in font control is to specify an entire font that will be downloaded. See Hour 19, "Using Dynamic Fonts," for an explanation of this feature.

Setting Font Size

The font-size property controls the size of letters. Its values can be a number, a percentage, or a generic value: small, medium, large, x-small, xx-small, x-large, xx-large. Additionally, you can use the values smaller or larger to set the size of an element relative to its parent element.

If you set a specific numeric size, you can set it to a percentage, a pixel value, or a point value. The following are examples of font size rules:

- P {font-size: 120%;} (percentage value; 120% of normal size)
- P {font-size: 10px;} (value in pixels)
- P {font-size: 12pt;} (value in points)
- P {font-size: 1.2em;} (value in em units; 120% of normal size)

Pixel and point values are typically used to set specific font sizes. A pixel value is more likely to display in the same size on different computers, although this will vary based on monitor resolution.

Using Bold, Italics, and Small Capitals

While you might think of bold and italics as similar ways to emphasize text, they are actually treated as two separate properties in CSS. Here are three properties that affect the appearance of the text:

- `font-style` can be set to `normal` (the default), `italic`, or `oblique` (slanted)

- `font-weight` can be set to `normal` (the default), `bold`, `bolder`, `lighter`, or a numeric weight from 100 to 900 in increments of 100. Whether some of these values are supported could depend on the fonts the user has installed, but you can be sure `normal` or `bold` will always work.

- `font-variant` can be set to `normal` (the default), or `small-caps` to display the text in small capital letters, with slightly larger capitals for uppercase letters.

Setting Margins and Borders

CSS includes a number of properties you can use to set margins and borders. You can use these properties to gain more control over text layout, and to center or indent objects within a Web page.

10

Properties for Margins

The following properties affect margins, borders, and the width and height of elements on the Web page:

- `margin-top`, `margin-bottom`, `margin-left`, `margin-right`—These properties specify the margins of the element. You can specify the margins as an exact number or as a percentage of the page's width. The default value, `auto`, lets the browser set the margins.

- `margin`—Allows you to specify a single value for all four of the margins, or four values separated by spaces for the top, right, bottom, and left values.

- `width`—Specifies the width of an element, such as an image. Can be set to `auto`, a percentage, or a numeric value.

- `height`—Specifies the height of an element. Can be set to `auto`, a percentage, or a numeric value.

- `float`—Allows the text to flow around an element. This is particularly useful with images or tables. Values include `left`, `right`, or `none`. The effect is similar to the `align=left` or `align=right` attributes for the `<img>` tag.

- `clear`—Specifies that the text should stop flowing around a floating image or element. Values include `none`, `left`, `right`, or `both`.

Border Properties

The following properties allow you to set up the border for an element:

- `border-width`—Allows you to specify a single value for the width of the border. You can also specify four values for the top, right, bottom, and left borders, separated by spaces.
- `left-border-width`, `right-border-width`, `bottom-border-width`, `top-border-width`—Allow you to set the four side borders individually.
- `padding`—Specifies the amount of space between the border and the content of the element. This can be one value for all four sides, or four values for top, right, bottom, and left borders, separated by spaces.
- `padding-left`, `padding-right`, `padding-top`, `padding-bottom`—Allow you to set the four padding values individually.
- `border-color`—Specifies the color for the border. You can specify one color value for all four borders, or four values for the top, right, bottom, and left borders.
- `border-style`—Sets the style of the border. Values include `none`, `dotted`, `dashed`, `solid`, `double`, `groove`, `ridge`, `inset`, and `outset`. You can specify one value for all four borders, or four separate values for top, right, bottom, and left borders.

Overflow and Clipping

Sometimes, when you've defined margins or a size for an object, its content will not all fit in the available area. The `overflow` property allows you to specify what happens to the content outside this area:

- `overflow:visible` shows the content outside the box.
- `overflow:hidden` hides the content outside the box.
- `overflow:scroll` displays scroll bars to allow the user to view all of the content.
- `overflow:auto` lets the browser decide how to handle overflow. Scroll bars are usually displayed.

Additionally, you can use the `clip` property to specify a different area for clipping than the default. This property's value specifies four coordinates to form a rectangle. The following example sets the clipping area of paragraphs at ten pixels in from the paragraph's edge on all sides:

```
P {clip:rect (10px, 10px, 10px, 10px); }
```

The four values for the rectangle specify the top, right, bottom, and left values.

Centering with CSS

When Netscape introduced the `<center>` tag, Web designers rejoiced as it created an easy way to center anything, but some objected as it's a tag for defining presentation rather than content. While `<center>` was added to the HTML specification, it's deprecated in HTML 4.0.

You might have noticed that there isn't an obvious replacement for the `<center>` tag in the CSS properties. There are actually two ways to center in CSS:

- For text elements, the `text-align` attribute can be set to `center`.
- For other elements, set the `margin-left` and `margin-right` values both to `auto`.

These methods of centering aren't supported consistently in all but the most recent browsers. One alternative for now is to simply use `<div align="center">` instead of the `<center>` tag.

10

Setting Other Style Attributes

You can also use CSS styles to set the styles for links, to control the mouse pointer's appearance, and to control the appearance of items within lists.

Setting Link Styles

Links are defined with the `<a>` tag, but not all `<a>` tags are links. The CSS standard includes four *pseudo-classes*, or special selectors, that you can use to define styles for links in various states:

- `a:link` defines default styles for links.
- `a:hover` defines styles for a link when the mouse pointer is over it.
- `a:active` defines styles for links when they are being clicked.
- `a:visited` defines styles for links that have been previously visited.

For example, this style sheet makes links blue by default, red when clicked, and highlights them with a yellow background when the mouse pointer hovers over them:

```
<style>
a:link {color: blue;}
a:active {color: red;}
a:hover {color: blue;
     background-color: yellow; }
</style>
```

Using the hover pseudo-class is a great way to create rollover effects without using JavaScript. However, these classes are supported only by Netscape 5.0 and later and Internet Explorer 4.0 and later.

Setting Cursor Styles

The cursor attribute allows you to set the style of the mouse cursor. The following values are available:

- auto is the default setting, and lets the browser change the mouse pointer according to standard user interface rules.
- none hides the mouse pointer.
- default is the default cursor for the operating system, usually an arrow.
- pointer is the pointer for links, usually a hand.
- move is the pointer for moving objects.
- text is a text cursor.
- wait is a waiting cursor, typically a watch or hourglass.
- help is a help cursor, typically a question mark.
- e-resize, w-resize, n-resize, s-resize, se-resize, sw-resize, ne-resize, and nw-resize are various cursors used for resizing objects, depending on the compass direction.

When you set this attribute for an element or class, the cursor will change to the shape you specified when the mouse pointer is over that element. For example, this style sheet changes the pointer to a question mark when it moves over any image:

```
<style>
img {cursor: help;}
</style>
```

The cursor styles are part of the CSS2 specification and are supported by Netscape 6.0 and later and Internet Explorer 4.0 and later.

Setting List Styles

The following style attributes can be applied to lists, such as the <ol> or <ul> tag, to set the style of list items:

- `list-style-type` —Sets the type of marker displayed before the list item. Values include `disc`, `circle`, and `square` for unordered lists, or `decimal`, `lower-roman`, `upper-roman`, `lower-alpha`, and `upper-alpha` for ordered lists.

- `list-style-image`—Specifies the URL of an image to be used as the list item marker. This overrides the `list-style-type` property.

- `list-style-position`—Specifies the position of the marker relative to the text. Values include `inside` to place lower rows of text and the marker at the same column, or `outside` to place all rows of text to the right of the marker.

- `list-style`—Provides a quick way of setting the previous three list properties. Values include the various marker types, a URL for the image, and `inside` or `outside` for positioning.

> The list styles apply to items with the `display` property value `list-item`. Items within HTML lists have this property set by default.

Workshop: Creating a Styled Document

To practice using the style sheet properties you've learned in this hour and the previous hour, you can create a styled document using an external style sheet. This keeps your HTML document short, and also makes it easy to link more than one document to the same style sheet.

> Rather than create style sheets manually, you can use a number of tools to automate the process. You'll find these listed in Appendix A, "Other JavaScript and DHTML Resources."

Creating the Style Sheet

As a first step, you can create a style sheet document that will be used with an HTML document. In practice, you'll probably find it useful to work on the style document and the HTML concurrently until you've created the look you're after.

Listing 10.1 shows the CSS file. To use it, save it as `style.css` or the name of your choice. You will link an HTML document to this style sheet in the next section.

The style sheet and HTML files for this example are available from this book's Web site: http://www.starlingtech.com/dhtml/.

LISTING 10.1   The External Style Sheet

```
body {font-family: Arial, Helvetica, sans-serif;
      font-size: 12pt;}
P {margin-left: 10%;
   margin-right: 10%;
   text-align: justify;
   text-indent: 3%;}
B {color: red;}
I {color: DarkViolet;}
H1 {font-size: 300%;
    text-align: center;
    text-transform: capitalize;}
UL {margin-left: 20%;
    margin-right: 20%;}
LI {margin-top: 10px;}
```

This style sheet sets the following properties:

- The body of the document is set to use a sans-serif font, with a 12-point size. These values will be inherited by all elements in the body unless we specify otherwise.

- Paragraphs using the <p> tag are set to have left and right margins of 10%, right-justified, and indented 3% at the first line.

- Bold text is set to be red in color.

- Italic text is set to be dark violet in color.

- Headings using the <h1> tag are set to be three times the normal size, centered, and capitalized.

- Bulleted lists using the <ul> tag are set to have left and right margins of 20%.

- Elements in bulleted lists using the <li> tag are set to have a top margin of 10 pixels, providing a space between list items.

Notice that the <style> tags aren't included in the style sheet document. They are not required in a CSS file, and could cause an error if included.

Creating the HTML Document

Now you can create an HTML document that uses the external style sheet you created. The most important part will be to include the `<link>` tag in your document, linking to the style sheet:

```
<link rel="stylesheet" href="style.css">
```

Listing 10.2 shows a complete example HTML document that links to this style sheet. Be sure that you save it in the same directory as the style sheet, and that the `<link>` statement's filename matches the name you used to save the style sheet.

LISTING 10.2   The HTML Document for the Style Sheet Example

```
<html>
<head>
<title>Style Sheet Example</title>
<link rel="stylesheet" href="style.css">
</head>
<body>
<h1>style sheet example</h1>
<p>This is a standard paragraph of text. It is displayed in a
12 point sans-serif font. The right and left margins are set at
10%, and the text is right-justified. Colors have been set for
<b>bold</b> and <i>italic</i> elements within paragraphs.
Paragraphs are also set to be indented.
</p>
<p>The H1 heading above has been set to a sans-serif font. It
is displayed centered, with a font size 300% of the normal size.
Each word in the heading has been capitalized by the style
sheet, even though the actual &lt;h1&gt; tag is in lowercase.
</p>
<ul>
<li>All of this was accomplished using an external style sheet.</li>
<li>Since the <b>font-family</b> value was set for the body
tag, the text in this bulleted list is displayed in that font. </li>
<li>The list has a margin of 20% on the left and right. These
were set for the &lt;ul&gt; tag, and are thus inherited by the
&lt;li&gt; tags nested within it.</li>
<li>We have added a top margin for the &lt;li&gt; tag to add
a bit of space in between each item in this bulleted list.</li>
</p>
</body>
</html>
```

10

Figure 10.1 shows the styled document as displayed in Netscape 6. It should display in a nearly identical way in Internet Explorer and other CSS-compliant browsers.

FIGURE **10.1**

Netscape displays the styled document.

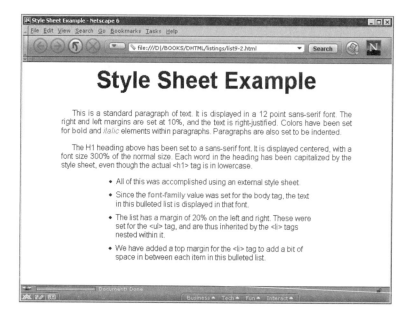

Summary

In this hour and the previous hour, you've learned the properties and values you can use in CSS style sheets. You should now know how to control color, font, position, and other attributes using style sheets.

In the next hour, you'll learn how you can dynamically control these properties using JavaScript, creating useful and sometimes dramatic effects.

Q&A

Q. How do I know which fonts each user has installed? Are there any fonts that are safe to use?

A. While you can never be sure which fonts are installed by your users, there are certain fonts included with the Windows and Macintosh operating systems that you can expect to find on most computers. Hour 12, "Creating Consistent Styles," includes a list of these fonts.

Q. What is a good font size for readable text on my page?

A. While a size of 10–12 points is typical for printed pages, you don't really know what text size will be displayed on each user's monitor, and some users might have different ideas than you of what's readable. It's best to avoid setting an exact size, and instead use the default size for the body, and percentages of this size for other elements.

Q. What is the difference between italic and oblique text styles?

A. While these are both basically slanted text, italics usually refers to a separate font that has been designed with a slant, and oblique text is a slanted version of the standard font produced by the computer.

Quiz

Test your knowledge of the material covered in this hour by answering the following questions.

Questions

1. Which of the following properties could you use to control the amount of space between paragraphs in a document?

   a. `paragraph-spacing`

   b. `word-spacing`

   c. `margin-top`

2. Which of the following could be used to center an image within the page?

   a. `text-align`

   b. `margin-auto`

   c. `margin-left` and `margin-right`

3. Which of the following is the correct rule to set H1 headings to have a font size of 24 pixels and a color of red?

   a. `H1 {font-size: 24px; color: red;}`

   b. `<H1> {font-size: 24px; color: red;}`

   c. `H1 {font-size: 24pt; color: red;}`

Answers

1. c. The `margin-top` property could be used to add space between paragraphs.

2. c. Setting `margin-left` and `margin-right` to `auto` is one way to center an image. The `text-align` property only works on text elements, such as paragraphs.

3. a. The correct rule is `H1 {font-size: 24px; color: red;}`. Choice B incorrectly uses angle brackets around `<H1>`, and choice C specifies points (`24pt`) instead of pixels (`24px`).

Exercises

If you'd like to gain a bit more experience with style sheets before you move on to the next hour, try the following exercises:

- Create another HTML document that links to the `styles.css` style sheet in Listing 10.1. Observe how the style rules format your document.

- In the style sheet in Listing 10.1, create a `.fineprint` class that has smaller than normal text and is displayed in italics. Assign one of the paragraphs in Listing 10.2 to this class.

HOUR 11

Controlling Styles with JavaScript

You have now learned many properties and values you can use to format pages using CSS. The DOM stores all of these values, and you can use JavaScript to manipulate them dynamically.

In this hour, you'll learn how you can use JavaScript and the DOM's style objects to change the colors, fonts, styles, and other aspects of a document—anything that you can control with style sheets.

This hour covers the following topics:

- Formatting properties for dynamic styles
- Controlling colors dynamically
- Changing text properties dynamically
- Dynamic styles in action

Dynamic Styles

In the previous hours of this book you've learned two things: how DHTML and the DOM can make pages dynamically, and how you can use CSS to control the formatting of your pages. In this hour, you'll learn to combine these two ideas and create documents that can be restyled dynamically.

Translating Property Names

The DOM includes objects that correspond with all of the style properties you learned about in the previous hours. These are stored under the `style` object for each HTML element. For example, suppose you have defined a heading with this HTML:

```
<h1 ID="head1">This is a Heading</h1>
```

You can use the following JavaScript statements to change the color of this heading:

```
h=document.getElementById("head1");
h.style.color="red";
```

In this case, the property name (`color`) is the same as the style property name. However, with any property name that includes two or more words, the DOM object has a slightly different name—it includes the same words, but with no spaces and with capitals on all but the first word. Here are a few examples:

- `text-align` becomes `style.textAlign`
- `margin-left` becomes `style.marginLeft`
- `font-family` becomes `style.fontFamily`
- `left-border-width` becomes `style.leftBorderWidth`

One exception to this pattern is the `float` property. Its corresponding JavaScript property name is `style.cssFloat`. This change is because `float` is a reserved word in JavaScript.

You've used some style properties already. Hour 5, "Understanding the DOM," includes an example using visibility properties, and Hour 6, "Creating Positionable Elements (Layers)," shows an example of the positioning properties.

Working with Colors

As one example of using style properties in JavaScript, you can change colors dynamically in a document. The following are the color and background properties available from the DOM:

- color—The text color for an element
- backgroundAttachment—The background scroll setting
- backgroundColor—The background color for an element or document
- backgroundImage—The background image for an element or document
- backgroundPosition—The offset of the background image position
- backgroundRepeat—The tile setting for the background image

> These properties are the same as the style properties, formatted as DOM properties. These properties are explained in detail in Hour 9, "Introducing Style Sheets."

11

Using Color Properties

One easy way to manipulate colors is to create a function to change the color of an object. This function changes the color of the heading with the ID attribute head1:

```
function HColor(c) {
  h=document.getElementById("head1");
  h.style.color=c;
}
```

This simply finds the object for the heading, and changes its color to the value specified in the function's parameter. You can also create a function to change the color for more than one object:

```
function PColor(c) {
  paras=document.getElementsByTagName("P");
  for (i=0; i<paras.length; i++) {
    if (paras[i].className=="para")
    paras[i].style.color=c;
  }
}
```

This example uses the document.getElementsByTagName method to get an array of objects for all of the paragraphs in the document. For each one, it checks for a CLASS attribute value of para, and if this value is found, it changes the color of the object to the value specified in the function's parameter.

Calling the Functions

Now that you have created two color-changing functions, you can easily call them from JavaScript. While you could use event handlers to do this, one simple way is to use `javascript:` links. For example, the following `<a>` tag defines a link that sets the heading's color to red:

```
<a href="javascript:HColor('red');">red</a>
```

The following example changes the color of the paragraphs to blue:

```
<a href="javascript:PColor('blue');">blue</a>
```

When using `javascript:` links, be sure to use double quotes around the entire `href` attribute of the `<a>` tag, and single quotes for any parameters within the JavaScript statement itself.

Changing Colors Dynamically

You can now create a simple HTML document that includes the functions you created and a variety of links that test the dynamic color functions. Listing 11.1 shows the complete document.

LISTING 11.1   The Complete Color Changing Example

```
<html>
<head>
<title>Dynamic Colors</title>
<script language="JavaScript">
function HColor(c) {
   h=document.getElementById("head1");
   h.style.color=c;
}
function PColor(c) {
   paras=document.getElementsByTagName("P");
   for (i=0; i<paras.length; i++) {
      if (paras[i].className=="para")
         paras[i].style.color=c;
   }
}
</script>
</head>
<body>
<h1 ID="head1">Dynamic Colors</h1>
<p CLASS="para">This document inclues a short script that
```

LISTING **11.1** continued

```
uses DHTML to change the colors of objects
by manipulating style properties.</p>
<p CLASS="para">You can change this page's heading to
<a href="javascript:HColor('red');">red</a>,
<a href="javascript:HColor('blue');">blue</a>,
or <a href="javascript:HColor('black');">black</a>.
You can also change the color of these two paragraphs
of text to <a href="javascript:PColor('red')">red</a>,
<a href="javascript:PColor('blue')">blue</a>, or
<a href="javascript:PColor('green')">green</a>.
</p>
<p>The paragraphs can all change color at once because
they are in the same class. This particular paragraph doesn't
change color since it doesn't have a CLASS attribute.</p>
</body>
</html>
```

To use this example, save it as an HTML document and load it into a browser. While this example requires Internet Explorer 5.0 or later or Netscape 6.0 or later, you can change some of the same properties in the 4.0 browsers using the techniques you'll learn in Hour 17, "Dealing with Browser Differences."

11

> This example quickly illustrates how the color properties work, but isn't too dramatic. The same concept is used to create rollovers in Hour 13, "Creating Drop-Down Menus," and to create blinking and fading text in Hour 15, "Creating DHTML Text Effects."

Here is a breakdown of how this listing works:

- The HColor function changes the color of the heading with the ID head1.
- The PColor function changes the color of all paragraphs with the CLASS attribute para.
- The <h1> tag defines a heading with the head1 identifier.
- The first two <p> tags define two paragraphs in the para class. These paragraphs also include links to manipulate the various parts of the document.

Internet Explorer's display of this example is shown in Figure 11.1.

FIGURE **11.1**

Internet Explorer displays the dynamic colors example.

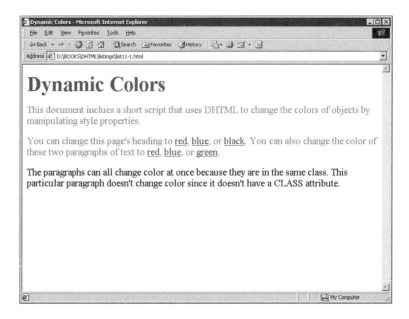

As usual, you can download this hour's examples from this book's Web site rather than typing them. Here's the URL:
http://www.starlingtech.com/dhtml/.

Changing Text Styles Dynamically

Colors aren't the only thing you can change dynamically. You can manipulate any style property in a script. For example, you can change fonts, alignment, and other text styles dynamically.

Suppose you have defined a paragraph with the ID para1 like this:

```
<p ID="para1">This is a paragraph.</p>
```

The following statements change the alignment and font for the paragraph:

```
p=document.getElementById("para1");
p.style.textAlign="center";
p.style.fontFamily="sans-serif";
p.style.fontSize="16px";
```

As with color properties, remember to translate the names: text-align becomes textAlign, and so on. Also, you should enclose any value that includes a unit (for example, 16px, 12pt, 200%) in quotation marks to avoid creating JavaScript errors.

Workshop: Using Dynamic Styles

As a more sophisticated example of dynamic styles, you can create an HTML document with a simple function that can easily change any style property. This provides an easy way for you to experiment with different property values and examine how they are displayed in the browser.

Creating the Function

Rather than working with any specific object, you can create a function that will change any property of any object. Sound complicated? Actually, it's much simpler than the functions you created earlier in this hour:

```
function Change(id,p,v) {
  if (!document.getElementById) return;
  obj=document.getElementById(id);
  obj.style[p]=v;
}
```

This function accepts three parameters: id, p, and v. It finds the object with the specified ID attribute, then sets the property p for that object to the value v.

Notice the brackets in the statement obj.style[p]=v. They simply indicate a child object: obj.style["color"] would be the same as obj.style.color. Using the brackets allows you to use a variable for the property name.

11

Creating the HTML Document

You can now create an HTML document that includes the function you created and a variety of links to test the function. Listing 11.2 shows the complete HTML document.

LISTING 11.2   An HTML Document Including Dynamic Style Functions

```
<html>
<head>
<title>Dynamic Styles</title>
<script language="JavaScript">
function Change(id,p,v) {
   if (!document.getElementById) return;
   obj=document.getElementById(id);
   obj.style[p]=v;
}
</script>
</head>
```

LISTING **11.2**   continued

```
<body>
<h1 ID="head1">Dynamic Styles</h1>
<p ID="para1">
This document includes a simple function that can change
any style property. For example, you can change this paragraph's
font size to
<a href="javascript:Change('para1','fontSize','50%');">small</a>,
<a href="javascript:Change('para1','fontSize','100%');">normal</a>, or
<a href="javascript:Change('para1','fontSize','200%');">large</a>.
</p>
<p ID="para2">
This paragraph's alignment can be changed to
<a href="javascript:Change('para2','textAlign','left');">left</a>,
<a href="javascript:Change('para2','textAlign','center');">center</a>,
<a href="javascript:Change('para2','textAlign','right');">right</a>, or
<a href="javascript:Change('para2','textAlign','justify');">justify</a>.
You can also change the font of this paragraph to
<a href="javascript:Change('para2','fontFamily','sans-serif');">
sans-serif</a>,
<a href="javascript:Change('para2','fontFamily','serif');">
serif</a>,
<a href="javascript:Change('para2','fontFamily','monospace');">
monospace</a>,
<a href="javascript:Change('para2','fontFamily','cursive');">
cursive</a>, or
<a href="javascript:Change('para2','fontFamily','fantasy');">
fantasy</a>. Try the links in different browsers and notice the
different choice of fonts.
</p>
<p>The weight of the heading at the top of the page can be set to
<a href="javascript:Change('head1','fontWeight','normal');">normal</a>,
<a href="javascript:Change('head1','fontWeight','bold');">bold</a>,
<a href="javascript:Change('head1','fontWeight','bolder');">bolder</a>, or
<a href="javascript:Change('head1','fontWeight','lighter');">lighter</a>.
Notice that bold is the default setting for a heading, and the
<b>lighter</b> value is the same as <b>normal</b> in the current
versions of Netscape and Internet Explorer.
</p>
</body>
</html>
```

This listing includes the Change function you created. The paragraphs and heading within the document have ID attributes, and include links that use the javascript: format to change various attributes.

To try this example, save it as an HTML document and load it into a browser. This example requires Netscape 6.0 or later or Internet Explorer 5.0 or later. Figure 11.2 shows Netscape's display of the document after a few changes have been made.

FIGURE 11.2

Netscape displays the dynamic styles example.

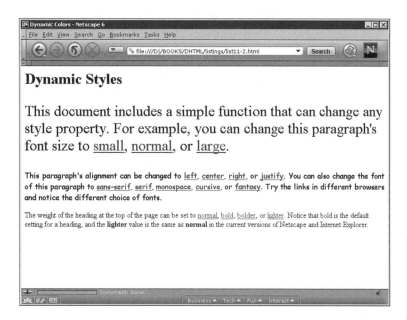

Summary

In this hour, you've learned how you can use JavaScript and the DOM to dynamically change text styles, colors, and other properties of your document. Combined with CSS, these give you sophisticated control of how users see your pages. You'll use these properties to create several practical examples in the remaining hours of this book.

In the next hour, you'll take a final look at CSS style sheets and learn the best ways to use them to create readable, browser-friendly Web pages. You'll also learn how to use JavaScript to enable and disable style sheets.

Q&A

Q. Why are the fonts different between Netscape and Internet Explorer? Neither `cursive` font is actually cursive, and Netscape's `fantasy` font looks normal.

A. The rules for CSS don't say exactly what these generic fonts should look like, so don't expect consistency. Fortunately, the basic `sans-serif`, `serif`, and `monospace` fonts are very similar.

Q. Are there any practical reasons to use dynamic styles?

A. Aside from special effects, style properties are an important part of many DHTML applications. You'll use them throughout the rest of this book, starting with the drop-down menu application in Hour 13.

Q. Are dynamic styles supported by all browsers?

A. Netscape 4.0 and later and Internet Explorer 4.0 and later support the styles discussed in this chapter, but no browser's support for style properties is perfect. You should test on several current browsers to be sure your styles have the effect you intended.

Quiz

Test your knowledge of the material covered in this hour by answering the following questions.

Questions

1. Which of the following is the correct way of referring to the `margin-right` style property for the `firstline` object within a script?

   a. `firstline.marginRight`

   b. `firstline.style.marginRight`

   c. `firstline.style.margin-right`

2. Which of the following properties are *not* included under the `style` object?

   a. Visibility

   b. Text alignment

   c. Child objects and siblings

3. Which of the following is the correct statement to change the `firstline` object's font size to 20 pixels?

   a. `firstline.style.fontSize="20px";`

   b. `firstline.fontsize=20;`

   c. `firstline.style.fontSize=20px;`

Answers

1. b. `firstline.style.marginRight` is the correct property.

2. c. The node relationship properties (child objects, siblings, and so on) are not stored under the `style` object. They are properties of each node itself.

3. a. The correct statement is `firstline.style.fontSize="20px"`. Since the pixel value isn't an integer, you must use quotation marks around it.

Exercises

If you'd like further practice using dynamic styles before you move on to the next hour, try the following exercises:

- Add a couple of paragraphs to Listing 11.2. Include links to change font style (normal or italic), text decoration, and any other properties you're curious about.

- Try your modified version of Listing 11.2 in at least two different browsers, and notice any differences in the way the properties are interpreted.

11

Hour 12

Creating Consistent Styles

You've now learned just about everything that can be done with style sheets. With powerful features like these, you should make sure you are not creating styles that will annoy your users.

In this hour, you'll learn some guidelines for using style sheets consistently and tastefully. You'll also learn how you can use JavaScript to give users a choice of different styles.

This hour covers the following topics:

- Using style sheets effectively
- Choosing appropriate colors
- Selecting fonts for Web pages
- Choosing margin and border sizes
- Supporting older browsers
- Creating multiple-choice styles

Using Restraint

The history of the Web is filled with events that put powerful tools in the hands of Web designers—and often they fell into the wrong hands. Netscape's <blink> tag, JavaScript scrolling messages, and the <font> tag resulted in an epidemic of bad Web pages.

Style sheets are a step in the right direction, but you still can use them to create poorly designed pages. In this hour, you'll learn some guidelines to help you create pages that fit three important criteria:

- Readability and Usability
- Consistency between browsers that support CSS
- Usability in older, non-CSS browsers

Usability Tips

Web *usability* is a relatively new concept, but an important one. As Web pages and sites become more complex, it's important to keep them readable and navigable. When you start adding CSS and DHTML to your pages, it's easier than ever to create a page that annoys or confuses visitors. Here are a few tips to avoid common usability mistakes:

- Know your audience. Styles that would fit perfectly well in a site that reviews video games would look garish and overdone on a site that offers financial reports for stockholders.
- Don't hide your links from visitors. You can use CSS to make links take any appearance, or use graphic links or other navigation methods—but when you do, make sure the links are immediately identifiable as links, and clearly state where they go.
- Make sure your most important links aren't buried in the site design, and are clearly labeled with text. Don't make users scan the mouse around the screen or decipher bizarre icons just to see what content is available on the site.
- Don't tell your visitors that they need a certain browser, screen resolution, or video mode to fully appreciate your site. Nobody will change these settings just for your site, and a good design will work with a wide range of settings.
- When you add graphics, styles, and dynamic features, make sure you're not increasing the time it takes visitors to load your site too much. Test your pages using a slow Internet connection and watch for long pauses.

Of course, there are exceptions to every rule, and your site might need to break a rule or two to look and work its best. Just make sure your audience is impressed by the styles and features you use, rather than annoyed or confused.

To know your audience better, talk to them. When you redesign a site, let users view the new version and give you their feedback before you replace the old version.

Choosing Colors

Color is a vital part of Web pages—anyone who was around when the first browsers came out knows that they displayed black text on a gray background by default, and there was no way for Web designers to use alternate colors. The Web has come a long way since then.

Of course, you've probably run into a few Web pages with such frightening color choices you've wished for black on gray. If you follow a few simple guidelines, you can avoid giving users headaches with your color choices.

Text and Background Colors

The text and background colors you choose greatly affect readability. Yellow text on a black background might look cool, and might fit right in with the design of the site you're working on, but there's a reason the vast majority of literature is printed in black on white: it's easier to read.

Black and white aren't the only choices. If you're careful, there are a number of equally readable choices: black on light blue, dark blue on light gray, or even white on dark blue. If you have to squint to read the text on your page, imagine how it must look for users with imperfect vision, or with monitors that aren't as clear as yours.

Of course, there are exceptions to any rule. If your site is graphically oriented and only has a few words of text per page, yellow on black would work just fine. Just keep readability in mind when you use colors.

Link Colors

If you've spent much time browsing the Web, you probably automatically think of blue text as a link, and purple text as a link you've visited. Your users think the same way, and if you've changed the color of links you can create confusion.

That doesn't mean you should avoid changing the link colors entirely, but if you do, be sure you are consistent throughout your site. Be sure both visited and non-visited links are different colors, and neither is the same as the regular text on your page.

Since most browsers display links as underlined text, you also can create confusion if you underline other text, or remove underlines from links. Avoid these changes whenever possible.

Background Images

If reading text displayed over a bright background color is hard, imagine trying to read text displayed over a brightly colored, detailed background image. While background images are a great way to give a page a unique style, they can make reading very difficult if you're not careful.

One way to avoid problems with background images is to use a very simple background: a texture with mostly a single color, or a solid color with a very faint, watermark-like company logo. Another way is to use a background that doesn't cover the entire page—use CSS positioning or a table to place your text in areas where the background is one solid color.

Choosing Fonts

The font options of CSS bring typography to the Web, and you can now choose fonts to match the design of your site. However, don't forget that with power comes responsibility—choosing the wrong fonts is another way to make a page virtually unreadable.

In general, there are three big mistakes you can make with your font choices:

- Choosing a difficult to read font—cursive fonts, handwriting-style fonts, and calligraphy are common examples
- Choosing a specific font that might not be available on all browsers or computers
- Using several different fonts in the same page, especially fonts that don't match (serif and sans-serif fonts, for example)

Common Font Choices

One way to avoid running into trouble with users who don't have the same fonts installed as you is to use a list of commonly available fonts. If you list a Windows font, a Macintosh font, and a generic font, you can be sure all users will see your page the way you intended.

Here are a few basic font lists you can use. Each includes a Windows font name, Macintosh font name, and generic CSS font name that are roughly equivalent.

- Arial, Helvetica, sans-serif
- MS Sans Serif, Geneva, sans-serif
- MS Serif, New York, serif
- Times New Roman, Times, serif
- Courier New, Courier, monospace

Available Windows and Macintosh Fonts

When choosing fonts, you might find it useful to know which fonts are commonly installed on Windows and Macintosh systems. While users can always add or remove fonts, the fonts in the lists below are installed by default and generally are available.

> Don't forget to enclose any font name that includes spaces in quotation marks when you use it from CSS or JavaScript.

Windows Fonts

The following fonts are installed by default in Windows 95 and later versions:

- Arial (sans-serif)
- MS Sans Serif (sans-serif)
- Copperplate Gothic Bold (serif)
- Copperplate Gothic Light (serif)
- Courier New (monospace)
- Terminal (monospace)
- Times New Roman (serif)

Macintosh Fonts

The following fonts are installed by default in Mac OS 7 and later versions:

- Chicago (sans-serif)
- Courier (monospace)
- Geneva (sans-serif)
- Helvetica (sans-serif)
- Monaco (monospace)

12

- New York (serif)
- Palatino (serif)
- Times (serif)

Choosing Font Sizes

You also should be careful when choosing font sizes. While anywhere from 10 to 14 point sizes will be readable, you should keep in mind that the actual size will depend on the browser and monitor in use, and different users will prefer different sizes. If you set an exact size, users who have carefully set their browsers' font size to their liking will be surprised.

The best advice about font sizes is not to set one. Instead, let the default size be used for body text, and use percentage sizes to set the size of any headings, fine print, or other special text. This way the fonts can be resized easily by the user.

Use relative units to specify font sizes. These include percentages, em units, and ex units. See Hour 9, "Introducing Style Sheets," for a discussion of the different units available.

Margins and Borders

Many Web designers have puzzled over the issue of what size of monitor to design for. While 640×480 resolution was common a couple of years ago, 800×600 is now the most popular size and higher resolutions are much more commonplace.

While these guidelines will help with graphics and other elements that can't be resized, you should allow your page to be resized whenever possible. This means avoiding using exact pixel amounts in margin, border, and width settings, and in the sizes for table columns.

If you avoid exact sizes, not only will users with lower-resolution screen be able to read your page, but users with higher-resolution screens will be able to take advantage of the space they have available and stretch your page to fit their browser width.

Supporting Older Browsers

Last, but not least, you should be sure that as you add CSS features to your pages, you don't create a page design that *requires* a CSS browser to be readable at all. While CSS is designed to avoid this problem, you still can cause problems through misuse of CSS.

For example, you can use CSS positioning to overlap several identical lines of text, creating a nifty shadow effect—but when you view the page in a non-CSS browser, the lines of text are all displayed one at a time.

To avoid problems like this, you should always test your pages that use CSS in an older browser that doesn't support CSS, or in your normal browser with style sheets turned off. If you design your pages carefully, they'll be readable whether your styles are used or not.

> It isn't just older browsers you should worry about—some users with current browsers might have style sheets turned off, or specify their own custom style sheet.

Workshop: Creating Multiple-Choice Styles

One way to avoid alienating users with your bold design choices is to give the user a choice. You can create a document with two or more style sheets defined, and use DHTML to enable only one of them based on the user's preference.

Creating the First Style Sheet

The first step in creating multiple-choice styles is to create the first style sheet. The style sheets will be external, so you should save them as css files. Remember that external style sheets do not require the <style> tags.

Listing 12.1 shows the first style sheet. This sets fonts, margins, and fonts for several HTML elements. Save this document as style1.css or a name of your choice.

LISTING 12.1   The First Style Sheet

```
body {font-family: Arial, Helvetica, sans-serif;
        font-size: 12pt;}
P {margin-left: 10%;
   margin-right: 10%;
   text-align: justify;
   text-indent: 3%;}
B {color: red;}
I {color: DarkViolet;}
H1 {font-size: 300%;
    text-align: center;
    text-transform: capitalize;}
UL {margin-left: 20%;
    margin-right: 20%;}
LI {margin-top: 10px;}
```

12

As usual, you can download the CSS and HTML files for this example from this book's Web site: http://www.starlingtech.com/dhtml/.

Creating the Second Style Sheet

Next, you'll need another style sheet that provides a second choice. This style sheet, shown in Listing 12.2, uses some more extreme style choices and probably isn't ideal for all users. This style sheet will be disabled by default in our example.

LISTING 12.2   The Second Style Sheet

```
body {font-family: Times, "Times New Roman", sans-serif;
        font-size: 14pt;}
P {margin-left: 20%;
   margin-right: 20%;
   text-align: left;
   text-indent: 0%;}
B {color: black;
background-color: aqua;}
I {color: red;}
H1 {font-size: 200%;
   text-align: right;
   text-transform: uppercase;}
UL {margin-left: 30%;
   margin-right: 30%;
   background-color: yellow;}
LI {margin-top: 20px;}
```

Save this style sheet as style2.css, or a name of your choice.

Creating the Function

Last, but not least, you need a way to switch style sheets dynamically. You can use an attribute of the <link> tag to accomplish this:

```
<link rel="stylesheet" href="style2.css" DISABLED>
```

This tag uses the DISABLED attribute of the <link> tag to define a style sheet that will not be used by default. You later can enable the style sheet using JavaScript.

The current version of Netscape 6 does not support the DISABLED attribute. However, you still can disable a style sheet using JavaScript, and the final script you create will work in both Netscape 6 and Internet Explorer 5 and later.

To enable and disable styles, you can use a simple DHTML function:

```
function Style(n,enable) {
  if (!document.getElementsByTagName) return;
  links=document.getElementsByTagName("link");
  links[n].disabled=!enable;
  links[1-n].disabled=true;
}
```

The `Style` function uses two parameters: n, the number of the stylesheet to enable (0 or 1), and enable, a flag to indicate whether to enable the style sheet. If enable is true, one of the style sheets is enabled; if enabled is false, both are disabled. This allows you to provide the user with the option of turning off style sheets altogether.

This function first checks for the `document.getElementsByTagName` property, since it will be used later. This prevents errors from occurring on browsers that do not support DHTML.

Next, the function uses the `getElementsByTagName` method to store an array of `<link>` objects for the document in the `links` variable. It assigns the link specified in the n parameter's `disabled` property to the opposite of the enable parameter, and assigns the disabled property of the other style sheet to true.

> The `disabled` property is a bit confusing. Remember that a value of `true` disables the style sheet and a value of `false` enables the style sheet.

Creating the HTML Document

Finally, you can create an HTML document that includes your `Style` function, some text to serve as an example, and links to allow the style sheet to be changed. Listing 12.3 shows the complete HTML document.

LISTING 12.3   The HTML Document for the Multiple Choice Styles Example

```
<html>
<head>
<title>Style Sheet Example</title>
<link rel="stylesheet" href="style1.css">
<link rel="stylesheet" href="style2.css" DISABLED>
<script language="javascript">
function Style(n,enable) {
  if (!document.getElementsByTagName) return;
  links=document.getElementsByTagName("link");
  links[n].disabled=!enable;
```

12

LISTING 12.3 continued

```
    links[1-n].disabled=true;
}
Style(0,true);
</script>
</head>
<body>
<h1>multiple-choice styles</h1>
<p>This is a standard paragraph of text. Its font, margins,
fonts, justification, and other attributes depend on the style
sheet you select. This paragraph includes some text in
<b>bold</b> and <i>italics</i>.
</p>
<p>You can select one of three styles for this document:
</p>
<ul>
<li><a href="javascript:Style(0,true);">Style sheet # 1</a></li>
<li><a href="javascript:Style(1,true);">Style sheet # 2</a></li>
<li><a href="javascript:Style(0,false);">No style sheet</a></li>
</ul>
<p>These links call a short JavaScript function that enables one
of this document's two linked external style sheets. You can edit
the style sheets to style this document in two different ways,
without changing any HTML.</p>
</body>
</html>
```

To test this document, be sure that the href attributes of the <link> tags match the filenames you used for the two style sheets, and save this document in the same directory. When you first load the document, it will be displayed using the first style sheet. Figure 12.1 shows Internet Explorer's display of this example with the default style.

Here is a breakdown of the components of this HTML document:

- The <link> tags include both external style sheets. The second style sheet is disabled by default.

- The Style function is defined in the <script> section.

- The last line in the <script> section calls the Style function to enable the first style sheet and disable the second when the page is displayed. This is necessary because Netscape 6 doesn't support the DISABLED property of the <link> tag.

- The list items in the <ul> section define three links that call the Style function: one for the first style sheet, one for the second, and a third to turn off both style sheets.

- The rest of the document includes a heading and paragraphs that will be styled according to the style sheet you select.

FIGURE 12.1

The multiple-choice styles example displayed with the first style sheet.

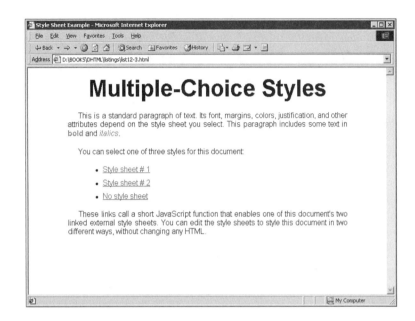

When you click the links, you should see the styles of the document change dynamically. Figure 12.2 shows the document styled with the second style sheet, and Figure 12.3 shows the document with the styles turned off.

FIGURE 12.2

The multiple-choice styles example displayed using the second style sheet.

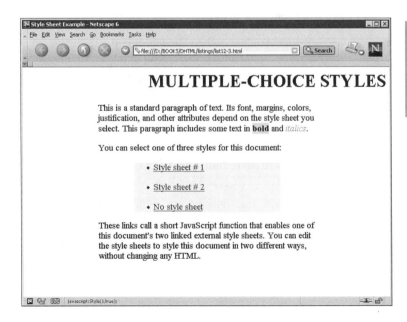

12

FIGURE **12.3**

The multiple-choice styles example displayed without styles.

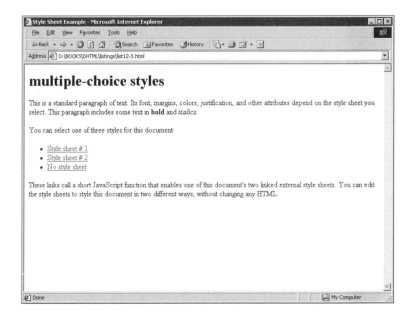

Summary

In this hour, you've learned some basic guidelines for using styles to create usable, readable pages that will display consistently on CSS browsers, and still will be readable on browsers without CSS support.

Congratulations! You've reached the end of Part III. In Part IV, you'll apply what you've learned so far to create several impressive and useful examples of DHTML in action. You'll begin in the next hour by using DHTML to create drop-down menus for site navigation.

Q&A

Q. Aren't there more fonts available on most computers than those listed here?

A. Yes. In particular, several are included with Windows 98 and later, and some are installed with Internet Explorer. Additional Mac fonts are installed by default in MacOS 8.5 and later. If you're really picky about fonts, you can assemble a much larger list, but be sure to provide alternatives from our basic list and generic CSS fonts.

Q. I've seen the `document.styleSheets` object used to disable style sheets. Why was this not used in the example in this hour?

A. This object is supported only by Internet Explorer 5 and 6. The technique in this hour using `<link>` tags is a bit more complex, but works in Internet Explorer 5 and later and Netscape 6.

Q. Can I enable or disable style sheets in Netscape 4 or Internet Explorer 4?

A. In Internet Explorer 4, you can use `document.all.tags('link')` instead of the `getElementsByTagName` method. Once you've obtained the array, the enable/disable script can work the same way. There is no way to do this in Netscape 4.

Quiz

Test your knowledge of the material covered in this hour by answering the following questions.

Questions

1. Which of the following lists includes three fonts that are roughly equivalent?

    a. Times New Roman, Helvetica, serif

    b. Arial, Helvetica, sans-serif

    c. Arial, Courier, sans-serif

2. Which of the following fonts is guaranteed to work on all CSS-compliant browsers?

    a. Courier

    b. Arial

    c. monospace

3. What is the name of the property of a `<link>` element you change to enable or disable an external style sheet?

    a. `enabled`

    b. `disabled`

    c. `stylesheet`

12

Answers

1. b. Arial, Helvetica, and the generic sans-serif are all sans-serif fonts.

2. c. Since monospace is a CSS generic font, it will work on all CSS-compliant browsers. Of course, its appearance isn't guaranteed to be identical between browsers.

3. b. You can use the `disabled` property of a `<link>` element to enable or disable an external style sheet.

Exercises

If you'd like some final practice using CSS style sheets before moving on, try the following exercise:

- Try creating your own page with multiple-choice styles, and two or more style sheets to switch between.

PART IV

Dynamic HTML in Action

Hour

HOUR 13

Creating Drop-Down Menus

Welcome to Part IV! You're halfway through this book, and should be comfortable with the basics of DHTML and CSS. In the next four hours, you'll apply what you've learned about DHTML to create some useful, practical examples.

In this hour, you'll begin by creating a menu-based navigation system for a Web page. This is a popular application of DHTML and isn't hard to accomplish.

This hour covers the following topics:

- Planning objects and events
- Creating the menu bar
- Creating menu layers
- Creating JavaScript functions
- Completing and testing the example

Overview

In this hour, you'll learn how you can use DHTML to create a user-friendly navigation system for a Web site. If you've used a Windows or Macintosh computer, you're familiar with the menu bar at the top of an application's window. You can create a similar menu for your site.

As an example in this hour, you will use the Figby Industries Web page that you created in Hour 2, "Reviewing HTML." The original page included several links to navigate to different sections of the site: Products, Sales, Service, and so on. Using DHTML, you can create a menu that offers several further choices under each item.

> In a site with only a few pages, a DHTML menu like this can create more confusion than it solves. In a large site with many pages, on the other hand, a well-organized menu makes the perfect navigation system.

Of course, if you're designing a menu system for a non-fictional site, there's another important step—plan the structure of the site and how the menu will be organized. A poorly organized menu system can actually be more confusing to users than a simple list of links.

Objects and Events

When planning a DHTML project like this, it's useful to get an idea beforehand of which HTML elements you'll be treating as objects. You then can be sure to use the ID attribute on these elements to make them easy to manipulate. In this example, you'll use objects for the following HTML elements:

- Each menu term will be displayed in a table cell, created with a <td> tag. You will use this tag's object to create a rollover effect, changing the menu term's color when the mouse pointer is over it. You also will use this object to determine the menu term's position within the browser window, so you can position the menu directly below the term.

- When the mouse is over one of the menu terms, a layer will be used to display the menu under the term. The menu itself will be a table, and each cell in this table also will be assigned an ID attribute. You can use this object to change each menu item's color as the mouse pointer moves over them.

Layers are a good choice for the menus because they will be small square areas that overlap the other content of the page. Using layers also will make it easier to make your menus compatible with the 4.0 browsers if you choose to do so later.

Event Handlers

As you might have guessed, this example will use the onMouseOver and onMouseOut event handlers. You will use these for two reasons:

- To open each menu when the mouse pointer is over the menu's term
- To highlight each menu term or item with a rollover effect

To accomplish this, both the menu terms and each item within each menu will need onMouseOver and onMouseOut event handlers.

Creating the HTML Document

This will be the largest DHTML application you've worked with so far, and it involves quite a bit of HTML and JavaScript. To make things easier, you can use the SRC attribute of the <script> tag to keep the JavaScript code in a separate document.

The following tag defines a script that is stored in the file menu.js, in the same directory as the HTML document:

```
<script language="JavaScript" src="menu.js">
```

You will create the HTML portion of the document in this section, then proceed to create the JavaScript portion.

Using a separate file for the JavaScript code also would make it easy to use the same code on several different pages, each with a different menu.

13

Creating the Menu HTML

The menu bar will simply be a horizontal group of links. To display them in a neat layout with a box around each link, you can organize them in a table. The table will begin with these tags:

```
<table border="0" cellpadding="4">
<tr>
```

The <table> tag starts the table. The border=0 attribute removes the standard border between table cells, and the cellpadding=4 attribute adds some padding around the menu text. The <tr> tag defines the table's single row. Each menu term will be a single table cell. For example, here is the definition for the Products term within the menu bar:

```
<td ID="menu-products" width="100" bgcolor="Silver"
   onMouseOver="Menu('products');" onMouseOut="Timeout('products');">
   <a href="products.html"><b>Products</b></a>
</td>
```

This code defines a table cell with the <td> tag. This tag defines a background color for the cell and has an explicit width specified, so all of the menu terms will have the same width (100 pixels).

The menu term (Products) is linked to an HTML document (products.html). This link can be used by older browsers that don't display the menu of more specific links. Each menu term uses two event handlers:

- onMouseOver calls the Menu function, which will open the menu under this term.
- onMouseOut calls the Timeout function, which will close the menu if it is no longer in use.

The menu will display as a simple bar across the top of the document. Figure 13.1 shows Internet Explorer's display of the example before any of the menus are opened.

FIGURE 13.1

The HTML document with menu bar.

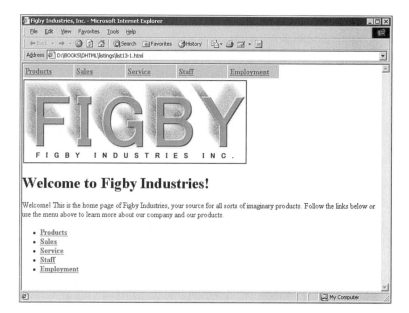

Defining the Layers

Next, you'll need to define the menus themselves. Each menu will be a layer, defined with the `<div>` tag. The layers will use the `visibility` style attribute set to `hidden`, so none of the menus will be displayed until the user moves the mouse over the menu terms.

For example, the following is the HTML code for the Products menu:

```
<div ID="products" STYLE="position:absolute; visibility: hidden">
  <table width="100%" border="0" cellpadding="4" cellspacing="0">
  <tr> <td width="100%" ID="p1"
    onMouseOver="Highlight('products','p1');"
    onMouseOut="UnHighlight('products','p1');">
  <a href="equip.html">Equipment</a></td></tr>
  <tr> <td width="100%" ID="p2"
    onMouseOver="Highlight('products','p2');"
    onMouseOut="UnHighlight('products','p2');">
  <a href="supplies.html">Supplies</a></td></tr>
  </table>
</div>
```

Within the `<div>` tag that defines the layer, the menu is defined as a table. Each table row contains a single cell with a menu item. In this example, there are two items in the Products menu.

Each item in the menu is defined with a `<td>` tag. Each `<td>` tag should have a unique `ID` attribute. Along with a link, each menu item has two event handlers:

- The `onMouseOver` event handler calls the `Highlight` function. This will change the menu item's background color.

- The `onMouseOut` event handler calls the `UnHighlight` function, which will return the background color to normal.

Finishing the HTML Document

You now can create the complete HTML document for the example. This will simply be a combination of the HTML components explained in the previous sections. Listing 13.1 shows the complete HTML document.

13

LISTING 13.1   The Complete HTML Document

```
<html>
<head>
<title>Figby Industries, Inc.</title>
<script language="JavaScript" src="menu.js">
</script>
```

LISTING 13.1   continued

```html
</head>
<body style="margin-left:0; margin-top:0;">
<table border="0" cellpadding="4">
<tr>
   <td ID="menu-products" width="100" bgcolor="Silver"
      onMouseOver="Menu('products');" onMouseOut="Timeout('products');">
    <a href="products.html"><b>Products</b></a>
   </td>
   <td ID="menu-sales" width="100" bgcolor="Silver"
      onMouseOver="Menu('sales');" onMouseOut="Timeout('sales');">
    <a href="sales.html"><b>Sales</b></a>
   </td>
   <td ID="menu-service" width="100" bgcolor="Silver"
      onMouseOver="Menu('service');" onMouseOut="Timeout('service');">
    <a href="service.html"><b>Service</b></a>
   </td>
   <td ID="menu-staff" width="100" bgcolor="Silver"
      onMouseOver="Menu('staff');" onMouseOut="Timeout('staff');">
    <a href="staff.html"><b>Staff</b></a>
   </td>
   <td ID="menu-jobs" width="100" bgcolor="Silver"
      onMouseOver="Menu('jobs');" onMouseOut="Timeout('jobs');">
    <a href="jobs.html"><b>Employment</b></a>
   </td>
</tr>
</table>
<div ID="products" STYLE="position:absolute; visibility: hidden">
   <table width="100%" border="0" cellpadding="4" cellspacing="0">
   <tr> <td width="100%" ID="p1"
      onMouseOver="Highlight('products','p1');"
      onMouseOut="UnHighlight('products','p1');">
   <a href="equip.html">Equipment</a></td></tr>
   <tr> <td width="100%" ID="p2"
      onMouseOver="Highlight('products','p2');"
      onMouseOut="UnHighlight('products','p2');">
   <a href="supplies.html">Supplies</a></td></tr>
   </table>
</div>
<div ID="sales" STYLE="position:absolute; visibility: hidden">
   <table width="100%" border="0" cellpadding="4" cellspacing="0">
   <tr> <td width="100%" ID="s1"
      onMouseOver="Highlight('sales','s1');"
      onMouseOut="UnHighlight('sales','s1');">
   <a href="prices.html">Price List</a></td></tr>
   <tr> <td width="100%" ID="s2"
      onMouseOver="Highlight('sales','s2');"
      onMouseOut="UnHighlight('sales','s2');">
   <a href="order.html">Order Form</a></td></tr>
   <tr> <td width="100%" ID="s3"
      onMouseOver="Highlight('sales','s3');"
```

LISTING 13.1   continued

```
          onMouseOut="UnHighlight('sales','s3');">
      <a href="specials.html">Specials</a></td></tr>
      </table>
   </div>
3. <div ID="service" STYLE="position:absolute; visibility: hidden">
      <table width="100%" border="0" cellpadding="4" cellspacing="0">
      <tr> <td width="100%" ID="r1"
         onMouseOver="Highlight('service','r1');"
         onMouseOut="UnHighlight('service','r1');">
      <a href="support.html">Support</a></td></tr>
      <tr> <td width="100%" ID="r2"
         onMouseOver="Highlight('service','r2');"
         onMouseOut="UnHighlight('service','r2');">
      <a href="cservice.html">Contact Us</a></td></tr>
      </table>
   </div>
4. <div ID="staff" STYLE="position:absolute; visibility: hidden">
      <table width="100%" border="0" cellpadding="4" cellspacing="0">
      <tr> <td width="100%" ID="t1"
         onMouseOver="Highlight('staff','t1');"
         onMouseOut="UnHighlight('staff','t1');">
      <a href="staff.html">Meet the Staff</a></td></tr>
      </table>
   </div>
5. <div ID="jobs" STYLE="position:absolute; visibility: hidden">
      <table width="100%" border="0" cellpadding="4" cellspacing="0">
      <tr> <td width="100%" ID="j1"
         onMouseOver="Highlight('jobs','j1');"
         onMouseOut="UnHighlight('jobs','j1');">
      <a href="jobs.html">Job Listings</a></td></tr>
      </table>
   </div>
   <img align="center" src="logo.gif" width="486" height="180" border="0"
   alt=""><br>
   <h1>Welcome to Figby Industries!</h1>
   <p>Welcome! This is the home page of Figby Industries,
   your source for all sorts of imaginary products. Follow the links
   below or use the menu above to learn more about our company
   and our products.
   </p>
   <ul>
     <li><a href="products.html"><b>Products</b></a></li>
     <li><a href="sales.html"><b>Sales</b></a></li>
     <li><a href="service.html"><b>Service</b></a></li>
     <li><a href="staff.html"><b>Staff</b></a></li>
     <li><a href="jobs.html"><b>Employment</b></a></li>
   </ul>
   </body>
   </html>
```

13

This example uses an image, logo.gif. You can download this image, along with the HTML and JavaScript files for this example, from this book's Web site: http://www.starlingtech.com/dhtml/.

While this is a long HTML document, it really just repeats the same familiar HTML code. The following are the components of this document:

- The <script> tag in the <head> section includes a script called menu.js. You will create this file in the next section with the required JavaScript functions.

- The menu bar is defined between the first <table> and </table> tags. The menu now has five terms: Products, Sales, Service, Staff, and Employment, each defined with a separate <td> tag.

- After the menu bar are five <div> sections that define the five menus. All of these will be hidden by default.

- After the menu is defined, the remainder of the body of the page includes a bulleted list of links to provide an alternative navigation system.

Save the HTML document now. You can load it into a browser to test, but the browser will display JavaScript error messages, since the JavaScript functions aren't available until you create the JavaScript file.

Creating the JavaScript Functions

Next, you'll need to create the JavaScript functions to open and close the menus, and to highlight menu items. You will assemble all of these functions into a JavaScript file in this hour's Workshop section.

Displaying a Menu

The Menu function will display a menu. Here is the beginning of the function:

```
function Menu(current) {
   if (!document.getElementById) return;
```

The function has one parameter, current. This will be the name of the menu to open. The if statement checks the document.getElementById object and exits the function if the browser does not support this needed W3C DOM function. The next portion of the function sets some variables to keep track of which menu is currently open:

```
inmenu=true;
oldmenu=lastmenu;
lastmenu=current;
if (oldmenu) Erase(oldmenu);
```

The `inmenu` variable is a global variable that indicates whether a menu is currently open or not, and the `lastmenu` global variable keeps track of the most recently opened menu. This portion of the function sets `inmenu` to `true`. It saves the previously opened menu name in the `oldmenu` variable, then sets the `lastmenu` variable to the new value.

If the `oldmenu` variable is set, the previous menu might still be displayed. We call the `Erase` function, which you'll create later, to erase the previous menu. Next, the function obtains the needed objects:

```
m=document.getElementById("menu-" + current);
box=document.getElementById(current);
```

The `m` object is the table cell for the menu term, and the `box` object is the layer for the appropriate menu. Next, we calculate the position where the menu should be displayed:

```
box.style.left= m.offsetLeft;
box.style.top= m.offsetTop + m.offsetHeight;
```

This sets the left position of the layer (`box`) to the same position as the menu term (`m`). The top position is set to the menu term's top position plus its height, so the layer should appear directly below the menu term. Next, we set some other style attributes:

```
box.style.visibility="visible";
m.style.backgroundColor="Aqua";
box.style.backgroundColor="Aqua";
box.style.width="108px";
}
```

The `visibility` attribute makes the layer appear. We also set its background color, highlight the menu term with the same background color, and set the width of the menu. This completes the `Menu` function.

13

> Although the menu terms have a width of 100 pixels, we use the value 108 here. This is because the `cellpadding=4` attribute in the menu bar's definition adds four pixels of padding on each side.

Erasing Menus

Next, you need a function to erase a menu when it's no longer in use. When the user moves the mouse pointer out of a menu term, the `Timeout` function is called:

```
function Timeout(current) {
   inmenu=false;
   window.setTimeout("Erase('" + current + "');",500);
}
```

This function simply sets the `inmenu` variable to `false`, and uses the `window.setTimeout` method to call the `Erase` function after a half-second delay. This delay is necessary because when the mouse pointer moves away from the menu term, it might be moving into the menu itself. If so, the menu shouldn't be erased.

Here's the `Erase` function:

```
function Erase(current) {
   if (!document.getElementById) return;
   if (inmenu && lastmenu==current) return;
   m=document.getElementById("menu-" + current);
   box=document.getElementById(current);
   box.style.visibility="hidden";
   m.style.backgroundColor="Silver";
}
```

This function uses an `if` statement to check the `inmenu` and `lastmenu` variables. These will be set each time the mouse pointer moves over a menu item. If they're set, the menu is still open, so the function aborts.

Next, it finds the `m` and `box` objects as in the `Menu` function. The layer is hidden, and the menu term's background color is returned to normal.

Highlighting Menu Items

Finally, you'll need two simple functions to highlight the menu items as the mouse pointer moves over them. First, the `Highlight` function:

```
function Highlight(menu,item) {
   if (!document.getElementById) return;
   inmenu=true;
   lastmenu=menu;
   obj=document.getElementById(item);
   obj.style.backgroundColor="Silver";
}
```

This function first sets the `inmenu` and `lastmenu` variables to ensure that the menu is not erased by the `Timeout` function. Next, it finds the object for the current menu item, and sets its background color. The `UnHighlight` function is equally simple:

```
function UnHighlight(menu,item) {
   if (!document.getElementById) return;
   Timeout(menu);
   obj=document.getElementById(item);
   obj.style.backgroundColor="Aqua";
}
```

This function calls the Timeout function for the current menu, because the mouse pointer might have moved out of the menu entirely. Next, it finds the object for the current menu item and returns its background color to normal.

Workshop: Creating the Complete Example

You now can combine all of the JavaScript functions you have created into a JavaScript file with the .js extension to complete the example. Save this file as menu.js in the same directory as the HTML document. Listing 13.2 shows the complete JavaScript file.

LISTING 13.2 The Complete JavaScript File

```
var inmenu=false;
var lastmenu=0;
function Menu(current) {
   if (!document.getElementById) return;
   inmenu=true;
   oldmenu=lastmenu;
   lastmenu=current;
   if (oldmenu) Erase(oldmenu);
   m=document.getElementById("menu-" + current);    // m: menu object
   box=document.getElementById(current);            // layer name.
   box.style.left= m.offsetLeft;
   box.style.top= m.offsetTop + m.offsetHeight;
   box.style.visibility="visible";
   m.style.backgroundColor="Aqua";
   box.style.backgroundColor="Aqua";
   box.style.width="108px";
}
function Erase(current) {
   if (!document.getElementById) return;
   if (inmenu && lastmenu==current) return;
   m=document.getElementById("menu-" + current);
   box=document.getElementById(current);
   box.style.visibility="hidden";
   m.style.backgroundColor="Silver";
}
function Timeout(current) {
   inmenu=false;
   window.setTimeout("Erase('" + current + "');",500);
}
function Highlight(menu,item) {
   if (!document.getElementById) return;
   inmenu=true;
   lastmenu=menu;
   obj=document.getElementById(item);
   obj.style.backgroundColor="Silver";
}
```

13

LISTING 13.2   continued

```
function UnHighlight(menu,item) {
   if (!document.getElementById) return;
   Timeout(menu);
   obj=document.getElementById(item);
   obj.style.backgroundColor="Aqua";
}
```

The first two lines of this document declare the global variables inmenu and lastmenu. The remainder of the document includes the Menu, Erase, Timeout, Highlight, and UnHighlight functions.

> Notice that the JavaScript file does not include <script> tags. These are included in the HTML document. You can use only JavaScript statements within the JavaScript file.

Now that you have completed the HTML document and the menu.js file, you can load the HTML document into a browser and test the menu. When you move the mouse pointer over a menu term, its corresponding menu should appear. Menu items should change color as you move over them, and the menu should be erased when you move away from it.

Figure 13.2 shows Netscape 6's display of the example. In the figure, the Sales menu is open and the Order Form link is currently selected.

> This example works in Internet Explorer 5.0 or later and Netscape 6 or later. However, it is possible to adapt it to work in 4.0 browsers. See Hour 17, "Dealing with Browser Differences," for details.

FIGURE 13.2
Netscape displays the menu in action.

Summary

In this hour, you've created a menu system using DHTML. This is one of the most popular uses of DHTML, and a great way to simplify navigation for a Web site.

In the next hour, you'll create another real-world DHTML example: a hierarchical menu tree with items that can expand and collapse.

Q&A

Q. Why does the example's <body> tag set the left and top margins to zero?

A. This is to avoid a discrepancy between Internet Explorer and Netscape. If the margins are non-zero, Internet Explorer's values for the offset properties will be measured from the edge of the browser window, but Netscape's values will be measured from the margins. The only way to avoid this issue is to use zero margins or to adjust the position of the menus based on the current browser.

Q. To customize this example for my site, can I have more than three items in a menu?

A. Yes. Just add additional <td> sections for each menu item. Be sure each one has a unique ID attribute.

13

Q. **In Netscape 6, when I click on an item within the menu nothing happens. What's wrong?**

A. You are most likely testing the document in a local file rather than on a Web server. When you click on a link to a file that does not exist, some versions of Netscape display an error message and others do nothing. In a real site, since the links would point to actual files, this wouldn't be a problem.

Quiz

Test your knowledge of the material covered in this hour by answering the following questions.

Questions

1. If you are placing JavaScript code in a separate file, which document contains the `<script>` tag?

    a. The HTML file

    b. The JavaScript file

    c. Neither file

2. Which of the following statements correctly makes a layer, defined by the box object, visible?

    a. `box.visibility="true";`

    b. `box.style.visibility=1;`

    c. `box.style.visibility="visible";`

3. Which HTML tags are typically used to define layers?

    a. `<div>` or `<body>`

    b. `<div>` or `<span>`

    c. `<span>` or `<script>`

Answers

1. a. The `<script>` tag, with the SRC attribute, should appear in the HTML document. The JavaScript file can contain only JavaScript statements, not HTML tags.

2. c. The correct statement assigns the value `"visible"` to the `box.style.visibility` property.

3. b. Layers are typically defined using the `<div>` or `<span>` tags.

Exercises

If you'd like to practice what you learned in this hour before moving on, try the following exercises:

- Add an additional item to the Products menu in the example.
- Combine the Staff and Employment menus in the example into a single menu.

13

Hour 14

Creating a Menu Tree

One of the major limitations of HTML is that it can't support dynamic navigation systems, such as those used in computer operating systems. HTML is limited to simple lists of links. Fortunately, DHTML can overcome this limitation—you created one kind of navigation system in the previous hour.

In this hour, you'll create a hierarchical, tree-style menu that could be used as a Web site's navigation system. This provides a way to view a map of the entire site at a glance.

Hour 14 covers the following topics:

- How the menu tree will appear
- Planning the objects for the menu
- Creating the HTML document
- Creating the JavaScript functions
- Finishing and testing the example

Overview

In this hour, you'll create a hierarchical tree of options for site navigation. You might have seen this technique used on the Web—and you've certainly seen it used on your PC. Windows, Macintosh, and X-Windows systems use a system like this to allow you to navigate through the directories and files on a disk.

Here's how this menu system works. At the top level, main categories are listed. Each has a [+] icon to its left indicating that the category can be expanded. When you click on the [+] icon, the items under the category are listed, and the icon changes to a [-] symbol. You can then click on the icon to return the category to its collapsed (hidden) state.

As an example, a section of the menu might look like this:

```
[+]Products
[-]Support
   Technical Support
   Support Forum
   Contact Support
```

This example shows two categories, Products and Support. The Products category is currently collapsed, and the Support category is currently displayed.

> You also can use images rather than [+] and [-] icons. In Hour 16, "Using DHTML for Animation," you'll create a menu tree that uses image icons.

Nested Categories

While this structure of categories and items provides a well-organized navigation system for small sites, in a larger site you might want to go further and create subcategories. For example, the Products category might look like this:

```
[-]Products
   Product List
   Order Form
   [-]Specifications
      Old Products
      New Products
   Price List
```

In this example, the Products category contains four items. One of these, Specifications, can be further expanded with two sub-items under the category.

The tree navigation system you will create in this hour can actually have any number of nested levels of categories.

Objects and Events

While this menu system might sound sophisticated, it's actually simple to create. You can create it by using a <div> element to enclose each category's contents. You'll use objects for two HTML elements to create the menu:

- Each <div> that contains a category will be assigned an ID attribute. You then can find its corresponding object and manipulate the style.display property to control whether the category is expanded or collapsed.

- Each [+] icon will be enclosed within a link element (<a> tag), and the <a> tag will be assigned an ID attribute. This will allow your script to manipulate the object's innerHTML property, and change the expand ([+]) icon to a collapse ([-]) icon when the category is expanded, and vice versa when the category is collapsed.

As you might have guessed, the user will interact with the navigation system in two ways: clicking the [+] and [-] icons, and clicking on the individual item links. The browser will handle the links in the normal way, and you can use javascript: links to call a script when the icons are clicked.

Creating the HTML Document

The first step in creating the menu tree is to create the HTML document. As with the previous hour's example, you will use the SRC attribute of the <script> tag to keep the JavaScript code in a separate file.

Defining the Menu Items

The bulk of the HTML document will consist of the menu items. Each item will include a linked [+] icon, the category name, and a <div> that defines the menu items. For example, here is the HTML code for the Support category:

```
<b><a ID="xsupport" href="javascript:Toggle('support');">[+]</a>
   Support</b><br>
   <div ID="support" style="display:none; margin-left:2em;">
      <a href="tech.html">Technical Support</a><br>
      <a href="sforum.html">Support Forum</a><br>
      <a href="sforum.html">Contact Support</a><br>
   </div>
```

14

The <div> is assigned the ID attribute support, and the Toggle('support') command calls a JavaScript function to expand or collapse the category. The [+] icon's <a> element is given the ID attribute xsupport.

Using a name based on the <div> tag's identifier will make it easy to find this object in your script. If you add additional items or customize the menu, make sure you create unique ID values for each <div>, and add x to the name of each for the ID of the corresponding link tag.

> The menu tree will be collapsed by default, showing only the category names. You can make it expanded by default by changing the display style property to the value block and the [+] icon to a [-] icon.

Completing the HTML Document

By combining several menu category definitions in the <body> section, you can create a complete HTML document. Listing 14.1 shows the complete HTML code for this example.

LISTING 14.1   The Complete HTML Document

```html
<html>
<head>
   <title>Creating a Navigation Tree</title>
   <style>
      A {text-decoration: none;}
   </style>
   <script language="javascript" src="tree.js">
   </script>
</head>
<body>
<h1>Navigation Tree Example</h1>
<p>The navigation tree below allows you to expand and
collapse items. You could use this in a frame to provide a
sophisticated navigation system for a site.</p>
<hr>
<b><a ID="xproducts" href="javascript:Toggle('products');">[+]</a>
   Products</b><br>
   <div ID="products" style="display:none; margin-left:2em;">
   <a href="prodlist.html">Product List</a><br>
   <a href="order.html">Order Form</a><br>
   <a ID="xspecs" href="javascript:Toggle('specs');">[+]</a>
   Specifications<br>
   <div ID="specs" style="display:none; margin-left:2em">
```

LISTING 14.1 continued

```
          <a href="specs1.html">Old Products</a><br>
          <a href="specs2.html">New Products</a><br>
        </div>
        <a href="pricelist.html">Price List</a><br>
      </div>
<b><a ID="xsupport" href="javascript:Toggle('support');">[+]</a>
    Support</b><br>
      <div ID="support" style="display:none; margin-left:2em;">
        <a href="tech.html">Technical Support</a><br>
        <a href="sforum.html">Support Forum</a><br>
        <a href="sforum.html">Contact Support</a><br>
      </div>
<b><a ID="xcontact" href="javascript:Toggle('contact');">[+]</a>
    Contact Us</b>
      <div ID="contact" style="display:none; margin-left:2em;">
        <a href="contact1.html">Sales Department</a><br>
        <a href="contact2.html">Service Department</a><br>
        <a href="contact3.html">Marketing Department</a><br>
      </div>
<p> </p>
<a href="javascript:Expand();">[Expand All]</a><br>
<a href="javascript:Collapse();">[Collapse All]</a>
</body>
</html>
```

Notice that the Products menu contains a subcategory, and defining this is as simple as nesting a <div> tag within the <div> for the Products menu. You can nest any amount of items in this manner.

To use this HTML document, save it using any name. Notice the <script> tag that references the JavaScript file tree.js. You will create this script file in the next section.

Creating the JavaScript Functions

The JavaScript functions for the menu tree are actually quite simple. You will use a single function to expand or collapse a category. You also can create links that expand or collapse all of the categories using simple JavaScript functions.

Hiding and Showing Menus

The Toggle function is called when the user clicks on the [+] or [-] icon. This function expands or collapses a menu item, and changes the icon appropriately. Here is the JavaScript code for the Toggle function:

14

```
function Toggle(item) {
   obj=document.getElementById(item);
   visible=(obj.style.display!="none")    // true or false
   key=document.getElementById("x" + item);
   if (visible) {                          // true.
     obj.style.display="none";
     key.innerHTML="[+]";
   } else {
     obj.style.display="block";
     key.innerHTML="[-]";
   }
}
```

This function first gets the object for the category's <div> element in the obj variable, and the object for the [+]icon in the key variable. The visible variable is assigned the value true if the category is currently displayed, and the value false if it is currently hidden.

If the category is currently visible, the script assigns the value none to the display property, hiding the contents of the <div> element. It also changes the icon to a [+] symbol.

If the category is currently hidden, the script assigns the value block to the display property, revealing the category's contents. It then changes the icon to the [-] symbol.

In this example, you use the display property to hide and show the menu items. When you use this property, the page expands and collapses as the items are revealed or hidden. The visibility property wouldn't work here because it would leave a blank space for all of the items that are not currently shown.

Expanding All Items

The HTML document you created already contains links for two additional functions:

```
<a href="javascript:Expand();">[Expand All]</a><br>
<a href="javascript:Collapse();">[Collapse All]</a>
```

These will provide an easy way to show or hide all of the menu items. The Expand function expands all of the categories:

```
function Expand() {
   divs=document.getElementsByTagName("DIV");
   for (i=0;i<divs.length;i++) {
     divs[i].style.display="block";
```

```
      key=document.getElementById("x" + divs[i].id);
      key.innerHTML="[-]";
   }
}
```

This function uses the `getElementsByTagName` method to get an array, `divs`, of all of the `<div>` elements in the document. It uses a `for` loop to iterate through each of these elements. It changes their display properties to `block`, gets the object for their corresponding icon, and changes it to the `[-]` symbol.

Collapsing All Items

The `Collapse` function will collapse all of the categories in the menu tree. It is very similar to the `Expand` function:

```
function Collapse() {
   divs=document.getElementsByTagName("DIV");
   for (i=0;i<divs.length;i++) {
     divs[i].style.display="none";
     key=document.getElementById("x" + divs[i].id);
     key.innerHTML="[+]";
   }
}
```

This function also uses an array of `<div>` elements. The only difference is that it assigns the value `none` to their `display` properties, and changes their corresponding icons to `[+]` symbols.

> For simplicity, the `Expand` and `Collapse` functions show or hide every `<div>` element in the document. This works for the example, but if you include the menu in a larger HTML document, it might affect other `<div>` elements on the page. Be sure you modify the functions to account for this.

Workshop: Finishing and Testing the Menu

To complete this example, you can combine the JavaScript functions you have created into a `.js` file. Listing 14.2 shows the complete JavaScript file.

LISTING 14.2   The JavaScript File for the Menu Tree

```
function Toggle(item) {
   obj=document.getElementById(item);
   visible=(obj.style.display!="none")
   key=document.getElementById("x" + item);
```

14

LISTING 14.2 continued

```
      if (visible) {
        obj.style.display="none";
        key.innerHTML="[+]";
      } else {
         obj.style.display="block";
         key.innerHTML="[-]";
      }
  }
  function Expand() {
     divs=document.getElementsByTagName("DIV");
     for (i=0;i<divs.length;i++) {
       divs[i].style.display="block";
       key=document.getElementById("x" + divs[i].id);
       key.innerHTML="[-]";
     }
  }
  function Collapse() {
     divs=document.getElementsByTagName("DIV");
     for (i=0;i<divs.length;i++) {
       divs[i].style.display="none";
       key=document.getElementById("x" + divs[i].id);
       key.innerHTML="[+]";
     }
  }
```

To test the example, save this JavaScript file as `tree.js`. If you use a different name, be sure you modify the SRC attribute of the <script> tag in the HTML document to use the same name. Save the JavaScript file in the same directory as the HTML document.

This example requires Internet Explorer 5 or later, or Netscape 6 or later. When you load the document into a browser, the main categories are displayed. You can expand or collapse categories using the icons. Figure 14.1 shows Internet Explorer's display of this document with several categories expanded.

Don't forget that you can download all of the listings for this book, including this hour's HTML and JavaScript files, from this book's Web site at `http://www.starlingtech.com/dhtml/`.

FIGURE **14.1**

The menu tree as displayed by Internet Explorer.

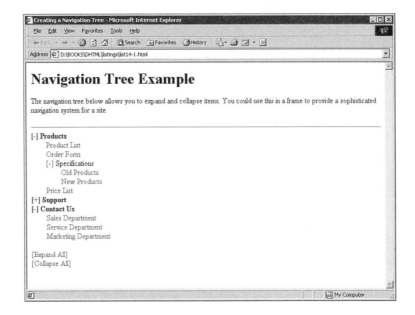

Summary

In this hour, you've created a tree-style navigation system that could easily be adapted to any Web site. This is easy to do with DHTML and provides an ideal navigation method for large Web sites.

In the next hour, you'll explore some more examples of DHTML in action. Specifically, you'll learn how to create various effects with text—moving, blinking, fading, and scrolling.

Q&A

Q. How can I use graphic symbols rather than the [+] and [-] icons?

A. Simply replace the icons in the HTML document with image tags, and change the `Toggle`, `Expand`, and `Collapse` functions to change the image sources. See Hour 16 for a modified version of this hour's example with images.

Q. If I use this form of navigation on my site, won't the entire content move up and down as the sections are expanded and collapsed?

A. Yes, if the entire site is in a single window. You can avoid this issue by placing the navigation system in a frame within the page, or even in a column of a table.

14

Q. **How can I prevent the `Expand` and `Collapse` functions from hiding or showing other `<div>` elements within my page?**

A. One easy way is to keep the navigation tree in its own frame. If that isn't practical, you can modify the `ID` attributes to have a common value: for instance, using a special character in the names that won't be expanded or collapsed. You then can modify the Expand and Collapse functions to check for that character in each division's `id` attribute before modifying it. Hour 16 includes a modified version of this hour's example that includes this feature.

Q. **Can this example be adapted to work in the version 4.0 browsers?**

A. Yes—see Hour 17, "Dealing with Browser Differences," for an explanation. However, the 4.0 browsers don't consistently support the `display` attribute, so you might run into problems.

Quiz

Test your knowledge of the material covered in this hour by answering the following questions.

Questions

1. Which of these properties can you use to hide or show an element of a document and have the remainder of the document expand or collapse accordingly?

   a. `style.visibility`

   b. `style.display`

   c. `style.collapse`

2. Which is the correct command to find objects for all of the `<div>` elements in a document and store them in an array?

   a. `divs=document.getElementsByTagName("DIV");`

   b. `divs=document.getArrayByTagName("DIV");`

   c. `divs=document.style.getElementsByTagName("DIV");`

3. Which of the following is the correct command to change the linked text within an `<a>` tag?

   a. `key.textValue="[+]";`

   b. `key.linkText="[+]";`

   c. `key.innerHTML="[+]";`

Answers

1. b. The `style.display` property allows you to expand or collapse the display of items within a Web document.

2. a. This is the correct statement: `divs=document.getElementsByTagName("DIV");`

3. c. The `innerHTML` property is one way to change the text within a link tag.

Exercises

If you'd like to work further with this example before moving on, try the following exercises:

- Create a menu for your own site, or a different imaginary site, using this hour's example as a basis. Test it in a browser and verify that it works correctly.

- Add "Show Menu" and "Hide Menu" links to the example in Listing 13.1. Create script functions to hide or show the entire menu. One easy way to do this is to place the entire menu in a <span> tag, and change that element's `display` property. See Hour 16 for a more complex example that uses animation to hide and show the menu.

14

Hour 15

Creating DHTML Text Effects

While DHTML can do complex things like setting up a navigation system for a site, it's also well-suited to simple tasks. You can add a bit of style or life to a Web page with a simple DHTML script.

In this hour, you'll explore some simple ways to use DHTML to draw attention to text within a page: blinking text, fading text, moving text, and scrolling messages.

This hour covers the following topics:

- Creating blinking text
- Moving text within a page
- Fading text in and out
- Creating a scrolling message

Creating Blinking Text

Netscape created quite a buzz when they introduced the `<blink>` tag in version 2.0. This tag, not part of the HTML standard, caused its contents to disappear and reappear at regular intervals. Between the proprietary nature of the tag and the headaches it caused, it quickly gained a well-deserved bad reputation.

Wisely, Internet Explorer never supported `<blink>`, and even Netscape stopped supporting it in Netscape 6. Nonetheless, there are a few situations in which you might still want blinking text, and you can easily accomplish this using DHTML.

> To avoid annoying your readers, you should avoid blinking text except when absolutely necessary—for example, in an error message or an online game. Remember, the title of your page is *not* important enough to blink.

Creating the Script

To make the text blink, you'll need a simple JavaScript function. The `Blink` function will toggle the text's `visibility` attribute, and then set a timer for the next blink:

```
function Blink() {
   obj=document.getElementById("blink");
   if (obj.style.visibility=="hidden") obj.style.visibility="visible";
      else obj.style.visibility="hidden";
   window.setTimeout("Blink();",500);
}
```

This function first finds the object for the text with the ID "blink". Next, it checks the text's `style.visibility` attribute. If the text is currently hidden, it is made visible; otherwise, it is hidden.

Finally, the `Blink` function uses the `window.setTimeout` method to repeat itself. This causes the function to be called again in 500 milliseconds (half a second).

> Change the `500` in this function to change the rate of blinking. Smaller numbers speed it up, and larger numbers slow it down. Be warned, though, text that blinks too quickly can give viewers headaches.

Completing the Blinking Text Example

To use the `Blink` function, all you need to do is include it in an HTML document and assign the `ID` attribute "blink" to some text. Listing 15.1 shows the complete example document.

LISTING 15.1 The Complete Blinking Text Example

```
<html>
<head>
   <title>Blinking Text Example</title>
<script language="javascript">
function Blink() {
   obj=document.getElementById("blink");
   if (obj.style.visibility=="hidden") obj.style.visibility="visible";
      else obj.style.visibility="hidden";
   window.setTimeout("Blink();",500);
}
</script>
</head>
<body onLoad="Blink();">
<h1>Blinking Text Example</h1>
<p>This is a quick example of blinking text.
<span ID="blink">This sentence is blinking</span> because a
DHTML script is manipulating its visibility property.</p>
</body>
</html>
```

This HTML document includes the `Blink` function you created, and the `onLoad` event handler for the `<body>` tag starts the blinking. The sentence that will blink is contained in a `<span>` tag with the ID attribute set to `"blink"`.

> The Blinking Text, Moving Text, and Fading text examples in this hour require Internet Explorer 5.0 or later or Netscape 6 or later, but they could easily be adapted to 4.0 browsers using the techniques in Hour 17, "Dealing with Browser Differences."

Moving Text

Another way to draw attention to text is to move it, and you can easily do this with DHTML. In Hour 6, "Creating Positionable Elements (Layers)," you learned the positioning properties that make this possible.

Creating the Script

Only a small script is required to move the text:

```
var pos=0;
var direction=1;
function Move() {
   obj=document.getElementById("head1");
   pos += direction;
   if (pos >= 100 || pos <= -100) direction = 0 - direction;
   obj.style.left=pos;
   window.setTimeout("Move();",25);
}
```

This script first declares two variables, pos and direction. The pos variable will store the current position of the heading, and the direction variable indicates the current direction of motion: 1 moves to the right, and -1 moves to the left.

The Move function handles the actual moving. It first finds the variable for the head1 object, which will be a heading on the page. Next, it increments or decrements pos by adding the direction variable. The if statement checks the position, which can range from -100 to 100. If the position reaches the edge of this boundary, it switches directions.

 The position of the text ranges from -100 to 100 because the heading will use relative positioning. When the position is -100, the heading will be 100 pixels to the left of its original position.

Finally, the Move function sets the style.left property for the heading to the pos value and uses the setTimeout method to repeat itself. The Move function will be called again every 25 milliseconds.

Completing the Moving Text Example

To use the moving text script, all you need to do is add it to an HTML document and assign the ID head1 to an object within the page. Listing 15.2 shows the complete moving text example.

LISTING 15.2   A Simple Example of Moving Text

```
<html>
<head>
<title>Moving Text Example</title>
<script language="javascript">
var pos=0;
```

LISTING 15.2   continued

```
var direction=1;
function Move() {
   obj=document.getElementById("head1");
   pos += direction;
   if (pos >= 100 || pos <= -100) direction = 0 - direction;
   obj.style.left=pos;
   window.setTimeout("Move();",25);
}
</script>
</head>
<body onLoad="Move();">
<h1 align="center" style="position:relative;" ID="head1">
  Moving Text Example</h1>
<p>The heading of this page moves back and forth
across the page. This is done using DHTML and the
style attributes that control positioning.</p>
</body>
</html>
```

The <h1> heading is assigned the ID head1. Its position style attribute has been set to relative so that the motion will be relative to its original (centered) position. The onLoad event handler for the <body> tag calls the Move function to start the motion.

Figure 15.1 shows this example running in Internet Explorer. In the figure, the message has just reached the right-hand side and is now moving to the left.

FIGURE 15.1

The moving text example in action.

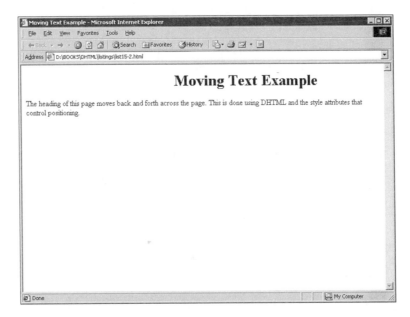

Fading Text

You also can draw attention to text by fading it in or out. This is easily accomplished in DHTML by changing the text color. You might recall using code like this to change a text color earlier in this book:

```
h=document.getElementById("head1");
h.style.color="Blue";
```

This example changes the color of the head1 object to blue. Along with color names, you also can use a hexadecimal number that specifies the red, green, and blue values. This example changes the color to green using a numeric value:

```
h=document.getElementById("head1");
h.style.color="#00FF00";
```

To fade text from white to black using shades of gray, you can cycle through color values that have equal red, green, and blue components. For example, #050505, #101010, and #F1F1F1 are three different shades of gray.

Creating the Script

You can create a simple script that allows text to be faded either in (white to black) or out (black to white):

```
var hcolor=255;
function Fade(direction) {
    obj=document.getElementById("head1");
    hcolor += direction;
    if (hcolor >= 0 && hcolor < 256) {
        hex=hcolor.toString(16);
        if (hex.length==1) hex="0" + hex;
        obj.style.color="#" + hex + hex + hex;
        window.setTimeout("Fade(" + direction + ");",1);
    }
}
```

This script first declares a global variable, hcolor, to store the current color of the heading. The Fade function handles the actual fading. This function's parameter, direction, specifies the direction of the fade: 1 for black to white, and –1 for white to black.

After finding the object for the head1 heading, the Fade function adds the direction value to hcolor. An if statement verifies that hcolor falls within the legal range of zero to 255. If it does, the function continues.

The hex variable is assigned to the hexadecimal equivalent of hcolor using the toString method. The function then builds a string with the # symbol followed by the same hexadecimal number three times, and changes the heading's color.

The if statement that checks hex.length is necessary because a single-digit value of hcolor, such as 5, would produce an invalid color string (#555). If the value has only one digit, an initial zero is added.

Last, but not least, the Fade function uses window.setTimeout to repeat itself in one millisecond. You can use a longer delay for a slower fade, or use larger values of direction for a faster fade that skips some shades.

Completing the Fading Text Example

To use the fading text script, simply add it to an HTML document, assign the identifier head1 to an object, and trigger the Fade function. Listing 15.3 shows the complete fading text example.

LISTING 15.3 The Complete Fading Text Example

```html
<html>
<head>
<title>Fading Text Example</title>
<script language="javascript">
var hcolor=255;
function Fade(direction) {
   obj=document.getElementById("head1");
   hcolor += direction;
   if (hcolor >= 0 && hcolor < 256) {
      hex=hcolor.toString(16);
      if (hex.length==1) hex="0" + hex;
      obj.style.color="#" + hex + hex + hex;
      window.setTimeout("Fade(" + direction + ");",1);
   }
}
</script>
</head>
<body onLoad="Fade(-1);">
<h1 ID="head1" style="color:#FFFFFF;">
Fading Text Example</h1>
<p>The heading of this page fades in gradually when you load the
page, and you can
<a href="javascript:Fade(1);">fade it out</a> or
<a href="javascript:Fade(-1);">back in</a> using these links.
This is accomplished by changing the color of the heading
using DHTML.</p>
</body>
</html>
```

This example creates an <h1> heading with the ID head1 to be faded. The onLoad event handler in the <body> tag fades the heading in when the page is loaded. You also can use the two links that call the Fade function directly to fade the text in or out.

Fading text can be a relatively tasteful effect, especially when it fades in and stops as in this example. Text that continues to fade in and out can be distracting.

Workshop: Creating a Scrolling Message

While not as dramatic (or annoying, depending on your opinion) as blinking text, scrolling messages have been a fixture on the Web since the advent of JavaScript. However, they have been traditionally limited to scrolling within the status line or a form field.

DHTML removes this limitation. Since the W3C DOM allows you to modify any text within the page, you easily can create a scrolling message within the contents of any HTML tag.

Creating the Script

The scrolling message will use a JavaScript function to handle each step of the scrolling. Here is the script:

```
msg = "This is an example of a scrolling message. ";
msg += "Notice that the actual message is larger ";
msg += "and only a portion is displayed at once. ";
pos = 0;
function ScrollMessage() {
    newtext = msg.substring(pos, msg.length) +
        "...  ..." + msg.substring(0, pos);
    newtext=newtext.substring(0,80);
    obj = document.getElementById("scroll");
    obj.firstChild.nodeValue = newtext;
    pos++;
    if (pos > msg.length) pos = 0;
    window.setTimeout("ScrollMessage()",150);
}
```

This script first defines the msg variable, containing the entire message to scroll, and the pos variable, which will store the current scrolling position. The ScrollMessage function handles the actual scrolling.

15

This function first assigns the `newtext` variable to the latest text for the scrolling area. This consists of the message from the `pos` position to the end, a spacer, and the message from the beginning to the `pos` position. The text is then limited to its first 80 characters to prevent the scrolling message from wrapping on the screen.

> Since this example modifies text within the Web page, it requires Internet Explorer 5.0 or later, or Netscape 6 or later. There is no easy way to achieve this effect in the 4.0 browsers.

The function then finds the object for the paragraph with the `ID` attribute "scroll" and assigns the value of its text node to the new text.

Next, the `ScrollMessage` function increments the `pos` variable. The `if` statement checks whether the end of the message has been reached, and if so, it starts `pos` over at zero. Finally, it uses the `window.setTimeout` method to repeat the `ScrollMessage` function every 150 milliseconds.

> As with the other examples in this hour, you can speed up or slow down the scrolling message by changing the `150` in the `window.setTimeout` method to a different value. Keep in mind that timeouts under 150 tend to create messages that move too fast to read.

Putting It All Together

To test the scrolling message script, you can add it to an HTML document and create a text object to scroll. This example will use a `<pre>` tag, since it displays the text in a monospace font. This makes the scrolling appear smoother.

Listing 15.4 shows the complete scrolling message example.

LISTING 15.4   The Complete Scrolling Message Example

```
<html>
<head>
<title>Scrolling Messages in DHTML</title>
<script language="javascript">
msg = "This is an example of a scrolling message. ";
```

LISTING 15.4 continued

```
msg += "Notice that the actual message is larger ";
msg += "and only a portion is displayed at once. ";
pos = 0;
function ScrollMessage() {
   newtext = msg.substring(pos, msg.length) +
      "...  ..." + msg.substring(0, pos);
   newtext=newtext.substring(0,80);
   obj = document.getElementById("scroll");
   obj.firstChild.nodeValue = newtext;
   pos++;
   if (pos > msg.length) pos = 0;
   window.setTimeout("ScrollMessage()",100);
}
</script>
</head>
<body onLoad="ScrollMessage();">
<h1>A DHTML Scrolling Message</h1>
<p>The text below is scrolled across the screen using DHTML.
This allows text to be scrolled directly in the body of the page
rather than within a form or the status line.</p>
<hr>
<pre ID="scroll">This text is required, but will be replaced.</pre>
</body>
</html>
```

The onLoad event handler in the <body> tag starts the scrolling message by calling the ScrollMessage function. The <pre> tag has been assigned an ID attribute of "scroll" and will contain the scrolling message.

Notice the text in the <pre> tag, which will be instantly replaced by the scrolling message. This is necessary because if you leave the <pre> tag empty, the browser won't create a text node to hold the scrolling message.

To test this example, load it into a browser. Figure 15.2 shows the scrolling message in action in Netscape 6.

FIGURE 15.2

FIGURE 15.2

The scrolling message example in action.

Summary

In this hour, you've explored some simple examples of using DHTML to add emphasis to text: blinking text, moving text, fading text, and a scrolling message. To keep your visitors sane, please use these techniques sparingly, and refrain from using them all on the same page.

In the next hour, you'll further explore how DHTML can be used for animation with a more complex example of animated graphics.

Q&A

Q. How can I speed up the moving text example?

A. If you reduce the delay in the window.setTimeout statement, the text will move faster. For an even faster display, change the initial value of the direction variable to a number greater than one.

Q. Why does the fading text example use timeouts instead of a simple for loop to fade the text?

A. While you could use a for loop to cycle the color through all of the shades of gray, it would happen very quickly—on a fast computer, it would look like the color instantly changed rather than faded. Using timeouts allows you to slow down the effect.

Q. Why doesn't the scrolling message look as good with proportional fonts?

A. Since these fonts have different widths for different letters, for example "i" and "W", the message appears to move at different rates depending on the letters in the message. With a monospace font, the letter widths—and the movements—are equal.

Q. Can I scroll a message vertically, like the credits at the end of a film?

A. Yes. This is a great way to scroll a longer message, or several, while keeping it readable. See Hour 24, "DHTML Tips and Tricks," for an example of vertical scrolling.

Quiz

Test your knowledge of the material covered in this hour by answering the following questions.

Questions

1. Which of the following is the correct command to set a timeout that calls the `Fade` function in half a second?

   a. `window.setTimeout(Fade();,.5);`

   b. `window.setTimeout(Fade();,500);`

   c. `window.setTimeout("Fade();",500);`

2. Which of the following browsers supports the `<blink>` tag?

   a. Netscape 6

   b. Netscape 4

   c. Internet Explorer 5

3. Which of the following timeouts in the scrolling message example would result in the fastest scrolling?

   a. `window.setTimeout("ScrollMessage()",200);`

   b. `window.setTimeout("ScrollMessage()",50);`

   c. `window.setTimeout("ScrollMessage()",1000);`

Answers

1. c. The correct statement uses quotation marks around the JavaScript statement to be executed, and the value of 500 milliseconds (half a second).

2. b. Netscape 4 supports the `<blink>` tag, but Internet Explorer and Netscape 6 do not.

3. b. Since shorter delays lead to faster scrolling, a delay of 50 milliseconds would scroll the message the fastest. Too fast to read, in fact.

Exercises

If you'd like to experiment further with this hour's examples before you move on, try the following exercises:

- Change the moving text example to move the heading vertically, instead of horizontally.

- Change the fading text example to fade through several different colors, instead of shades of gray.

Hour **16**

Using DHTML for Animation

One of the most dramatic applications of DHTML is in the area of animation. By repeatedly changing object positions, you can create a moving object within a Web page, or add stylish animation to other dynamic tasks.

In this hour, you'll explore the use of DHTML for animation by creating two examples: a simple animated graphic, and a menu bar that can be shown or hidden using animation.

This hour covers the following topics:

- Choosing appropriate animation methods
- Creating JavaScript functions for animation
- Completing a simple animation example
- Creating an animated navigation bar

Methods of Web Animation

There are many reasons to use animation: novelties and games, technical illustrations that show a process, or stylish transitions, to name a few.

There are also many ways to create animation for the Web. While DHTML is ideal for some types of animation, it isn't always the best choice. Before you create animations using DHTML, it would be useful to review the different ways Web pages can be animated.

Animated GIF Images

The GIF image standard supports animated images, and this was the first type of animation supported by Web browsers. Animated GIF images consist of two or more images that are rotated over time. At its simplest, this effect creates most of the flashing advertising banners that distract you from your favorite sites.

GIF animations can be more complex—you can even display a series of photographs within the animated GIF, creating a primitive movie. However, this creates a large graphic file, and the GIF format doesn't support full-color graphics.

JavaScript Image Animation

You can use JavaScript to create animations similar to animated GIF images, simply by replacing one image with another on the page. This can be done using the `images` array, part of the Level 0 DOM, and is supported by Netscape 2.0 and later, and Internet Explorer 3.0 and later.

This technique is handy for animating small drawings. Unlike GIF animations, JavaScript animations can interact with the user—for example, a button can become animated when the mouse pointer moves across it.

Dynamic HTML

You've already learned how to use the DOM's positioning properties to move layers or other objects using DHTML. By repeatedly moving an object, you can create a simple animation. The examples in this hour will demonstrate this.

You also can combine DHTML positioning animation with JavaScript image-swapping to create more complicated animations. Hour 22, "Creating Complex Animations," demonstrates an example of this technique.

Flash

Macromedia's Flash plug-in is becoming ubiquitous on the Web, and is supported by the latest browsers. Like animated GIFs, its most popular use is in advertising banners, but Flash can create some much more impressive animations.

Flash has one important advantage over animated GIFs and JavaScript animations: it's vector-based. This means that rather than storing a series of bitmap images, the animation can simply be a set of instructions for drawing the parts of the animation.

Using vector-based graphics allows complicated animations to be performed with low-bandwidth files. It also allows the animation to easily be shown at different screen resolutions while maintaining a size.

For more information about Flash, see Macromedia's Web site, `http://www.macromedia.com/`.

Java

Sun's Java language provides a sophisticated way of creating animations, but is rarely the easiest choice unless the animation needs to interact with the user or with data on the Web. For example, Java could be used to create an animated stock ticker. For more information about Java, see Sun's Web site, `http://java.sun.com/`.

Movies

Last, but not least, Web browsers support movies using Microsoft's AVI format and Apple's QuickTime format. If you need a full-scale movie, rather than a simple animation, these are much better choices.

Creating a Simple Animation

As a simple example of animation using DHTML, you can create a graphic that moves across the screen. You can place the graphic within a layer and repeatedly change the layer's position, effectively moving the graphic across the page.

You also can assign an ID attribute to the image itself and move it, rather than using a layer. However, using a layer makes it easy to adapt this example to work with older browsers. Hour 17, "Dealing with Browser Differences," includes a version of this example that works on both 4.0 browsers and newer browsers.

The graphic for this example, `mouse.gif`, is available at this book's Web site: `http://www.starlingtech.com/dhtml/`. If you're a better artist than me—most people are—you can also substitute the graphic of your choice.

Creating the Animation Function

You can animate the mouse graphic using a single function. Here is the `Move` function:

```
function Move() {
   position += 1;
   if (position > 650) position = 0;
    document.getElementById("mouse").style.left = position;
    window.setTimeout("Move();",10);
}
```

This function increments the `position` variable by one, and if it has passed 650, resets it to zero. It then finds the object for the mouse graphic, and sets its `style.left` property to the `position` value. Finally, the `Move` function uses the `setTimeout` method to call itself again in 10 milliseconds.

Completing the HTML Document

To complete the animation example, you simply need to include the `Move` function in an HTML document and initialize it. Listing 16.1 shows the complete HTML document.

LISTING 16.1   The Complete HTML Document for the Simple Animation Example

```
<html>
<head>
<title>Animation with Dynamic HTML</title>
<script language="javascript">
var position=0;
function Move() {
   position += 1;
   if (position > 650) position = 0;
   document.getElementById("mouse").style.left = position;
   window.setTimeout("Move();",10);
}
</script>
 </head>
 <body onLoad="Move();">
 <H1>Animation with Dynamic HTML</H1>
 <HR>
<div ID="mouse" STYLE="position:absolute; left:0; top:100;
  width:100; height:100; visibility:show">
  <img src="mouse.gif" width=100 height=100 alt="" border="0">
</div>
</body>
</html>
```

This HTML document includes a `<script>` section that first initializes the `position` variable, then declares the `Move` function. The `onLoad` event handler in the `<body>` tag starts the animation by calling the `Move` function. The `<div>` section in the body of the page declares the layer that contains the graphic.

To try the example, save it and load it into a browser. This example requires Netscape 6 or later or Internet Explorer 5.0 or later. Figure 16.1 shows Netscape's display of this example as the mouse image moves across the screen.

FIGURE **16.1**

The simple animation example in action.

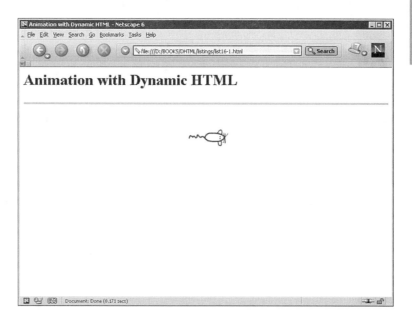

Workshop: Creating an Animated Navigation Bar

Another use for animation is to add a touch of style to more useful DHTML features. One feature that can be animated is the process of showing or hiding a section of the page, such as a navigation bar.

In Hour 14, "Creating a Menu Tree," you created a DHTML navigation tree with items that can be expanded or collapsed. As another example of animation, you can move the menu tree to a navigation bar on the left side of the page, and use animation to show or hide it.

This version of the menu tree also adds another feature: graphic icons instead of the [+] and [-] symbols.

Creating the HTML Document

The HTML document for this example is largely the same as the original in Hour 14. The main differences are that the navigation bar and the body text have been enclosed within <div> tags to allow them to be positioned, and images are used instead of [+] and [-] icons.

Listing 16.2 shows the complete HTML document. The script functions will be contained in a separate JavaScript file, animenu.js.

LISTING 16.2 The HTML Document for the Animated Navigation Bar

```
<html>
<head>
   <title>Animated Navigation Tree</title>
   <style>
     A {text-decoration: none;}
   </style>
   <script language="javascript" src="list16-3.js">
   </script>
</head>
<body>
<div id="_tree"
style="position: absolute; left:0; height:100%; background-color:aqua;">
<b><a ID="icon" href="javascript: ShowHide();">&gt;&gt;&gt;</a></b><br>
<div id="_indented" style="margin-left:31px">
   <b><a ID="xproducts" href="javascript:Toggle('products');">
     <img name="xproducts" width="20" height="20"
     src="minus.gif" border="0" align="middle">
   </a>Products</b><br>
   <div ID="products" style="display:block; margin-left:2em;">
    <a href="prodlist.html">Product List</a><br>
    <a href="order.html">Order Form</a><br>
    <a href="javascript:Toggle('specs');">
    <img name="xspecs" width="20" height="20"
     src="minus.gif" border="0" align="middle">
    </a>Specifications<br>
      <div ID="specs" style="display:block; margin-left:2em">
        <a href="specs1.html">Old Products</a><br>
        <a href="specs2.html">New Products</a><br>
      </div>
    <a href="pricelist.html">Price List</a><br>
```

LISTING 16.2   continued

```
   </div>
   <b><a href="javascript:Toggle('support');">
    <img name="xsupport" width="20" height="20"
    src="minus.gif" border="0" align="middle">
   </a>Support</b><br>
   <div ID="support" style="display:block; margin-left:2em;">
    <a href="tech.html">Technical Support</a><br>
    <a href="sforum.html">Support Forum</a><br>
    <a href="sforum.html">Contact Support</a><br>
   </div>
   <b><a href="javascript:Toggle('contact');">
     <img name="xcontact" width="20" height="20"
     src="minus.gif" border="0" align="middle">
    </a>Contact Us</b>
    <div ID="contact" style="display:block; margin-left:2em;">
     <a href="contact1.html">Sales Department</a><br>
     <a href="contact2.html">Service Department</a><br>
     <a href="contact3.html">Marketing Department</a><br>
    </div>
  <p> </p>
  <a href="javascript:Expand();">[Expand All]</a><br>
  <a href="javascript:Collapse();">[Collapse All]</a>
</div>
</div>
<div ID="_text"
style="position:absolute; left:30px; height:100%; background-color:white;">
<h1>Animated Navigation Tree Example</h1>
<p>The navigation tree to the left allows you to expand and
collapse items. You can hide or show the menu iteself using the
&lt;&lt;&lt; or &gt;&gt;&gt; icons.</p>
</div>
</body>
</html>
```

To use this example, save it as an HTML file. You can test it in a browser, but the dynamic functions won't work until you add the JavaScript in the following sections. Figure 16.2 shows Internet Explorer's initial display of the HTML document, with the menu hidden.

Notice that when you first load the document, the body text layer is positioned to cover most of the navigation bar. The animation you add later will move the body text layer to the right or left, revealing or hiding the navigation bar.

FIGURE 16.2

The animated naviga-tion bar example with the menu hidden.

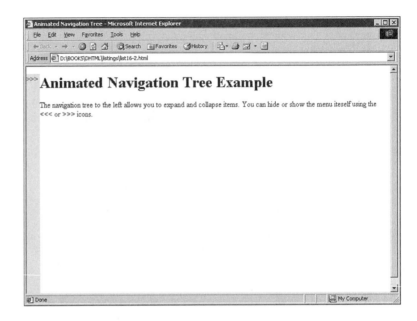

Planning Layers

If you examine the HTML document in Listing 16.2, you'll notice that it uses several nested <div> elements to create layers that can be hidden or positioned. Since this structure can be confusing, here's a breakdown of the different <div> sections used:

- The _tree layer contains the entire navigation tree. This layer will be hidden under the body text layer and revealed using animation.
- The _indented layer contains all of the menu items and their menus. This layer is indented so that no part of the menu is visible until the user chooses to show it.
- The products, support, and contact layers each contain a menu that can be shown or hidden. Additionally, the products layer has a submenu, specs.
- The _text layer contains the body text. This layer will be animated to hide and reveal the navigation tree.

Figure 16.3 is a diagram showing how these layers are nested.

The text layer has been assigned a white background using the background-color style property. Setting a color is necessary because otherwise the layer would be transparent, and would be shown merged with the navigation bar layer underneath.

16

FIGURE 16.3

The menu tree uses several nested layers.

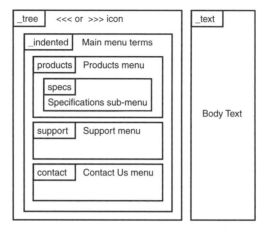

Expanding or Collapsing Items

The Toggle function is called when the [+] or [-] icons are clicked. This function is only slightly different from Hour 14's example:

```
function Toggle(item) {
  obj=document.getElementById(item);
  visible=(obj.style.display!="none")
  key="x" + item;
  if (visible) {
    obj.style.display="none";
    document.images[key].src="plus.gif";
  } else {
    obj.style.display="block";
    document.images[key].src="minus.gif";
  }
}
```

This function first checks whether the item is currently visible, and assigns the visible variable accordingly. Depending on this value, it either shows or hides the item using its display property, and resets the icon.

This time, the images array, part of the Level 0 DOM, is used to change the src attribute of the image for the [+] or [-] icon. Depending on the status of the menu, either plus.gif or minus.gif is assigned as the image source.

The images for the [+] and [-] icons are available at this book's Web site, http://www.starlingtech.com/dhtml/.

Expand and Collapse All

The Expand and Collapse functions expand or collapse the entire menu tree at once. In Hour 14's example, these functions simply used a loop to work on every <div> element in the entire document. Since you are now using some <div> elements for other purposes, you need to add a statement to differentiate the two:

```
if (divs[i].id.indexOf("_") >-1) continue;
```

> The indexOf string method searches for a character within a string. It returns an index if it is found, and -1 if it is not found.

This statement checks whether the underscore (_) character appears in the ID attribute for each division. If it is there, the loop continues with the next item. In the HTML document you created earlier, the <div> elements that are not part of the menu tree have been assigned names beginning with the underscore character.

Here are the Expand and Collapse functions with the added if statements, and the changes needed to work with the graphic [+] and [-] icons:

```
function Expand() {
   divs=document.getElementsByTagName("DIV");
   for (i=0;i<divs.length;i++) {
      if (divs[i].id.indexOf("_") >-1) continue;
      divs[i].style.display="block";
      key="x" + divs[i].id;
      document.images[key].src="minus.gif";
   }
}
function Collapse() {
   divs=document.getElementsByTagName("DIV");
   for (i=0;i<divs.length;i++) {
      if (divs[i].id.indexOf("_") >-1) continue;
      divs[i].style.display="none";
      key="x" + divs[i].id;
      document.images[key].src="plus.gif";
   }
}
```

The ShowHide Function

The ShowHide function will be called when the <<< or >>> icon is clicked, to show or hide the entire menu using animation. Here is the JavaScript code for this function:

```
function ShowHide() {
   if (!document.getElementById) return;
   thetext=document.getElementById("_text");
   thetree=document.getElementById("_tree");
   theicon=document.getElementById("icon");
   if (thetext.offsetLeft<40) {
      MoveRight();
      theicon.innerHTML="&lt;&lt;&lt;";
   }
   else {
      MoveLeft();
      theicon.innerHTML="&gt;&gt;&gt;";
   }
}
```

16

This function first finds objects for three elements: the body text layer (_text), the menu tree layer (_tree) and the <<< or >>> icon (icon). It then uses an if statement to determine the body text's current location.

If the body text is currently covering the menu, the MoveRight function is called to slide it to the right, and the icon is changed to <<<. If the menu is already showing, the MoveLeft function is called to slide the text back over the menu, and the icon is changed to >>>.

The MoveRight Function

When the body text layer moves to the right, it should start at its current position and move until it is on the right side of the menu tree. You can use the offsetWidth property to determine the right edge of the menu tree. The final destination of the animation will be 10 pixels to the right of the menu tree's right edge:

```
thetree.offsetWidth + 10
```

The MoveRight function moves the body text to the right step-by-step, gradually revealing the menu tree. Here is the MoveRight function:

```
function MoveRight() {
   thetext=document.getElementById("_text");
   thetree=document.getElementById("_tree");
   position +=10;
   thetext.style.left=position;
   if (position < thetree.offsetWidth + 10) {
      window.setTimeout("MoveRight();",3);
   }
}
```

This function first finds objects for the body text and the menu tree. It increments the `position` variable by 10 pixels. This global variable will keep track of the body text layer's current position.

The `MoveRight` function then sets the text layer's `style.left` attribute to the `position` value. The `if` statement checks whether the layer has reached its final destination. If not, it uses the `setTimeout` method to call itself again after a 3-millisecond delay.

> The speed of the animation is controlled by two values: the increment in the `position += 10` statement, and the timeout value in the `setTimeout` statement. Use a larger increment or a smaller timeout to speed things up.

The `MoveLeft` Function

The `MoveLeft` function moves the body text layer to the left step-by-step, hiding the menu tree. This function is the opposite of the `MoveRight` function:

```
function MoveLeft() {
   thetext=document.getElementById("_text");
   thetree=document.getElementById("_tree");
   position -=10;
   thetext.style.left=position;
   if (position > 30) {
      window.setTimeout("MoveLeft();",3);
   }
}
```

This function subtracts 10 from the `position` variable each time it runs. If the body text layer has not yet reached its final destination of 30 pixels from the edge, `MoveLeft` is called again using a timeout.

Putting It All Together

To complete the animated navigation bar example, you simply need to create a JavaScript file with the functions you have created. Listing 16.3 shows the complete JavaScript file.

LISTING 16.3   The JavaScript File for the Animated Navigation Bar

```
var position=30;
function Toggle(item) {
   obj=document.getElementById(item);
   visible=(obj.style.display!="none")
   key="x" + item;
```

LISTING 16.3 continued

```
    if (visible) {
      obj.style.display="none";
      document.images[key].src="plus.gif";
    } else {
       obj.style.display="block";
       document.images[key].src="minus.gif";
    }
}
function Expand() {
    divs=document.getElementsByTagName("DIV");
    for (i=0;i<divs.length;i++) {
      if (divs[i].id.indexOf("_") >-1) continue;
      divs[i].style.display="block";
      key="x" + divs[i].id;
      document.images[key].src="minus.gif";
    }
}
function Collapse() {
    divs=document.getElementsByTagName("DIV");
    for (i=0;i<divs.length;i++) {
      if (divs[i].id.indexOf("_") >-1) continue;
      divs[i].style.display="none";
      key="x" + divs[i].id;
      document.images[key].src="plus.gif";
    }
}
function ShowHide() {
    if (!document.getElementById) return;
    thetext=document.getElementById("_text");
    thetree=document.getElementById("_tree");
    theicon=document.getElementById("icon");
    if (thetext.offsetLeft<40) {
      MoveRight();
      theicon.innerHTML="&lt;&lt;&lt;";
    }
    else {
      MoveLeft();
      theicon.innerHTML="&gt;&gt;&gt;";
    }
}
function MoveRight() {
    thetext=document.getElementById("_text");
    thetree=document.getElementById("_tree");
    position +=10;
    thetext.style.left=position;
    if (position < thetree.offsetWidth + 10) {
      window.setTimeout("MoveRight();",3);
    }
```

16

LISTING 16.3 continued

```
}
function MoveLeft() {
   thetext=document.getElementById("_text");
   thetree=document.getElementById("_tree");
   position -=10;
   thetext.style.left=position;
   if (position > 30) {
      window.setTimeout("MoveLeft();",3);
   }
}
```

This JavaScript file simply consists of the functions you have created, with the addition of a var statement on the first line to set the initial value for the position global variable.

To use this file, save it as animenu.js in the same directory as the HTML document you created earlier, and load the HTML document into a browser. Figure 16.4 shows the result in Netscape 6 after the move to the right has completed, with the navigation bar completely revealed.

FIGURE 16.4

The example after the navigation bar has been revealed.

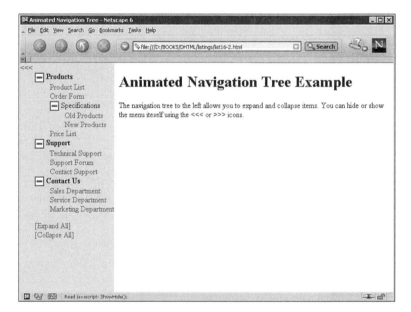

Summary

In this hour, you've learned how DHTML's positioning features can be used to create animation. You've created a simple example, and a more complex example that hides and shows a navigation bar.

Congratulations—you've reached the end of Part IV! In Part V, "Learning Advanced Techniques," you'll learn some advanced DHTML techniques, including dealing with older browsers, creating dynamic forms, using downloadable fonts, and troubleshooting.

16

Q&A

Q. Can I animate more than one object at once?

A. Yes. Simply create separate `position` variables for each object and update them all in the `Move` function. You also can move an object vertically, as well as horizontally, by using a separate variable for the vertical position.

Q. Can objects be animated in the version 4.0 browsers?

A. Yes, although you'll need separate animation functions for Netscape and Internet Explorer. Hour 17 includes a modified version of this hour's simple animation example that works in the 4.0 browsers.

Q. Why does the example in Listings 16.2 and 16.3 use `&gt;` and `&lt;` instead of the > and < symbols?

A. Since the < and > (greater-than and less-than) symbols are used in the formatting of HTML tags, such as `<body>`, HTML requires that you use coded versions when you want to display the actual symbols.

Quiz

Test your knowledge of the material covered in this hour by answering the following questions.

Questions

1. Which JavaScript method is typically used to repeat an animation function?

    a. `window.repeat`

    b. `window.setTimeout`

    c. `window.animate`

2. Which of the following is the correct command to set the horizontal position of a layer to the 100th pixel from the left?

    a. `layer.style.left=100;`

    b. `layer.left=100;`

    c. `layer.x=100;`

3. What causes the body text layer to obscure the navigation layer in Listing 16.2?

    a. The `z-index` properties are set explicitly.

    b. It is defined last.

    c. It has a lighter background color.

Answers

1. b. The `window.setTimeout` method is typically used to repeat animation functions.

2. a. The `style.left` property determines a layer or other object's horizontal position.

3. b. Since the example doesn't explicitly set the `z-index` properties of the layers, the layer defined second (the body text layer) appears on top.

Exercises

If you'd like more practice with DHTML before you move on to Part V, try the following exercises:

- Modify Listing 16.1 to place two mice on the screen on different rows, each with a different speed.

- Create a simplified version of Listing 16.3 that shows or hides the navigation bar without animation.

PART V

Learning Advanced Techniques

Hour

Hour **17**

Dealing with Browser Differences

The W3C DOM has revolutionized DHTML by making a single standard that both Netscape and Microsoft have committed to support. Nevertheless, neither supports it perfectly yet, and many users use older browsers. If your page relies on DHTML, you will need to account for all of these possibilities.

Welcome to Part V! In the next four hours, you'll learn some advanced aspects of DHTML. In this hour, you'll learn how to understand the basic differences between the DHTML browsers, and how to write scripts that detect the current browser. You'll also learn how to adapt DHTML applications to work on the version 4.0 browsers.

This hour covers the following topics:

- Differences between DHTML browsers
- Detecting the current browser
- Detecting feature support
- Writing cross-browser DHTML scripts

- Supporting older browsers
- Creating cross-browser animation

DHTML Browser Differences

Back when the version 4.0 browsers were the latest thing, there were major differences between their support for DHTML. If you wrote an application using DHTML for Internet Explorer 4.0, there was no chance at all it would work on Netscape 4.0.

Things are different now with the W3C DOM. Since both Internet Explorer 5 and later, and Netscape 6 and later are based on this standard, if you write an application for one of these browsers the chances are good it will work on the other.

However, neither browser supports 100% of the W3C DOM standard. As you use more specific properties and attributes, the chance increases that you'll run into a difference between the browsers.

There are two key things you can do to make sure the latest DHTML browsers support your scripts: First, test your script in as many different browsers as possible. At the very least, you should have the latest versions of Netscape and Internet Explorer available.

Second, you can use JavaScript to detect the user's current browser or the features it supports, and deal with differences by writing code for different browsers. Using this technique, you can support older browsers, as well as the latest.

Detecting Browsers

If you plan to support more than one browser—or even if you're restricting your page to certain browsers—you'll need a way to detect which browser is in use. You can do this in one of two ways:

- Detecting the exact browser in use (*browser sensing*)
- Detecting whether a feature is supported (*feature sensing*)

Browser Sensing

The most obvious way to detect which browser is in use is to use the `navigator` object, which is supposed to contain a concise list of information about the user's browser. Listing 17.1 shows a simple script that displays the values of several `navigator` properties.

LISTING 17.1 Displaying Information About the Browser

```html
<html>
<head>
<title>Browser Information</title>
</head>
<body>
<h1>Browser Information</h1>
<hr>
<p>
The <b>navigator</b> object contains the following information
about the browser you are using.
</p>
<ul>
<script LANGUAGE="JavaScript">
document.write("<li><b>Code Name:</b> " + navigator.appCodeName);
document.write("<li><b>App Name:</b> " + navigator.appName);
document.write("<li><b>App Version:</b> " + navigator.appVersion);
document.write("<li><b>User Agent:</b> " + navigator.userAgent);
document.write("<li><b>Language:</b> " + navigator.language);
document.write("<li><b>Platform:</b> " + navigator.platform);
</script>
</ul>
<hr>
</body>
</html>
```

17

To test this example, save it and load it into a browser. Try at least two different browsers and notice the differences in the display. Figure 17.1 shows this example as displayed by Internet Explorer 5.5.

 You can try this example online, or download the listings for this hour, at this book's Web site: http://www.starlingtech.com/dhtml/.

If you haven't used the navigator object before, you might think that the code name, app name, version, and other properties would differ with each browser you tried. Unfortunately, you have only to look at Internet Explorer's display of the example to realize that something's amiss. Today's browsers have strange ways of supporting the navigator properties:

- Internet Explorer 4 and later list their code name as Mozilla, Netscape's code-name, and their user agent as Mozilla/4.0 (compatible), followed by the correct application and version information.

- Internet Explorer 5 and later list their app version and user agent as version 4.0, although the correct version number appears in parentheses.
- Netscape 6 lists its version number as 5.0. (Netscape 5, also known as Mozilla, is the open-source project that Netscape 6 is based upon.)

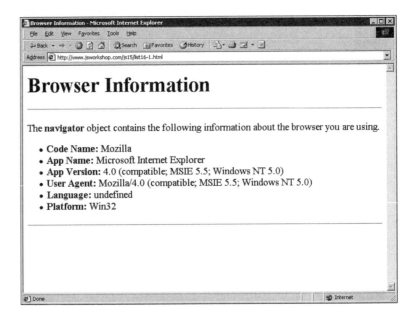

The **navigator** object contains the following information about the browser you are using.

- **Code Name:** Mozilla
- **App Name:** Microsoft Internet Explorer
- **App Version:** 4.0 (compatible; MSIE 5.5; Windows NT 5.0)
- **User Agent:** Mozilla/4.0 (compatible; MSIE 5.5; Windows NT 5.0)
- **Language:** undefined
- **Platform:** Win32

> The reasons for Internet Explorer's strange `navigator` values are rooted in the browser wars. With the advent of frames, DHTML, and other features, many Web designers made their pages check specifically for Netscape. When Microsoft supported these features, it made Internet Explorer's user agent similar to Netscape's to allow these pages to work without modification.

Although you can write a script to deal with these quirks, you can see that browser sensing isn't the easiest way to support different DHTML browsers. Nonetheless, it's sometimes necessary to use this technique when dealing with cutting-edge DHTML.

Feature Sensing

Suppose you've used browser sensing to check for Internet Explorer 5 or Netscape 6. Now suppose that Netscape has released version 7, Internet Explorer has released version 7.5, and Opera has released a version that supports DHTML better than either one. Chances are, one or more of these new browsers wouldn't work with your script.

To account for situations like these, you can use feature sensing rather than browser sensing. By detecting the specific DHTML features you plan to use, you can determine whether the current browser supports them—without necessarily knowing which browser it is.

You've already seen an example of browser sensing in several of the examples in this book:

```
if (!document.getElementById) return;
```

This statement checks whether the document.getElementById method exists. If it doesn't exist, it returns from a function. You can also use this technique to create a version of the script for older browsers, as you'll see later in this hour.

> While actually using the document.getElementById method on an older browser will cause an error, checking for it in this manner will not. Be sure you don't include any parentheses or parameters to avoid calling the function.

If you include a statement like this before you actually use the document.getElementById method, you can avoid error messages in older browsers. You can use the same technique with document.getElementsByTagName, or any other method or object your script will use.

Using Feature Sensing

Using feature sensing, you can create a simple script that checks whether the current browser supports the W3C DOM or one of the older DHTML standards. Listing 17.2 shows the feature sensing example.

LISTING 17.2   Using Feature Sensing

```
<html>
<head>
<title>Browser Feature Sensing</title>
</head>
<body>
<h1>Browser Features</h1>
<hr>
<p>The information below was obtained using feature sensing:
</p>
<ul>
```

LISTING 17.2   continued

```
<script LANGUAGE="JavaScript">
if (document.getElementById) {
   document.write("<li>This browser supports getElementById");
   document.write(", and appears to support the W3C DOM.</li>");
} else document.write("<li>The W3C DOM is not supported.</li>");
if (document.layers) {
   document.write("<li>This browser supports the layers array");
   document.write(", and is most likely Netscape 4.");
} else document.write("<li>The layers array is not supported.</li>");
if (document.all) {
   document.write("<li>This browser supports the document.all array");
   document.write(", and is most likely Internet Explorer.");
} else document.write("<li>document.all is not supported.</li>");
</script>
</ul>
<hr>
</body>
</html>
```

This example checks for three features: the document.getElementById method for
DOM-compliant browsers, the document.layers array supported by Netscape 4, and the
document.all array supported by Internet Explorer 4. Figure 17.2 shows Netscape 6's
display of this example.

FIGURE 17.2

*The feature sensing
example as displayed
by Netscape 6.*

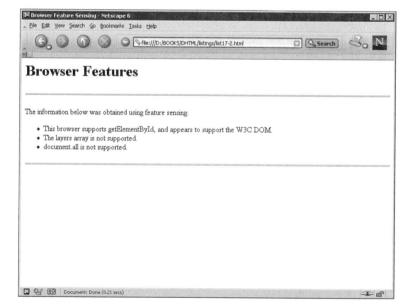

Writing Cross-Browser DHTML

Before you embark on a DHTML project, you should consider which browsers to support. At the very least, you should support the latest Internet Explorer and Netscape versions, and be sure your pages work with limited functionality in older versions.

While the W3C DOM standard allows you to create DHTML scripts that will work on both Internet Explorer 5 and Netscape 6 and later, there are still differences between these browsers. In fact, there are differences between browsers of the same version on different platforms, such as Windows and Macintosh.

Testing in Multiple Browsers

A big part of writing cross-browser DHTML is testing your scripts in multiple browsers. Even if you follow the W3C standards, you can run into trouble with one browser or another. It's easy to set up Netscape 4, Netscape 6, and Internet Explorer 5 on the same computer, to allow you to test your pages in these browsers.

17

Unfortunately, it's difficult to set up multiple versions of Internet Explorer on the same computer, and it's hard to test Macintosh, Windows, and Unix versions of browsers. One easy way around this is to publish a beta version of your Web site and allow users on different browsers and platforms to test it and give you feedback before you release the final version.

Accommodating Older Browsers

While the latest DOM-compliant browsers are popular and dominate the market, there are still a number of users out there using Netscape 4 or Internet Explorer 4. To avoid crashing browsers, you should make sure your DHTML scripts account for the 4.0 browsers.

As a bare minimum, you can use feature sensing to determine whether the DOM is supported, and make your script inactive if it is not supported. This is simple to do, prevents error messages, and allows users with older browsers to use your page without its dynamic features.

If you wish, you can go one step further. Both Netscape 4.0 and Internet Explorer 4.0 include limited DHTML features, and with a small amount of extra programming, you can add support for these browsers to your scripts.

Netscape 4 DHTML

When DHTML was first introduced in Netscape, it centered on the use of layers. Netscape 4 includes a `<layer>` tag to define layers, but fortunately it also supports the CSS positioning standard—using `<div>` or `<span>` elements with positioning attributes to define layers.

 Hour 6, "Creating Positionable Elements (Layers)," introduces layers and the methods of defining them and working with their properties.

If you use a `<div>` or `<span>` tag to define a layer, Netscape 4 will recognize it as well as newer browsers. However, Netscape 4 doesn't support the W3C DOM or the `getElementById` method. Instead, it stores information about each defined layer in the `document.layers` array.

For example, suppose you have defined a layer in a `<div>` tag with the ID attribute "page2". The following statement would find the object for the layer in DOM-compliant browsers:

```
obj=document.getElementById("page2");
```

The Netscape 4 equivalent is to look up the element with the name "page2" in the `layers` array:

```
obj=document.layers["page2"];
```

The other key difference is that Netscape does not use the `style` object under the layer object. For example, the `visibility` property of the layer referenced above would be `obj.visibility`, rather than `obj.style.visibility`.

Internet Explorer 4 DHTML

Internet Explorer 4 was the first version to include DHTML features, and Microsoft chose to create their own standard. Rather than using Netscape's `layers` array, Internet Explorer 4 includes the `document.all` array.

The `document.all` array includes elements for every object on the page. While this includes `<div>` and `<span>` elements like Netscape 4, it also includes other objects on the page and is not limited to layers.

For example, to find the object for a layer or other element with the ID attribute `"page2"` in Internet Explorer 4, you can look up the ID attribute in the `document.all` array:

```
obj=document.all["page2"];
```

Unlike Netscape 4, Internet Explorer 4 supports the `style` object. You could control the visibility of the object in this example using the `obj.style.visibility` property.

> If you've previously created a DHTML script for Internet Explorer 4, you can simulate the `document.all` array in the DOM-compliant browsers by using `document.getElementsByTagName("*");`.

Creating Cross-Browser Functions

17

There are some things that the 4.0 browsers simply can't do: for example, adding or deleting nodes from the DOM. But if you can use layers for your application, it's easy to adapt the script to support both older and newer browsers.

Finding Layer Objects

In DHTML scripts for W3C DOM browsers, the `getElemementById` function is often used to find objects. You can create an alternative function that works the same way, but also supports the 4.0 browsers. Here is the code for the `GetObject` function:

```
function GetObject(id) {
  if (document.getElementById)
    return document.getElementById(id);
  else if (document.layers)
    return document.layers[id];
  else if (document.all)
    return document.all[id];
  else {
    alert("DHTML support not found.");
    return false;
  }
}
```

> Internet Explorer 5.0 and 5.5 support the `document.all` array for backward compatibility. Since this function checks for the `getElementById` method first, it won't attempt to use `document.all` on these newer browsers.

This function accepts the ID attribute of a layer as its parameter, and uses a series of if statements and feature sensing to return one of three values:

- For DOM-compliant browsers, it returns the result of the getElementById method.
- For Netscape 4, it returns the appropriate object from the document.layers array.
- For Internet Explorer 4, it returns the appropriate object from the document.all array.

If none of these features are detected, the function displays an error message and returns a false value. Otherwise, it returns an object that can be used just like the getElementById result.

> For DHTML scripts that use the getElementsByTagName method, the document.all array provides the same functionality for Internet Explorer 4. There is no way to obtain a list of HTML elements in Netscape 4, since only layers are stored in the layers array.

Finding Style Objects

While the GetObject function above will work in some cases, often you need to deal with style properties. For example, if you need to change the horizontal position of the object obj, the correct properties are:

- obj.style.left (Internet Explorer 4 or later, Netscape 6 or later)
- obj.left (Netscape 4)

Since the style object isn't used by Netscape 4, you can't simply add style to the result of the GetObject function. An easy alternative is to create a GetStyleObject function that returns the appropriate object for the style properties:

```
function GetStyleObject(id) {
  if (document.getElementById)
    return document.getElementById(id).style;
  else if (document.layers)
    return document.layers[id];
  else if (document.all)
    return document.all[id].style;
  else {
    alert("DHTML support not found.");
    return false;
  }
}
```

This function is similar to the `GetObject` function, but returns the `style` object for DOM browsers or Internet Explorer 4, and returns the layer object directly for Netscape 4. Thus, if you include this function in a document, you can change the horizontal position of the `layer1` layer with two simple statements:

```
obj=GetStyleObject("layer1");
obj.left=300;
```

By including the `GetObject` or `GetStyleObject` functions, or both if needed, you can easily work with layers for both 4.0 browsers and newer DOM-compliant browsers.

Workshop: Supporting Old and New Browsers

As a demonstration of the `GetStyleObject` function, you can use it to make a version of the simple animation example from Hour 16, "Using DHTML for Animation," that works on both 4.0 browsers and newer browsers.

The example already uses a layer to enclose the `mouse.gif` graphic. This makes it easy to support the 4.0 browsers: simply add the `GetStyleObject` function to the `<script>` section in the header, and use this function instead of the `getElementById` method. Listing 17.3 shows the cross-browser version of the animation example.

LISTING 17.3   The Complete Cross-Browser Animation Example

```
<html>
<head>
<title>Animation with Dynamic HTML</title>
<script language="javascript">
var position=0;
function GetStyleObject(id) {
  if (document.getElementById)
    return document.getElementById(id).style;
  else if (document.layers)
    return document.layers[id];
  else if (document.all)
    return document.all[id].style;
  else {
    alert("DHTML support not found.");
    return false;
  }
}
function Move() {
  position += 1;
  if (position > 650) position = 0;
```

17

LISTING 17.3   continued

```
        obj = GetStyleObject("mouse");
        obj.left = position;
        window.setTimeout("Move();",10);
}
</script>
 </head>
 <body onLoad="Move();">
 <H1>Animation with Dynamic HTML</H1>
 <HR>
<div ID="mouse" STYLE="position:absolute; left:0; top:100;
  width:100; height:100; visibility:show">
  <img src="mouse.gif" width=100 height=100 alt="" border="0">
</div>
</body>
</html>
```

In this listing, the GetStyleObject function is defined at the beginning of the <script> section. The Move function uses GetStyleObject to get the appropriate object for the current browser, and sets the animation to its next position.

This modified example should work in a nearly identical fashion on Netscape 4.0, Internet Explorer 4.0, and the new DOM-compliant browsers. Figure 17.3 shows Netscape 4's display of the animation.

FIGURE 17.3

Netscape 4 shows the cross-browser animation example in action.

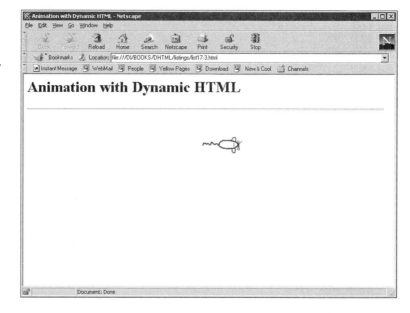

Summary

In this hour, you've learned how to deal with differences between browsers, including the latest DHTML browsers, as well as older browsers with limited DHTML support. You've also adapted an animation example to work on older browsers, as well as the latest ones.

In the next hour, you'll learn how DHTML can be used with forms. This will allow you to change a form dynamically based on information the user enters, a useful technique for online order forms.

Q&A

Q. Aren't there any other browsers that support DHTML?

A. Yes. Opera, `http://www.opera.com/`, has limited DHTML support. If you use feature sensing rather than browser sensing, you can support this browser in your DHTML scripts.

Q. I know exactly which browsers support the feature I'm using. What's wrong with using browser sensing?

A. The main problem is that the list of browsers that support a feature can change with every browser release, and you would have to modify your script each time.

Q. Does anyone really still use the version 4.0 browsers?

A. According to Internet.com's statistics at this writing, nearly 20% of Web users are still using Netscape 4 or Internet Explorer 4. Statistics vary for different sites, but chances are enough of your users use older browsers that you shouldn't ignore them.

Quiz

Test your knowledge of the material covered in this hour by answering the following questions.

Questions

1. Which of the following is the best all-around technique for determining which type of DHTML to use in a script?

   a. Browser sensing

   b. Feature sensing

   c. Assume everyone uses Internet Explorer

2. Which browser supports the `layers` array?

    a. Internet Explorer 4

    b. Netscape 4

    c. Netscape 6

3. What would be the `navigator.appCodeName` value for Internet Explorer 5.5 under Windows?

    a. Mozilla

    b. IE5

    c. IE4

Answers

1. b. Feature sensing is the best way to quickly determine which type of DHTML to use.

2. b. Only Netscape 4 supports the `layers` array.

3. a. Internet Explorer 4.0 and later report the code name `Mozilla` to indicate compatibility with Netscape.

Exercises

If you'd like to practice cross-browser scripting before you move on to the next hour, try the following exercise:

- There is an example of using JavaScript to position layers in the Workshop section of Hour 6. Use the functions you created in this chapter to modify that example to work with version 4.0 browsers.

HOUR 18

Using DHTML with Forms

In the previous hours of this book, you've learned how DHTML can make dramatic changes to Web pages in real time. Forms, some of the most common Web page elements, also can make use of DHTML.

In this hour, you'll learn some ideas for making forms dynamic using DHTML, and create several examples of forms that can be modified automatically depending on the user's choices.

This hour covers the following topics:

- Using dynamic forms
- Modifying form elements
- Adding elements to a form
- Creating a dynamic order form

Dynamic Forms

While forms are hardly the most exciting thing the Web can do, they're one of the most practical. Order forms, feedback forms, and registration forms abound on the Web.

Forms are also considered one of the uglier parts of the Web by designers. A page filled with white blanks isn't the best example of effective design, and many aspects of form appearance can't be controlled using style sheets.

You can alleviate some of the boredom of forms using DHTML. Your forms can show only the fields that are needed based on a choice the user makes, and can expand and shrink as needed.

> When using DHTML with forms, you can easily create a form that relies on DHTML, and won't work in older browsers. If you do, be sure to provide an alternative for browsers that don't support DHTML.

Modifying Form Elements

One problem that traditional Web forms share with printed paper forms is that they can't change to ask only for the required information. For example, suppose a response form asks the user whether they wish to be contacted by mail, by e-mail, or by phone. The form would need separate fields for the mailing address, e-mail address, and phone number, even though all of them won't be used.

Using DHTML, you can create a form that prompts for this information and displays only the needed fields.

Creating the JavaScript Function

To create a dynamic form, you will use three separate `<div>` elements, one for each of the contact options. The changes to the form will be made by the `Display` function. This function accepts the name of one of the `<div>` elements, shows it, and hides the others.

```
function Display(which) {
  ma=document.getElementById("mail");
  em=document.getElementById("email");
  ph=document.getElementById("phone");
  if (which=="mail") ma.style.display="block";
    else ma.style.display="none";
  if (which=="email") em.style.display="block";
    else em.style.display="none";
  if (which=="phone") ph.style.display="block";
    else ph.style.display="none";
}
```

This function accepts a parameter, which, and tests it. The if statements set the display property for the selected element to block, and the display properties for the other elements to none.

Creating the HTML Document

To complete the example, you need an HTML document with the three `<div>` elements and a way for the user to choose which one to display. Listing 18.1 shows the complete HTML document.

> As usual, you can download the HTML documents for the examples in this hour from this book's Web site: http://www.starlingtech.com/dhtml/.

LISTING 18.1 The HTML Document for the Dynamic Form

```html
<html>
<head>
<title>Modifying Forms with DHTML</title>
<script language="javascript">
function Display(which) {
  ma=document.getElementById("mail");
  em=document.getElementById("email");
  ph=document.getElementById("phone");
  if (which=="mail") ma.style.display="block";
    else ma.style.display="none";
  if (which=="email") em.style.display="block";
    else em.style.display="none";
  if (which=="phone") ph.style.display="block";
    else ph.style.display="none";
}
</script>
</head>
<body>
<h1>Modifying Forms with DHTML</h1>
<p>The form below changes depending on the radio button
selected.</p>
<hr>
<form name="form1">
<p>How would you like us to contact you?</p>
<input type="radio" name="type" value="mail" checked
 onClick="Display('mail');">
 By mail
<input type="radio" name="type" value="email"
 onClick="Display('email');">
 By email
```

18

LISTING 18.1   continued

```
<input type="radio" name="type" value="phone"
 onClick="Display('phone');">
 By phone
<br>
<div ID="mail" style="display:block;">
<b>Address 1:</b> <input type="text" name="address1" size="25">
<br>
<b>Address 2:</b> <input type="text" name="address2" size="25">
<br>
<b>City:</b> <input type="text" name="city" size="14">
<b>State:</b> <input type="text" name="state" size="5">
<b>Zip:</b> <input type="text" name="zip" size="9">
</div>
<div ID="email" style="display:none">
<b>Email address:</b>
<input type="text" name="email" size="25">
</div>
<div ID="phone" style="display:none">
<b>Phone:</b>
<input type="text" name="phone" size="15">
</div>
</form>
</body>
</html>
```

This document includes a set of radio buttons with onClick event handlers that call the Display function. It also includes the three <div> elements—mail, email, and phone.

To test this document, load it into a Web browser. This example requires Netscape 6 or later, or Internet Explorer 5 or later, although it could be adapted to work with older browsers.

> If you use a form like this, keep in mind that some of the form fields won't be available to users on non-DHTML browsers. Make sure you provide an alternative form for these browsers.

Figure 18.1 shows Netscape's display of the document while the By Mail option is selected. As you select other options, the bottom portion of the form changes accordingly.

FIGURE **18.1**

*The dynamic form
example in action.*

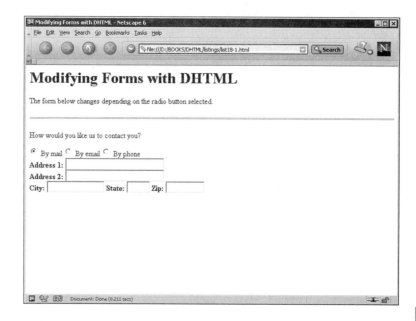

FIGURE **18.1**

*The dynamic form
example in action.*

Adding Form Elements

18

Using DHTML, you also can create forms that expand to fit the quantity of information
the user wishes to enter. As an example, you can create a simple form that allows fields
to be added at the click of a button.

Creating the JavaScript Function

The form will initially be displayed with one text field, labeled Item 1. A button will
allow the user to add one or more similar text fields. The following JavaScript code
declares a variable, items, to keep track of the number of items, and defines the AddItem
function to add items:

```
var items=1;
function AddItem() {
  div=document.getElementById("items");
  button=document.getElementById("add");
  items++;
  newitem="<b>Item " + items + ": </b>";
  newitem+="<input type=\"text\" name=\"item" + items;
  newitem+="\" size=\"45\"><br>";
  newnode=document.createElement("span");
  newnode.innerHTML=newitem;
  div.insertBefore(newnode,button);
}
```

The AddItem function first finds the object for the <div> element with the ID attribute "items". It also finds the object for the add items button, which will be inside the <div> element. It next increments the items variable.

Next, the newitem string is created with the HTML for the new item, including a label and the <input> tag. The createElement method is used to create a new <span> element containing the HTML in newitem, and the insertBefore method inserts the new node into the <div> element.

> The insertBefore method has two parameters: the new child node to insert, and the existing child node it should be inserted before. See Hour 7, "Working with DOM Properties and Methods," for more information about this method.

Completing the HTML Document

To complete this example, you need to create an HTML document that defines the form, including the <div> element to add items to, and the button that allows the user to add items. Listing 18.2 shows the complete HTML document.

LISTING 18.2   The Complete Example of Adding Form Elements

```
<html>
<head>
<title>Adding elements to a form</title>
<script language="javascript">
var items=1;
function AddItem() {
  div=document.getElementById("items");
  button=document.getElementById("add");
  items++;
  newitem="<b>Item " + items + ": </b>";
  newitem+="<input type=\"text\" name=\"item" + items;
  newitem+="\" size=\"45\"><br>";
  newnode=document.createElement("span");
  newnode.innerHTML=newitem;
  div.insertBefore(newnode,button);
}
</script>
</head>
<body>
<h1>Adding Form Elements</h1>
<p>The form below allows you to add elements dynamically.</p>
```

LISTING 18.2 continued

```
<hr>
<form name="form1">
<div ID="items">
<b>Item 1:</b>
<input type="text" name="item1" size="45">
<br>
<input type="button" value="Add an Item"
onClick="AddItem();" ID="add">
</div>
</form>
</body>
</html>
```

The `<script>` section in this document initializes the `items` variable and defines the `AddItem` function. The `<form>` section includes the `<div>` with the ID attribute `"items"`, containing the first item field and the Add an Item button. This button's `onClick` event handler calls the `AddItem` function.

Figure 18.2 shows Internet Explorer's display of this example after several items have been added to the form.

18

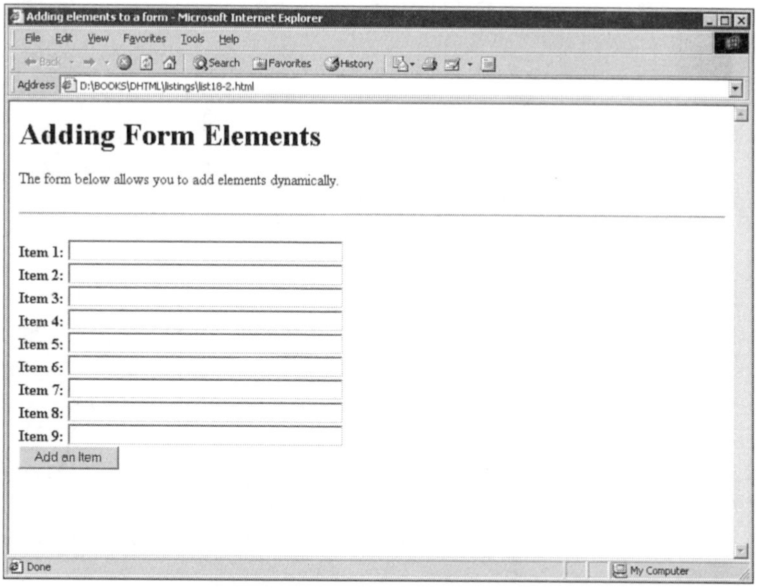

FIGURE 18.2

The form with added items.

Accepting Data from Forms

While you can use DHTML and JavaScript to add interactive features to forms as in this hour's examples, you also need a way to accept the data from the form. Since JavaScript and DHTML work on the client, they don't provide a way to accept data from forms. Typically, you would use a CGI (common gateway interface) script or program to accept the data.

CGI isn't a language, but rather a standard for executing scripts on Web servers. To use a CGI script, you need certain components in your HTML document:

- An `action` attribute in the `<form>` tag that specifies the URL of the CGI program.
- A `method` attribute in the `<form>` tag that specifies one of the two methods for communicating with CGI scripts, `GET` or `POST`. Which one you use depends on the needs of the CGI script.
- A Submit button, created with the `<input type="submit">` tag. When this button is clicked, the CGI script will execute on the server and receive the data from the form.

CGI programs can be written in any language supported by the server. Popular CGI languages include the open-source Perl and PHP languages, Microsoft's ASP (Active Server Pages), and Sun's JSP (JavaServer Pages). There's even a server-side version of JavaScript that can be used for this purpose.

> If you'd like to learn more about Perl, PHP, and other server-side languages, you'll find a list of useful Web sites in Appendix A, "Other JavaScript and DHTML Resources."

If you'd rather not learn a whole new language just to accept data from your forms, there are thousands of free CGI scripts available. Some can be downloaded and used on your server, while others are set up as services that you can use on their servers. You can find an excellent collection of links to these resources at the CGI Resource Index:

`http://cgi.resourceindex.com/`

If you'd like to learn more about CGI, a number of books are available. One good one to get started with is *Sams Teach Yourself CGI in 24 Hours*, by Rafe Colburn.

Workshop: Creating a Dynamic Order Form

As a final demonstration of the power of DHTML in working with forms, you can create a dynamic order form. This form will have two dynamic components: the ability to add items, as in the previous example, and a ship-to address form that displays only when it is needed.

Adding Items to the Form

The AddItems function is similar to the one in Listing 18.2, but this time the newitem variable includes HTML to define a quantity field as well as an item field for each new item:

```
var items=1;
function AddItem() {
  div=document.getElementById("items");
  button=document.getElementById("add");
  items++;
  newitem="<b>Qty: </b>";
  newitem+="<input type=\"text\" name=\"qty" + items;
  newitem+="\" size=\"3\"> ";
  newitem+="<b>Item: </b>";
  newitem+="<input type=\"text\" name=\"item" + items;
  newitem+="\" size=\"45\"><br>";
  newnode=document.createElement("span");
  newnode.innerHTML=newitem;
  div.insertBefore(newnode,button);
}
```

As before, the createElement method is used to create a new <span> element containing the HTML. The insertBefore method then is used to add the item immediately before the button.

Showing the Ship-to Address

Hiding or showing the ship-to address is simple. The Show function accepts a parameter indicating whether to show or hide the ship-to fields:

```
function Show(a) {
  obj=document.getElementById("shipto");
  if (a) obj.style.display="block";
    else obj.style.display="none";
}
```

The <div> element with the ID attribute "shipto" will contain the address fields. The if statements change the display property for the <div> element to block or none, depending on the value of the parameter (a).

18

Completing the HTML Document

To complete this example, all you need to do is add the JavaScript functions you created to an HTML document, and add the form elements. Listing 18.3 shows the complete HTML document.

LISTING 18.3   The Complete Dynamic Order Form

```html
<html>
<head>
<title>Dynamic Order Form</title>
<script language="JavaScript">
var items=1;
function AddItem() {
  div=document.getElementById("items");
  button=document.getElementById("add");
  items++;
  newitem="<b>Qty: </b>";
  newitem+="<input type='text' name='qty" + items;
  newitem+=" ' size='3'> ";
  newitem+="<b>Item: </b>";
  newitem+="<input type=\"text\" name=\"item" + items;
  newitem+="\" size=\"45\"><br>";
  newnode=document.createElement("span");
  newnode.innerHTML=newitem;
  div.insertBefore(newnode,button);
}
function Show(a) {
  obj=document.getElementById("shipto");
  if (a) obj.style.display="block";
    else obj.style.display="none";
}
</script>
</head>
<body>
<h1>Order Form</h1>
<hr>
<form name="form1">
<b>Bill to:</b><br>
<b>Name:</b> <input type="text" name="customer" size="20"><br>
<b>Address 1:</b> <input type="text" name="addr1" size="20"><br>
<b>Address 2:</b> <input type="text" name="addr2" size="20"><br>
<b>City:</b> <input type="text" name="city" size="15">
<b>State:</b> <input type="text" name="state" size="4">
<b>Zip:</b> <input type="text" name="zip" size="9">
<hr>
<b>Ship to:</b><br>
```

Listing 18.3 continued

```
<input type="radio" name="shipopt" value="same" checked onClick="Show(0);">
<b>Same Address</b>
<input type="radio" name="shipopt" value="other" onClick="Show(1);">
<b>Other Address</b>
<div ID="shipto" style="display:none;">
<br>
<b>Name:</b> <input type="text" name="shipname" size="20"><br>
<b>Address 1:</b> <input type="text" name="shipaddr1" size="20"><br>
<b>Address 2:</b> <input type="text" name="shipaddr2" size="20"><br>
<b>City:</b> <input type="text" name="shipcity" size="15">
<b>State:</b> <input type="text" name="shipstate" size="4">
<b>Zip:</b> <input type="text" name="shipzip" size="9">
</div>
<hr>
<div ID="items">
<b>Qty:</b>
<input type="text" name="qty1" size="3">
<b>Item:</b>
<input type="text" name="item1" size="45">
<br>
<input type="button" value="Add an Item"
onClick="AddItem();" ID="add">
</div>
<hr>
<input type="submit" value="Continue...">
</form>
</body>
</html>
```

The `<script>` section of this document defines the `AddItem` and `Show` functions. The `<form>` section defines two radio buttons that call the `Show` function. The ship-to fields are enclosed in a `<div>` element with the `style` attribute `display:none`, hidden by default.

The first item field and the Add an Item button are enclosed in the `<div>` element with the ID attribute `"items"`. The button's `onClick` event handler calls the `AddItem` function to add another item. Figure 18.3 shows the dynamic order form in action.

To test this script, load it into a browser. This example requires Netscape 6 or later, or Internet Explorer 5.0 or later. While you can test the interactive DHTML features, to use this example on a live site, you'll need a CGI script to handle the form submission when the `Continue` button is clicked.

18

FIGURE **18.3**

The dynamic order form in action.

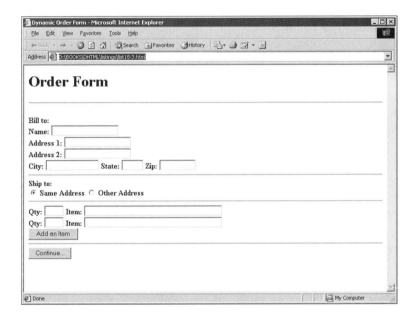

Summary

In this hour, you've learned some ways DHTML can be used to add functionality to Web forms. You've created simple examples including a dynamic order form.

In the next hour, you'll learn how to use dynamic fonts, a feature of the CSS standard that allows you to customize fonts and allow them to be downloaded with your HTML documents.

Q&A

Q. Can I create a script that adds items to a form that works in the version 4.0 browsers?

A. No. Since this example manipulates the DOM, it will only work in DOM-compliant browsers.

Q. How do I store the results of a form in a file or database?

A. This isn't something JavaScript or DHTML can do. You'll need a CGI script or other server-side application to accept the results of a form.

Q. Why is the combination \" used in the examples?

A. This is JavaScript's way of *escaping* the quotation character, meaning JavaScript doesn't interpret it as a quotation mark. It is used to include quotation marks within a string.

Quiz

Test your knowledge of the material covered in this hour by answering the following questions.

Questions

1. Which of the following is the correct command to insert the `newnode` object in the `div` object, immediately before the `button` object?

    a. `button.insertBefore(newnode);`

    b. `div.insertBefore(newnode,button);`

    c. `div.insertBefore(newnode);`

2. Which two values are used in an object's `display` property to display it or hide it?

    a. `display` and `none`

    b. `block` and `none`

    c. `1` and `0`

3. Which event handler is called when a radio button is selected?

    a. `onClick`

    b. `onSelect`

    c. `onRadio`

Answers

1. b. The `insertBefore` method is used on the container to insert the new object into it, and its parameters are the new node and the object to insert it before.

2. b. The `display` property accepts the value `block` to display an object in the default way, and `none` to hide it.

3. a. The `onClick` event handler is called when a radio button is selected.

18

Exercises

If you'd like further practice creating dynamic forms before you move on, try the following exercises:

- Add a fourth choice to the radio buttons in Listing 18.1, and create a section of the form to be displayed when that choice is selected.

- Add a Payment section to the form in Listing 18.3. Include radio buttons to choose credit card or check payment, and make the form dynamically display either a credit card number field or a check number field according to the selected option.

Hour 19

Using Dynamic Fonts

In Part III of this book, you learned how CSS style sheets can give you powerful, standardized control over the fonts, sizes, margins, spacing, and other aspects of your Web pages' appearance.

In this hour, you'll learn how to go one step further by using dynamic fonts, which can be downloaded with a Web page. These give you total control over fonts, although the current state of browsers makes the use of this feature a bit risky.

This hour covers the following topics:

- The basics of dynamic fonts
- The two dynamic font standards
- Defining dynamic fonts
- Using Microsoft's WEFT program
- Using dynamic fonts in Web pages

How Dynamic Fonts Work

While CSS allows you a great deal of versatility in selecting fonts for your Web pages, you're still relying on every user having the fonts you use available. Both Netscape and Microsoft have developed ways to escape this limitation.

Part of the original buzz in Netscape's debut of dynamic HTML was the dynamic fonts feature. Dynamic fonts, also known as downloadable or embedded fonts, are fonts that can be linked within a Web page, similar to the way you link an external style sheet. They can then be used by name in CSS styles, in the same way as built-in fonts.

Unfortunately, while this sounds like a grand idea, Netscape and Microsoft developed completely different standards for dynamic fonts, and some versions of both of their browsers don't support them at all.

In this hour, you'll learn how to embed fonts using both of the standards. You'll also learn which browsers support dynamic fonts, and some of the problems you might encounter when using them.

Dynamic Fonts and Browsers

Unlike the DOM, which has been standardized by the W3C, neither of the major browsers supports a cross-browser standard for dynamic fonts. Instead, two standards have emerged: Truedoc, from Netscape and Bitstream, and Microsoft's Web Embedding Fonts Tool (WEFT).

Unfortunately, each standard doesn't correspond to a line of browsers as you might expect—and some major browsers don't support dynamic fonts at all. Here's a summary of what's supported for the current browsers:

- **Netscape:** Versions 4.03 through 4.72 support Truedoc fonts. Netscape 6 and 6.1 don't support downloadable fonts at all.

- **Internet Explorer:** Versions 4.0 and later for Windows support WEFT fonts. These Windows versions can also support Truedoc fonts with a downloadable player from Bitstream. Internet Explorer for Macintosh doesn't support download-able fonts.

As you can see, progress will have to be made before you can rely on dynamic fonts. Nonetheless, it makes a nice luxury for those browsers that do support it when used carefully. The following sections describe the two major standards for dynamic fonts.

> The dynamic font situation might have changed since this writing. Be sure to check the Truedoc site at `http://www.truedoc.com/` and Microsoft's font site at `http://www.microsoft.com/typography` for the latest details.

Netscape (Truedoc) Fonts

The Truedoc standard was developed by Netscape and Bitstream. This format requires that the Bitstream Font Displayer be installed. This displayer is built in to Netscape 4.72 for Windows and MacOS.

Earlier versions of Netscape can support Truedoc fonts by downloading the font displayer from `http://www.truedoc.com/`. Internet Explorer 4.0 and later can also use these fonts with the font displayer installed.

Bitstream has a number of fonts available for public use at the `http://www.truedoc.com/` Web site. To create custom fonts, you have to purchase Bitstream's Web Font Wizard. This program creates dynamic fonts from TrueType or Postscript fonts.

> A demo version of Web Font Wizard is available at Bitstream's Web site, `http://www.truedoc.com/`. This version works for up to 10 days and creates up to 10 dynamic fonts.

19

Internet Explorer Dynamic Fonts

Microsoft's system of dynamic fonts is a bit easier to use, since the software for creating them (WEFT) is available as a free download. However, these fonts are supported strictly by Internet Explorer, and only on Windows platforms.

Microsoft's WEFT program creates *font objects*, files with the `.eot` extension. These objects don't include an entire font—rather, they include only the characters used by a document or set of documents you analyze.

> While including only certain characters makes embedded fonts smaller to download, the disadvantage is that you might need to re-create the font object when you add a page or edit an existing page.

Defining Dynamic Fonts

Defining fonts for use in your Web page is similar for the two downloadable font standards. In the sections below, you'll learn how to use both standards, and also take a look at Bitstream's Web Font Wizard and Microsoft's WEFT tool for creating font objects.

Using Truedoc Fonts

The Truedoc standard is easy to experiment with, since you can freely use the font definitions on Bitstream's Web site. The first step in embedding a Truedoc font is to specify the location of the `.pfr` file using a `<link>` tag in the header of your page:

```
<link REL="FONTDEF" SRC="http://www.truedoc.com/pfrs/EngraversGothic.pfr">
```

This tag is similar to the one you use to link an external style sheet. This tag is recognized by Netscape 4, which includes the Bitstream Font Displayer.

You can also support Truedoc fonts in Internet Explorer 4.0 and later by adding another bit of code to the header of your page:

```
<script LANGUAGE="JavaScript" src="http://www.truedoc.com/activex/tdserver.js">
</script>
<link>
```

This is a `<script>` tag that references an external JavaScript file. In this case, the file is stored on Bitstream's server. The first time an Internet Explorer user views your page, they might be prompted as to whether to run the font displayer application.

> The extra `<link>` tag is part of Bitstream's recommended code for including `.pfr` files, and is included to prevent bugs in some browser versions.

Once you've embedded the font, you can refer to it in the same way as other fonts, in the deprecated `<font>` tag or in a style sheet. The following is a brief style sheet that uses the font embedded above for paragraphs within a page:

```
<style type="text/css">
P {font-family: "EngraversGothic BT"}
</style>
```

> Notice that the font name for the `font-family` attribute isn't the same as the name of the `.pfr` file. The name is actually the original name of the font. If you use the fonts at the `truedoc.com` site, their names are specified there.

Using the Web Font Wizard

You can create .pfr files using Bitstream's Web Font Wizard. This program is available for Windows or Macintosh platforms. When you run the Web Font Wizard, it presents a series of dialogs to create a Web font:

1. The wizard displays an introductory message. Click Next to continue.

2. Select the font family and style (Regular, Bold, or Italic) for the Web font. You can choose any font that is installed on the local computer. This dialog is shown in Figure 19.1. Click Next to continue.

3. Select a set of characters to include in the font file: a standard alphanumeric set, a complete set of all characters in the font, or a custom set of the characters you specify. Click Next to continue.

4. Choose one or more URL paths where the dynamic font will be used. The font will work only when stored at a URL matching this list. Partial URLs are allowed. Click Next to continue.

5. Choose a filename for the new .pfr file. Click Finish to create the file. Along with the .pfr file, an HTML file will be created with an example of the font and instructions for using it on your site.

FIGURE 19.1

The Web Font Wizard displays the font selection dialog.

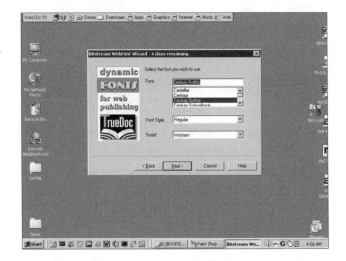

19

Many fonts are copyrighted, and you might be violating the copyright by using them on your site. Be sure to check the copyright status of any font you use as a dynamic font.

Using Microsoft Fonts

You use Microsoft's WEFT fonts by adding an @font-face selector within a style sheet. This specifies the URL of the embedded font object and the font family it corresponds with. Here is an example:

```
<STYLE TYPE="text/css">
  @font-face {
    font-family: Arial;
    font-style:  normal;
    font-weight: normal;
    src: url(http://www.starlingtech.com/dhtml/examples/ARIAL0.eot);
  }
</STYLE>
```

> Microsoft's WEFT application, described in the next section, can create the required style sheet code for your embedded font objects automatically.

Using Microsoft's WEFT Tool

To create a font object, you use Microsoft's WEFT (Web Embedding Fonts Tool) to analyze your Web documents and add the desired fonts to them. This tool is available for download from Microsoft's site at http://www.microsoft.com/typography/.

WEFT is available for Windows platforms only. Once you've downloaded and installed it, you can run it from the Start menu. When you run WEFT, a wizard guides you through the process of setting up an embedded font:

1. You are prompted for your name and e-mail address to identify the font object.

2. You are prompted for the URL or file location for one or more Web pages to analyze. This screen is shown in Figure 19.2.

3. After WEFT analyzes your pages, you are asked to list the fonts to embed. The default list includes a list of fonts that were used in the Web pages you specified for analysis.

4. You are prompted for a location to store the new font objects. This can be a local file or a path to a Web server directory. If you have trouble saving to a Web server, try saving a local file. You must also specify the URL where the objects will be used.

5. Finally, the wizard offers to insert links to the new font objects in your Web documents. You can also do this manually, as explained above.

FIGURE **19.2**

WEFT prompts you for
Web page URLs.

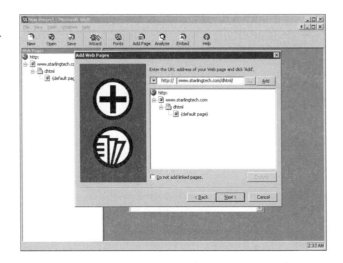

WEFT embedded fonts are locked to the URLs you specify when creating font
objects. They can't be used from another URL unless you re-create them.

Workshop: Using Dynamic Fonts

Although you should be cautious as dynamic fonts are not yet standardized between
browsers, you can still take advantage of them in your pages. The following examples
demonstrate how to use both types of downloadable fonts in Web pages.

Using a WEFT Font

First, you can try using Microsoft's WEFT standard for embedded fonts. Listing 19.1
shows a simple example that uses an embedded WEFT font.

LISTING 19.1   Using an Embedded Microsoft Font

```
<html>
<head>
<title>Dynamic fonts: Microsoft WEFT</title>
<STYLE TYPE="text/css">
  @font-face {
    font-family: "Freestyle Script";
    font-style:  normal;
    font-weight: normal;
```

19

LISTING 19.1   continued

```
    src: url(http://www.starlingtech.com/dhtml/examples/FREESTY0.eot);
  }
  P {font-family: "Freestyle Script";
  font-size: 34pt;}
</STYLE>
</head>
<body>
<h1>Embedded Fonts Example</h1>
<p>This is a simple example of dynamic fonts using
Microsoft's WEFT application. The text in this paragraph
is displayed in large letters in a script font that was
embedded into the document's style sheet.</p>
</body>
</html>
```

To use this example, save it as an HTML document and load it into Internet Explorer 4.0 or later. If you test this example on your local computer, it will work with the .eot file from this book's Web site.

Since the file is locked to a specific URL, you can't copy the .eot file from this book's Web site to use on your own machine. To use this example on your own server, you'll need to use the WEFT utility to create an .eot file for the FreeStyle Script font, or the font of your choice.

> You can try this example online or download the listings for this hour from this book's Web site, http://www.starlingtech.com/dhtml/.

This example will only work in Internet Explorer 4.0 or later for Windows. Figure 19.3 shows Internet Explorer's display of the example.

Using a Truedoc Font

Next, you can try using an embedded Truedoc font. Since Bitstream allows you to use the fonts from their site, you don't need a copy of the .pfr files. Listing 19.2 shows the Truedoc example.

FIGURE 19.3
The embedded WEFT font example in action.

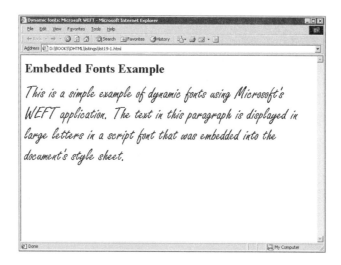

LISTING 19.2 Using an Embedded Truedoc Font

```html
<html>
<head>
<title>Dynamic fonts: Truedoc</title>
<LINK REL="fontdef" SRC="http://www.truedoc.com/pfrs/EngraversGothic.pfr">
<SCRIPT LANGUAGE="JavaScript" SRC="http://www.truedoc.com/activex/tdserver.js">
</SCRIPT>
<link>
<style type="text/css">
P {font-family: "EngraversGothic BT";
    font-size: 34pt;}
</style>
</head>
<body>
<h1>Embedded Truedoc Fonts</h1>
<p>This is a simple example of dynamic fonts using
Bitstream's Truedoc standard. The text in this paragraph
is displayed in large letters in the Engraver's Gothic font,
downloaded from Bitstream's site.</p>
</body>
</html>
```

19

To use this example, save it as an HTML document and upload it to a server. For reasons only Bitstream can explain, Truedoc fonts won't work in Netscape if your HTML document is stored on your local hard disk. If you don't have a Web server handy, try the online version on this book's Web site.

This example will work in Netscape 4 (but not Netscape 6) or Internet Explorer 4.0 or later. Internet Explorer will prompt you to download the Bitstream Font Displayer. Figure 19.4 shows Netscape 4's display of the example in action.

> Although Bitstream's Web site says that Truedoc fonts work in Netscape 4.03 and later, Netscape 6 does not currently support these fonts. With any luck, Bitstream will release a font displayer for Netscape 6, and Truedoc will become a true cross-browser method of using dynamic fonts.

FIGURE 19.4

The Truedoc font example in action.

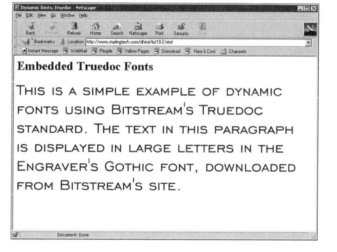

Summary

In this hour, you've learned about the two conflicting standards for downloadable, dynamic fonts. You've learned how to use both of these, and learned not to rely on them since there is not yet a consistent cross-browser standard.

As you create more advanced DHTML applications, you're bound to run into errors, and you should know how to deal with them. In the next hour, you'll take a look at some useful troubleshooting techniques for your DHTML scripts.

Q&A

Q. Which of the dynamic font standards is the best choice for my pages?

A. It depends on your audience. For intranet sites where Internet Explorer is the only browser used, Microsoft's WEFT standard is ideal. For public Web sites, there isn't currently an ideal choice, although the Truedoc standard will be when it's supported by Netscape 6. There will still be less popular browsers without support for these fonts, however.

Q. Has the W3C considered a standard for dynamic fonts?

A. Yes, as a matter of fact the `@font-face` method used for Internet Explorer's embedded fonts is a CSS2 standard. However, the W3C doesn't define a standard data format for fonts, so a common font format would be needed for cross-browser downloadable fonts.

Q. What happens if I specify a downloadable font and the user already has an installed font of the same name?

A. Browsers use the existing font rather than downloading a font whenever possible. This allows you to use downloadable fonts to provide a last-resort alternative when you specify a font that not everyone has available.

Quiz

Test your knowledge of the material covered in this hour by answering the following questions.

Questions

1. Which of the following is the extension used for font files created by Microsoft's WEFT program?

    a. `.weft`

    b. `.eot`

    c. `.pfr`

2. Which of the following font formats is supported by Netscape 4?

    a. Truedoc

    b. WEFT

    c. Postscript

19

3. Which CSS attribute do you use to assign text to a downloadable font you have embedded?

    a. `font-face`

    b. `font-family`

    c. `font-file`

Answers

1. b. Microsoft's WEFT program creates font object files with the `.eot` extension.

2. a. Netscape 4 supports the Truedoc system for dynamic fonts.

3. b. The `font-family` attribute is used to assign a font you've embedded to a section of text within the page.

Exercises

If you'd like to experiment further with dynamic fonts before moving on, try the following exercises:

- Use Microsoft's WEFT program to create a font file to go with Listing 19.1, linked to your server or local computer's URL.

- Look at the list of fonts at `http://www.truedoc.com/` and try adding another dynamic font to the example in Listing 19.2.

- Download the trial version of the Web Font Wizard from `http://www.truedoc.com/` and try creating a `.pfr` file.

Hour **20**

Troubleshooting DHTML

Throughout this book, you've learned how to use DHTML to create increasingly complex applications, and in the remaining hours you'll create some larger-scale examples. When you're dealing with this much HTML and JavaScript code, you're bound to run into errors here and there.

In this hour, you'll learn how to avoid some of the most common pitfalls when creating DHTML applications, and learn how to find and eliminate errors when they do occur.

This hour covers the following topics:

- Following good DHTML practices
- Avoiding common mistakes
- Displaying and analyzing error messages
- Testing dynamic documents
- Testing in multiple browsers
- Debugging an example document

Tips for Error-free DHTML

When you create DHTML applications, you're actually dealing with three separate languages: HTML, JavaScript, and the syntax of DOM objects. Sometimes your document will also use CSS styles, which have their own language. Each of these languages has rules and restrictions, and a small mistake in any of them can render your DHTML useless.

While every programmer runs into bugs on a regular basis, you can avoid some errors by making sure you follow consistent practices when creating DHTML scripts. Here are a few guidelines for creating error-free scripts:

- Format your scripts neatly for readability. Use indenting to separate sections, and separate each statement onto its own line.

- Use meaningful variable and function names. This way when you look at your script later, you'll remember how it works.

- Use JavaScript comments (begin a line with // or enclose comments between /* and */ characters) and HTML comments (begin with <!-- and end with -->) to document your scripts.

- End all JavaScript statements with semicolons. Although this is optional, it makes the script easier to read and makes it easier for the browser to display meaningful error messages.

- Divide complex scripts into functions, and divide large functions into smaller functions. This makes it easy to take a divide-and-conquer approach to debugging.

- When developing with an application, start with a simple version and add features, testing regularly to make sure everything works so far.

- Check your browser for error messages—these aren't always displayed unless you ask for them. You'll learn how to display these errors later this hour.

Avoiding Common Mistakes

While it's not hard to come up with an original mistake, you might also run into mistakes that are common and easy to make. The following are some of the most common errors in HTML, CSS, JavaScript, and DHTML.

Common HTML Mistakes

The HTML language is pretty forgiving, but when you add DHTML, your HTML syntax becomes even more crucial. The following are some common HTML errors:

- Forgetting to end sections. Except for special cases such as `<hr>` and `<br>`, HTML tags require an ending tag.
- Nesting tags improperly: for example, `<p><b>Hello</p></b>`. While this won't crash browsers, it can cause trouble with DHTML.
- Confusing the `ID` and `name` attributes. ID should be used with any tag that will be manipulated using DHTML, while `name` is used for form elements that will be read using a CGI program or manipulated using the Level 0 DOM.

Common CSS Mistakes

CSS style sheets aren't always crucial to the functioning of your application, but CSS errors might give your document an incorrect appearance and can cause trouble with DHTML. Here are some common CSS mistakes:

- Using style attributes as regular attributes. For example, `<p color=blue>` should be `<p style="color:blue">`.
- Including the `<style>` tag or other HTML tags in an external style sheet file. These files should contain only CSS directives.
- Confusing the `ID` and `class` attributes. An `ID` can be used for only one element, while a `class` can be assigned to several elements.
- Using incorrect selector syntax. A selector without punctuation (`Body`) refers to an HTML element; one beginning with a pound sign (`#table`) refers to an element's `ID` attribute; one beginning with a period (`.links`) refers to a `class` attribute.

Common JavaScript Mistakes

The JavaScript language is pretty simple, but it too has some common mistakes. The following are some of them you might run into:

- Getting case-sensitive keywords wrong. For example, `function` is lowercase, and properties such as `style.backgroundColor` have extra capital letters.
- Using HTML tags, such as `<script>`, in external JavaScript files. These files can contain only JavaScript statements.
- Confusing assignment (`=`) and equality (`==`) operators. For example, the statement `if (a=5)` will always return true, and worse, will set the variable a's value to five, potentially causing other errors. The correct statement is `if (a==5)`.
- Confusing local and global variables. If a variable is created outside a function, it's global; if it's created inside a function, it's local. Use the `var` keyword inside functions to ensure that you create a local variable if you use the same name as an existing global variable—or better yet, avoid using the same name for two variables at all.

20

Common DHTML Mistakes

Last but not least, common mistakes abound with the DOM objects used in DHTML. Here are a few mistakes you might run into:

- Getting case-sensitive objects and methods wrong. The getElementById method is the most common source of confusion—remember that the initial g and the final d are lowercase.

- Using objects incorrectly. Remember to use document.getElementById rather than simply getElementById.

- Attempting to use older DHTML syntax, such as the <layer> tag or the document.all collection. These should only be used if you're creating a compatible version for 4.0 browsers.

- Attempting to access an object without first finding the object. When you've assigned an ID attribute, you can't use it directly—use the result of getElementById instead.

Analyzing Errors

In an ideal world, any time something went wrong in your DHTML script, the browser would display an error message. Unfortunately, this is often not the case—an error can cause nothing to happen at all, cause the wrong result, or even cause the browser to crash.

Fortunately, both major browsers will at least let you know when syntax errors occur in your scripts, or when you refer to objects, properties, or methods that don't exist. To troubleshoot your DHTML applications, you should make sure your browser is configured to display errors.

Displaying Errors in Netscape

Some earlier versions of Netscape display JavaScript errors automatically by default. In Netscape 6 and some versions of Netscape 4, errors are not displayed by default.

To display the errors, you can simply look at the JavaScript console. To access this window, type javascript: into the browser's location bar. The console window, shown in Figure 20.1, displays a list of the most recent errors. You can keep the window open and clear it when you're about to test a new function.

Some versions of Netscape 6 don't accept the `javascript:` command. An alternate way of displaying the JavaScript console in Netscape 6 is to select Tasks, Tools, JavaScript Console from the menu.

FIGURE 20.1

Netscape's JavaScript console displays a list of recent errors.

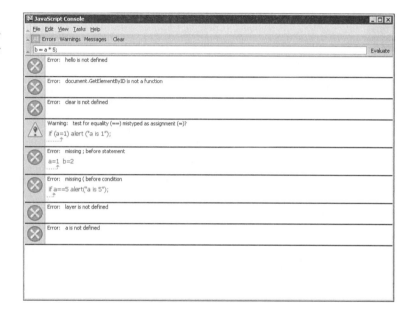

Displaying Errors in Internet Explorer

Some versions of Internet Explorer display an alert box for each JavaScript error by default, while other versions suppress the error by default. This is nice when you're browsing the Web and don't want to know about every JavaScript error you encounter, but when you're creating your own scripts, you'll want to make sure errors are displayed.

To display JavaScript errors in Internet Explorer 4.0 and later, select Tools, Internet Options from the menu. Select the Advanced tab, then uncheck the *Disable Script Debugging* option and check the *Display a notification about every script error* option.

20

When the display of errors is disabled, Internet Explorer will display an error icon on the status line. You can double-click this icon to display the error message.

Testing Dynamic Documents

An important part of the troubleshooting process is testing. While many errors are obvious—making an error message appear immediately when the page loads, or making the script not work at all—others are harder to notice.

To make sure your script is bug-free, you should test it thoroughly. If it interacts with the user, act like the worst possible user to see if you can find any errors. Enter the wrong information, click the wrong links, and so on.

> Don't just test your scripts by making what you believe to be typical user mistakes. Play piano on the keyboard and enter totally random information. You'll probably still be amazed at the mistakes users come up with.

Once an error occurs, you'll usually know which area of your script to look at, based on what you were doing at the time. After you've fixed the error, continue testing to make sure there are no others.

Testing Browser Compatibility

On top of the many places a bug might appear in your DHTML script, browsers have bugs too—not to mention inconsistencies, incompatibilities, and quirks. Often you'll develop an application that works perfectly, until you try it in a different browser.

To avoid surprises like this, you should keep at least a couple of different browsers (the latest Netscape and the latest Internet Explorer) handy. If you are designing scripts to work with older browsers, you'll need to test in each of those too.

Don't forget alternative browsers. Two good ones to test are Opera (`http://www.opera.com/`), a browser that supports many operating systems and languages, and Lynx (`http://lynx.browser.org/`), a text-based browser still in wide use.

> It's difficult, if not impossible, to keep two different versions of Internet Explorer installed on a Windows system. Sometimes you need to use a separate computer, or boot to a different operating system, to test in Internet Explorer 4.

Using Debugging Tools

While you can do most debugging using only a text editor and browser, sometimes software tools can save you time. Here are a few tools you might wish to use as you develop and debug larger DHTML applications:

- HTML validators can check your HTML documents to see if they meet the HTML standard. The validation process can also help you find errors in your HTML. The W3C has a validator online at `http://validator.w3.org/`.

- Netscape's JavaScript debugger allows you to set breakpoints, display variable values, and perform other debugging tasks. You can download the debugger at this URL: `http://developer.netscape.com/software/jsdebug.html`. The debugger does not yet support Netscape 6, but a version is in development: `http://www.mozilla.org/projects/venkman/`.

- Microsoft Script Debugger is similar, but works with Internet Explorer. It is available from this url: `http://msdn.microsoft.com/library/en-us/sdbug/Html/sdbug_1.asp`.

- While text and HTML editors are good basic editing tools, they can also help with debugging by displaying line numbers and using color codes to indicate valid commands.

> Appendix A, "Other JavaScript and DHTML Resources," includes links to HTML validators, editors, and other debugging tools.

Workshop: Debugging a Document

As an example of the process you'll go through when debugging a DHTML application, Listing 24.1 shows a document with HTML, JavaScript, and CSS, that uses DHTML to display a clock on the screen. However, this version of the document doesn't work—this hour's topic is troubleshooting, after all.

20

> You can download this hour's example, in working and non-working versions, from this book's Web site: `http://www.starlingtech.com/dhtml/`.

LISTING 20.1   The Clock Application, with Errors

```html
<html>
<head>
<title>DHTML Clock</title>
<script language="JavaScript">
function Clock() {
  if (!document.getElementById) return;
  theclock=document.getElementById("clock");
  now = new Date();
  hours=now.getHours();
  mins=now.getMinutes();
  secs=now.getSeconds();
  theclock.innerHTML = hours + ":" + mins + ":" + secs;
  window.setTimeout("Clock();",250);
}
</script>
<style type="text/css">
#clock {
    backgroundColor: yellow;
    position: absolute;
    left: 5px;
    top: 5px;
    font-family: monospace;
    font-size: 20pt;
    font-weight: bold;
}
</style>
</head>
<body onLoad="clock();">
<h1 align="center">DHTML Clock Example</h1>
<p>This example uses DHTML to display a clock in the
upper-left corner of the browser window. The clock
updates continuously to show the current time.</p>
<div ID="clock">
00:00:00
</div>
</body>
</html>
```

To test this document, save it as an HTML file and load it into a browser. Notice what happens, and if you feel ambitious, try to find the errors and get it working before you move on.

When it's working, the clock example will require Netscape 6 or later or Internet Explorer 5.0 or later. However, similar clocks can be created using layers to work with the 4.0 browsers.

Fixing Major Errors

When you first load the clock example into a browser, you'll immediately notice two major problems:

- A JavaScript error occurs when the page is first loaded, and the clock display remains at `00:00:00`.
- All of the HTML text fails to display, with the exception of the clock.

Now that you've found the errors, you can begin to fix them. Start with the most severe error, the JavaScript error on loading.

Netscape's display of this error reads `Error: clock is not defined`, and Internet Explorer's reads `Object expected, Line 28, Character 1`. While neither of these is a perfect clue, they should both lead you to this HTML tag:

```
<body onLoad="clock();">
```

In this tag, the `Clock` function isn't capitalized as it should be, since the `function` keyword defines it as `Clock`. After you've fixed this error, try loading the document again.

This time, the clock still doesn't work. Netscape displays the error message `theclock has no properties`, and Internet Explorer says `'theclock' is null or not an object`. Both of these are referring to this statement:

```
theclock=document.getElementById("clock");
```

This statement looks fine—`getElementById` is even spelled correctly. So the next step is to look for an HTML error near the `<div>` tag with the `ID` attribute "clock". If you look through the HTML document, you'll find that the heading is actually the problem:

```
<h1 align="center>DHTML Clock Example</h1>
```

In this line, the closing quotation mark is missing from `align="center"`. The result is that the quoted string encloses the rest of the document, and the `<div>` never gets defined. This also explains why most of the HTML content wasn't displayed!

Fixing Minor Errors

After adding the missing quotation mark, things are much better—the entire HTML content displays, and the clock actually acts like a clock. Now only two minor problems remain:

- The clock doesn't have the yellow background color that was specified in the style sheet.
- The clock doesn't display leading zeros: for example, `11:01:03` is displayed as `11:1:3`.

20

Since these are minor functional problems, don't expect the browser to give you any error messages. Instead, you'll have to look through the document. First, look at the crucial part of the style sheet for the background color:

```
backgroundColor: yellow;
```

While this might look correct at first glance, take a quick look at a DHTML reference, such as Hour 9, "Introducing Style Sheets," in this book. You'll discover that the correct property is `background-color`, not `backgroundColor`. Fix this error, and the background will display correctly.

Finally, the clock needs to display two-digit numbers. Since JavaScript displays numbers lower than ten as single digits, you'll have to manually add the zeros. Adding two `if` statements before the line that displays the clock takes care of this:

```
if (secs < 10) secs= "0" + secs;
if (mins < 10) mins= "0" + mins;
```

The Debugged Document

Now that you've found the HTML errors, JavaScript errors, and CSS errors and fixed them, you should have a working document. Listing 24.2 shows the debugged clock example.

LISTING 20.2   The Working Version of the Clock Application

```
<html>
<head>
<title>DHTML Clock</title>
<script language="JavaScript">
function Clock() {
  if (!document.getElementById) return;
  theclock=document.getElementById("clock");
  now = new Date();
  hours=now.getHours();
  mins=now.getMinutes();
  secs=now.getSeconds();
  if (secs < 10) secs= "0" + secs;
  if (mins < 10) mins= "0" + mins;
  theclock.innerHTML = hours + ":" + mins + ":" + secs;
  window.setTimeout("Clock();",250);
}
</script>
<style type="text/css">
#clock {
    background-color: yellow;
    position: absolute;
    left: 5px;
```

LISTING 20.2 continued

```
      top: 5px;
      font-family: monospace;
      font-size: 20pt;
      font-weight: bold;
}
</style>
</head>
<body onLoad="Clock();">
<h1 align="center">DHTML Clock Example</h1>
<p>This example uses DHTML to display a clock in the
upper-left corner of the browser window. The clock
updates continously to show the current time.</p>
<div ID="clock">
00:00:00
</div>
</body>
</html>
```

To test this document, save it as an HTML file and try it again in the browser. You should find that the clock is now fully functional. Figure 20.2 shows Internet Explorer's display of the working example.

FIGURE 20.2

The working version of the clock example.

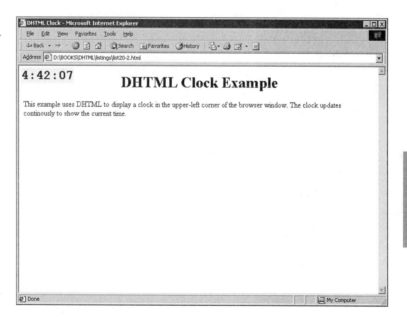

20

You've now completed the process of debugging a DHTML application. Fortunately, this was a worst-case scenario, and you won't usually have this much trouble with a simple example—but as you move on to more complex applications, you'll quickly gain more troubleshooting experience.

Summary

Congratulations—you've reached the end of Part V! In this hour, you've learned how to avoid common mistakes in DHTML, CSS, HTML, and JavaScript, and how to find and fix any errors that appear in your DHTML applications.

In the final four hours of this book, you'll explore more examples of what can be done with DHTML, ranging from a company Web page with multiple dynamic functions to a complete game application.

Q&A

Q. Do browsers always display JavaScript error messages when the page is first loaded?

A. No. Sometimes an error doesn't happen until a particular part of your script executes, and the error message is displayed then.

Q. Is there an easier way to find HTML errors?

A. Yes. See Appendix A for a list of applications you can use to *validate*, or test the syntax of, your HTML documents. Along with finding errors, this will let you know any areas where you've deviated from the W3C's HTML standard.

Q. Which time zone does the clock display the time in?

A. The clock is in local time, or the current browser's internal clock. Different users will see different times depending on their time zone and their computer's clock setting.

Q. Why does the SetTimeout method in the clock example repeat the function every 250 milliseconds, rather than once per second?

A. This makes the clock a bit more accurate. Since the timeout won't run the function each time the seconds value of the time changes, it runs four times per second and quickly updates the clock when the seconds have changed.

Quiz

Test your knowledge of the material covered in this hour by answering the following questions.

Questions

1. Which of the following JavaScript statements *does not* contain an error?

    a. `if (score==10) alert("You win!");`

    b. `if (score=10) alert("You win!");`

    c. `If (score==10) alert("You win!");`

2. Which of these statements *does not* contain an error?

    a. `a = document.getElementByID("layer");`

    b. `a == document.getElementById("layer");`

    c. `a = document.getElementById("layer");`

3. Which of the following is the correct command to enter into Netscape's location bar to display the JavaScript console?

    a. `console:`

    b. `http://www.netscape.com/javascript`

    c. `javascript:`

Answers

1. a. This statement is correct. In answer B's statement, the assignment operator (=) is used instead of the equality operator (==). In answer C, the `if` statement is improperly capitalized.

2. c. This statement is correct. In answer A, the `getElementById` method is capitalized incorrectly. In answer B, the equality operator (==) is used where the assignment operator (=) belongs.

3. c. The correct command is `javascript:`.

20

Exercises

If you'd like more practice troubleshooting before you move on to more complex applications, try the following exercises:

- Modify the working clock example, Listing 20.2, to create various errors, and see how the browser responds.
- Modify the clock example to flash the time on and off each second as it counts. Find and fix any errors you run into.

PART VI

Putting It All Together

Hour

HOUR 21

Creating a Dynamic Site

Welcome to Part VI! In the final part of this book, you'll take a look at some more complex DHTML examples, and learn some useful tips for use with large-scale DHTML applications.

In this hour, you'll see how easily you can combine two or more dynamic features on a single page. You'll create an example company Web site with menus and a scrolling message.

This hour covers the following topics:

- Guidelines for complex DHTML sites
- Creating the basic HTML document
- Creating the JavaScript file for menus
- Adding a scrolling message

Creating Complex DHTML Sites

While the examples in this book generally show a single DHTML feature in use at a time, you will frequently want to combine several dynamic features within the same site. Fortunately, this is as easy as including the appropriate HTML and JavaScript for each feature.

To avoid creating a huge and cumbersome HTML document, follow these tips when combining features:

- Carefully consider whether each feature is necessary, or whether it will make the page unnecessarily complex.
- Use separate JavaScript files whenever possible.
- Avoid using global variables in the DHTML functions except when absolutely necessary. Be sure that the same variable name is not used for two different global variables.
- Implement one feature at a time, and test each one to make sure it works correctly before adding additional features.

Creating the HTML Document

As an example of combining DHTML features, you will create a new version of the Figby Industries home page in this hour. This page will include two dynamic features:

- A menu system, similar to the one you created in Hour 13, "Creating Drop-Down Menus." However, this menu will be set up to work vertically instead of horizontally.
- A scrolling message, using the same function you used in Hour 15, "Creating DHTML Text Effects."

The first step in this process is to create the HTML document. Most of the dynamic features will be included in separate JavaScript files.

Laying Out the Page

In Hour 13, you created a Web site menu system. You can create an alternate version of this menu that works from a column at the left side of the page instead of the top. The first step is to define a table to lay out the body of the page and the menu column.

Here is the basic layout of the table. The two <td> sections will contain the menu column and the body of the page.

```
<table cellspacing="0" cellpadding="0" align="left">
<tr><td valign="top">
<!-- Menu bar goes here -->
</td>
<td>
<!-- Body of page goes here -->
</td></tr>
</table>
```

Defining the Menu

The menu itself is defined in another table, with each menu item appearing on its own row of the table. The following is a simplified menu with only two items:

```
<table border="0" cellpadding="4"> <!-- menu table -->
<tr>
   <td ID="menu-products" width="100" bgcolor="Silver"
     onMouseOver="Menu('products');" onMouseOut="Timeout('products');">
    <a href="products.html"><b>Products</b></a>
   </td>
</tr>
<tr>
   <td ID="menu-sales" width="100" bgcolor="Silver"
     onMouseOver="Menu('sales');" onMouseOut="Timeout('sales');">
    <a href="sales.html"><b>Sales</b></a>
   </td>
</tr>
</table>  <!-- end of menu table -->
```

The final menu will include five items. Each item has onMouseOver and onMouseOut tags to call the Menu and Timeout JavaScript functions, which will handle the opening and closing of menus.

Defining Layers

The final part of the HTML document for the menu system is a series of layers, each of which contains one of the menus that will be displayed when the mouse moves over a menu term. The following is the structure of one of the layers:

```
<div ID="products" STYLE="position:absolute; visibility: hidden">
  <table width="100%" border="0" cellpadding="4" cellspacing="0">
  <tr> <td width="100%" ID="p1"
     onMouseOver="Highlight('products','p1');"
     onMouseOut="UnHighlight('products','p1');">
   <a href="equip.html">Equipment</a></td></tr>
  <tr> <td width="100%" ID="p2"
     onMouseOver="Highlight('products','p2');"
     onMouseOut="UnHighlight('products','p2');">
   <a href="supplies.html">Supplies</a></td></tr>
  </table>
</div>
```

21

This layer will be made visible when the mouse is over the Products menu. It consists of a table to lay out the items, with a menu item in each row. This menu includes two items, Equipment and Supplies. The final HTML document will include five such layers, one for each menu term.

> You can add another menu by adding a row to the menu table with the appropriate links, and adding a corresponding `<div>` section with the menu itself.

Each item in the menu includes an `onMouseOver` event handler that calls the `Highlight` function. This function will change the background color of the item the mouse is over, and ensure that the menu continues to display.

Conversely, the `onMouseOut` event handler will call the `UnHighlight` function. This function will return the background color to normal and allow the display of the menu to time out.

Completing the HTML Document

To complete the HTML document, you need to complete the menu table and the layers for each menu, and combine them with the layout table and the body of the page. Listing 21.1 shows the complete HTML document.

LISTING 21.1 The Complete HTML Document

```
<html>
<head>
<title>Figby Industries, Inc.</title>
<script language="JavaScript" src="menu2.js">
</script>
</head>
<body style="margin-left:0; margin-top:0;" >
<table cellspacing="0" cellpadding="0" align="left"> <!-- layout table -->
<tr><td valign="top">  <!-- menu on left side -->
<table border="0" cellpadding="4"> <!-- menu table -->
<tr>
   <td ID="menu-products" width="100" bgcolor="Silver"
      onMouseOver="Menu('products');" onMouseOut="Timeout('products');">
    <a href="products.html"><b>Products</b></a>
   </td>
</tr>
<tr>
```

LISTING 21.1   continued

```
        <td ID="menu-sales" width="100" bgcolor="Silver"
           onMouseOver="Menu('sales');" onMouseOut="Timeout('sales');">
           <a href="sales.html"><b>Sales</b></a>
        </td>
     </tr>
     <tr>
        <td ID="menu-service" width="100" bgcolor="Silver"
           onMouseOver="Menu('service');" onMouseOut="Timeout('service');">
           <a href="service.html"><b>Service</b></a>
        </td>
     </tr>
     <tr>
        <td ID="menu-staff" width="100" bgcolor="Silver"
           onMouseOver="Menu('staff');" onMouseOut="Timeout('staff');">
           <a href="staff.html"><b>Staff</b></a>
        </td>
     </tr>
     <tr>
        <td ID="menu-jobs" width="100" bgcolor="Silver"
           onMouseOver="Menu('jobs');" onMouseOut="Timeout('jobs');">
           <a href="jobs.html"><b>Employment</b></a>
        </td>
     </tr>
     </table>   <!-- end of menu table -->
     <div ID="products" STYLE="position:absolute; visibility: hidden">
       <table width="100%" border="0" cellpadding="4" cellspacing="0">
       <tr> <td width="100%" ID="p1"
          onMouseOver="Highlight('products','p1');"
          onMouseOut="UnHighlight('products','p1');">
       <a href="equip.html">Equipment</a></td></tr>
       <tr> <td width="100%" ID="p2"
          onMouseOver="Highlight('products','p2');"
          onMouseOut="UnHighlight('products','p2');">
       <a href="supplies.html">Supplies</a></td></tr>
       </table>
     </div>
     <div ID="sales" STYLE="position:absolute; visibility: hidden">
       <table width="100%" border="0" cellpadding="4" cellspacing="0">
       <tr> <td width="100%" ID="s1"
          onMouseOver="Highlight('sales','s1');"
          onMouseOut="UnHighlight('sales','s1');">
       <a href="prices.html">Price List</a></td></tr>
       <tr> <td width="100%" ID="s2"
          onMouseOver="Highlight('sales','s2');"
          onMouseOut="UnHighlight('sales','s2');">
       <a href="order.html">Order Form</a></td></tr>
       <tr> <td width="100%" ID="s3"
          onMouseOver="Highlight('sales','s3');"
          onMouseOut="UnHighlight('sales','s3');">
```

21

LISTING 21.1   continued

```
      <a href="specials.html">Specials</a></td></tr>
      </table>
 </div>
 <div ID="service" STYLE="position:absolute; visibility: hidden">
      <table width="100%" border="0" cellpadding="4" cellspacing="0">
      <tr> <td width="100%" ID="r1"
         onMouseOver="Highlight('service','r1');"
         onMouseOut="UnHighlight('service','r1');">
      <a href="support.html">Support</a></td></tr>
      <tr> <td width="100%" ID="r2"
         onMouseOver="Highlight('service','r2');"
         onMouseOut="UnHighlight('service','r2');">
      <a href="cservice.html">Contact Us</a></td></tr>
      </table>
 </div>
 <div ID="staff" STYLE="position:absolute; visibility: hidden">
      <table width="100%" border="0" cellpadding="4" cellspacing="0">
      <tr> <td width="100%" ID="t1"
         onMouseOver="Highlight('staff','t1');"
         onMouseOut="UnHighlight('staff','t1');">
      <a href="staff.html">Meet the Staff</a></td></tr>
      </table>
 </div>
 <div ID="jobs" STYLE="position:absolute; visibility: hidden">
      <table width="100%" border="0" cellpadding="4" cellspacing="0">
      <tr> <td width="100%" ID="j1"
         onMouseOver="Highlight('jobs','j1');"
         onMouseOut="UnHighlight('jobs','j1');">
      <a href="jobs.html">Job Listings</a></td></tr>
      </table>
 </div>
 </td>
 <td>  <!-- body of page on right side -->
 <img align="center" src="logo.gif" width="486" height="180" border="0"><br>
 <h1>Welcome to Figby Industries!</h1>
 <p>Welcome! This is the home page of Figby Industries,
 your source for all sorts of imaginary products. Follow the links
 below or use the menu on the left to learn more about our company
 and our products.
 </p>
 <ul>
      <li><a href="products.html"><b>Products</b></a></li>
      <li><a href="sales.html"><b>Sales</b></a></li>
      <li><a href="service.html"><b>Service</b></a></li>
      <li><a href="staff.html"><b>Staff</b></a></li>
      <li><a href="jobs.html"><b>Employment</b></a></li>
 </ul>
 <pre>(c) 2002 Figby Industries</pre>
```

LISTING 21.1   continued

```
</td></tr>
</table>  <!-- end of layout table -->
</body>
</html>
```

To use this example, save it as an HTML document. You can view it in a browser, but the dynamic functions won't work until you add the JavaScript functions in the next section.

Notice the HTML comment tags in this example, <!-- and -->. These define comments that make it clear where the different sections of the layout table begin. In an example like this with several nested tables, comments can help you keep track of the different tags and avoid creating HTML errors.

This example requires a graphic, logo.gif. You can download it, along with the HTML and JavaScript files for this hour, from this book's Web site: http://www.starlingtech.com/dhtml/.

Creating the JavaScript File

The next step in creating the page is to add the JavaScript functions that will manage the menu. Since this is a complex document already, it's best to keep the JavaScript functions in a separate file. The HTML document already includes a <script> tag that references the file menu2.js:

```
<script language="JavaScript" src="menu2.js">
</script>
```

The JavaScript functions for the menu will be similar to those you used for the horizontally-oriented menu in Hour 13.

Modifying the Menu Function

The Menu function will be called by the onMouseOver event handlers for menu terms, and will open the menu requested by its parameter, current. The following is the Menu function:

```
function Menu(current) {
   if (!document.getElementById) return;
   inmenu=true;
   oldmenu=lastmenu;
   lastmenu=current;
```

21

```
if (oldmenu) Erase(oldmenu);
m=document.getElementById("menu-" + current);
box=document.getElementById(current);
box.style.left= m.offsetLeft + m.offsetWidth + 2;
box.style.top= m.offsetTop;
box.style.visibility="visible";
m.style.backgroundColor="Aqua";
box.style.backgroundColor="Silver";
box.style.width="100px";
}
```

This function first uses an `if` statement to verify that the browser has the necessary DOM support. It then sets the global `inmenu` and `lastmenu` variables to keep track of the current menu. It erases the previously displayed menu, if any, by calling the `Erase` function.

The difference between this function and the version for the horizontal menu is in the positioning of the menu. The `style.top` position is set to the top position of the menu term, and the `style.left` position is set to the menu term's position plus its width and a 2-pixel offset.

Completing the JavaScript File

The complete JavaScript file includes the modified `Menu` function as well as the `Erase`, `Timeout`, `Highlight`, and `UnHighlight` functions. These four functions are unchanged from those in Hour 13.

Listing 21.2 shows the complete JavaScript file for this example.

LISTING 21.2   The Complete JavaScript File

```
var inmenu=false;
var lastmenu=0;
function Menu(current) {
   if (!document.getElementById) return;
   inmenu=true;
   oldmenu=lastmenu;
   lastmenu=current;
   if (oldmenu) Erase(oldmenu);
   m=document.getElementById("menu-" + current);
   box=document.getElementById(current);
   box.style.left= m.offsetLeft + m.offsetWidth + 2;
   box.style.top= m.offsetTop;
   box.style.visibility="visible";
   m.style.backgroundColor="Aqua";
```

LISTING 21.2   continued

```
        box.style.backgroundColor="Silver";
        box.style.width="100px";
    }
    function Erase(current) {
        if (!document.getElementById) return;
        if (inmenu && lastmenu==current) return;
        m=document.getElementById("menu-" + current);
        box=document.getElementById(current);
        box.style.visibility="hidden";
        m.style.backgroundColor="Silver";
    }
    function Timeout(current) {
        inmenu=false;
        window.setTimeout("Erase('" + current + "');",500);
    }
    function Highlight(menu,item) {
        if (!document.getElementById) return;
        inmenu=true;
        lastmenu=menu;
        obj=document.getElementById(item);
        obj.style.backgroundColor="Aqua";
    }
    function UnHighlight(menu,item) {
        if (!document.getElementById) return;
        Timeout(menu);
        obj=document.getElementById(item);
        obj.style.backgroundColor="Silver";
    }
```

To use this file, save it as menu2.js, or the name you used in the <script src> tag in the HTML file. It should be saved in the same directory as the HTML document.

Once both files have been placed in the same directory, you can test the menu by loading the HTML document into a browser. Figure 21.1 shows Netscape 6's display of the menu in action, with the Sales menu currently selected.

This example uses the W3C DOM, and thus requires Netscape 6 or later or Internet Explorer 5 or later. However, since it uses layers, it could be adapted to work in the 4.0 browsers. See Hour 17, "Dealing with Browser Differences," for information about this process.

21

FIGURE 21.1

The menu in action, as shown by Netscape.

Workshop: Adding a Scrolling Message

As an example of how DHTML functions can be combined, you can add a scrolling message, similar to the one you created in Hour 15, to the Web page. To do this, you can simply create a JavaScript file to handle the scrolling functions and modify the HTML document to include this file.

Creating the JavaScript File

The JavaScript code for the scrolling message is identical to that used in Hour 13, except that the scrolling message itself has been changed and it will be stored in a separate JavaScript file. Listing 21.3 shows the complete JavaScript file.

LISTING 21.3 The JavaScript File for the Scrolling Message

```
msg = "Welcome to our site! ";
msg += "Be sure to check out our snazzy DHTML menu ";
msg += "and our daily specials. ";
pos = 0;
function ScrollMessage() {
   newtext = msg.substring(pos, msg.length) +
      "...  ..." + msg.substring(0, pos);
   newtext=newtext.substring(0,80);
   obj = document.getElementById("scroll");
```

LISTING 21.3   continued

```
    obj.firstChild.nodeValue = newtext;
    pos++;
    if (pos > msg.length) pos = 0;
    window.setTimeout("ScrollMessage()",100);
}
```

To use this JavaScript file, save it as scroll2.js in the same directory as the existing HTML and JavaScript files.

Modifying the HTML Document

Next, you need to modify the HTML document to include the new JavaScript file. First, you'll need to add a <script> tag that references the file:

```
<script language="JavaScript" src="scroll2.js">
</script>
```

You can add this <script> tag in the <head> section of the document, after the closing </script> tag for the menu script.

> You could also combine these JavaScript functions into the JavaScript file you created earlier and include them with a single <script> tag. However, it's useful to keep related functions in their own files for a modular approach.

Next, you'll need to create a place for the message to scroll. There is already a <pre> section at the end of the document containing a copyright notice. Assign it the ID attribute "scroll" to place the scrolling message there:

```
<pre ID="scroll">(c) 2002 Figby Industries</pre>
```

Last but not least, you need to start the scrolling message. Add an onLoad event handler to the <body> tag to start the ScrollMessage function. Here's the modified <body> tag:

```
<body style="margin-left:0; margin-top:0;" onLoad="ScrollMessage();">
```

Testing the Modified Example

Now that these changes are in place, you can load the HTML document into a browser. Once you load it, the message should begin to scroll, and the menu will continue to work as before. Figure 21.2 shows Internet Explorer's display of the example in action with the menu closed and the message scrolling.

21

FIGURE 21.2

*Internet Explorer
shows the scrolling
message in action.*

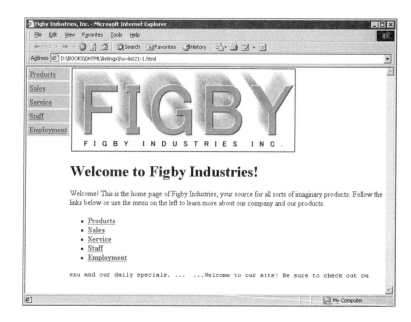

Summary

In this hour, you've seen how you can combine multiple JavaScript files to create a page that supports multiple dynamic features using DHTML. You can use this same technique to combine whichever features you need onto a single page, or onto all of the pages within a site.

In the next hour, you'll explore another larger DHTML example—this time, you'll create a more complex DHTML animation that uses dynamic graphics combined with DHTML positioning.

Q&A

Q. Can I position the menu somewhere other than the upper-left corner?

A. Yes. However, there is a difference in the way current browsers interpret the `offsetTop` and `offsetLeft` properties. Netscape measures these properties from the edge of the browser window, while Internet Explorer measures them from the edge of the table cell. To deal with a menu anywhere other than the top of the page, you'll need to change the positioning based on the current browser.

Q. How can I modify the menu to work in the version 4.0 browsers?

A. The key difference is to use a browser-independent version of the `getElementById` method, as discussed in Hour 17. You will also need to change the way menu items are positioned, since the `offset` properties don't work in the 4.0 browsers.

Q. Is there a limit to the number of `<script>` tags I can use that reference external files?

A. No, but adding additional files increases the browser's delay when loading the HTML document. To avoid this delay, combine functions into a single JavaScript file, or avoid using unneeded DHTML functions.

Quiz

Test your knowledge of the material covered in this hour by answering the following questions.

Questions

1. Which of the following is the typical extension used for external JavaScript files?

    a. `.script`

    b. `.js`

    c. `.jsc`

2. When starting an animation or scrolling message, which is a way to call the function whenever the browser displays the page?

    a. an `onLoad` event handler in the `<body>` tag

    b. an `onLoad` event handler anywhere

    c. a `<script>` tag in the header of the page

3. Which of the following is the property you use to set the left-hand position of a layer with the object `box`?

    a. `box.offsetLeft`

    b. `box.style.offsetLeft`

    c. `box.style.left`

21

Answers

1. b. JavaScript files typically end with the .js extension.

2. a. An onLoad event handler in the <body> tag will start a function as soon as the page loads.

3. c. You can use the box.style.left property to assign the left-hand position of a layer or other object.

Exercises

If you'd like to work further with this example before moving on, try the following exercises:

- Modify Listing 21.1 to personalize the menu system for your own site, or an example site of your choosing.

- Try adding a link or button within the page that can disable the scrolling message. You should set a global variable as a flag, then change the ScrollMessage function to check that variable before it continues the scrolling.

HOUR **22**

Creating Complex Animations

As you've explored in the earlier hours of this book, DHTML provides a simple way to position and animate objects. This can be used for entertaining animations as well as practical purposes, such as animated navigation features.

In this hour, you'll create some more complex examples of DHTML animation. You will also learn how to combine DHTML animation with JavaScript image source changes to create better animations.

This hour covers the following topics:

- Following the mouse pointer's position
- Creating an animation that tracks the mouse
- Animating with multiple images
- Creating JavaScript functions
- Completing the animation example

Following the Mouse Pointer

In Hour 16, "Using DHTML for Animation," you created a simple animation that moved a picture of a mouse across the Web page. In this hour, you'll improve upon this example by making the graphic mouse follow the mouse pointer across the screen.

First, you'll create a simpler version of the animation that follows the mouse pointer directly. Later, you'll create a more sophisticated version that uses multiple images.

Creating the HTML Document

To begin creating this example, you'll need an HTML document. The following is the basic HTML document:

```
<html>
<head>
<title>Follow that Mouse!</title>
</head>
<body onLoad="Setup();">
<h1>Animation in DHTML</h1>
<div ID="mouse" style="position:absolute; left:150; top:150;">
<img ID="mouseimg" src="mouse.gif" width="100" height="100" border="0">
</div>
</body>
</html>
```

This document defines a layer with the ID attribute "mouse" using a <div> tag. You will add JavaScript functions to this HTML document to animate the mouse.

> Notice that the <img> tag also has an ID attribute defined. You will use this later this hour to make the image change dynamically.

Detecting the Browser Type

Although this example will use cross-browser DHTML, the methods for detecting and following mouse movement are different in Netscape and Internet explorer. To make it easier to address these differences, you can include this line at the beginning of the script:

```
var Netscape=(navigator.appName.indexOf("Netscape") != -1);
```

This statement sets a variable, Netscape, which will be true if the browser is a version of Netscape, and false if it is not.

Capturing Events

The Setup function will be called by the `<body>` tag's onLoad event handler, and will set up event capturing so that the onMouseMove event can be detected. This is necessary because the onMouseMove event is generated frequently and is not detected by default. Here is the Setup function:

```
function Setup() {
  if (!document.getElementById) return;
  if (Netscape)
    document.captureEvents(Event.MOUSEMOVE);
  document.onmousemove=Move;
}
```

This function first verifies that the getElementById method is supported by the browser, since it will be used in other functions. Next, the Netscape variable is tested and the document.captureEvents property is set for Netscape browsers. This property tells Netscape which events can be captured.

Finally, the function assigns the onMouseMove event handler for the document to the Move function. Because the event handler is assigned using JavaScript, an onMouseMove attribute is unnecessary within the body of the HTML document.

> For details on how event capturing works in Internet Explorer and Netscape, see Hour 8, "Responding to Events."

Creating the Move Function

Now that event capturing is set up, the Move function will be called each time the mouse moves over the Web page. This function will update the position of the layer to track the mouse pointer.

```
function Move(e) {
  if (!document.getElementById) return;
  obj=document.getElementById("mouse");
  if (Netscape)
    event=e;
  if (event.pageX) { // Netscape...
    xpointer=event.pageX;
    ypointer=event.pageY;
  }
```

22

```
  else if (event.x) { // Internet Explorer...
    xpointer=event.x;
    ypointer=event.y;
  }
  obj.style.left=xpointer - 50;
  obj.style.top=ypointer - 50;
}
```

This function first finds the object for the layer and stores it in the `obj` variable. Next, since Netscape does not set the `event` variable automatically, it assigns it to the `Move` function's argument.

Next, the function finds the current mouse pointer position and stores it in the `xpointer` and `ypointer` variables. Depending on the browser, the position is found either in the `event.x` and `event.y` properties, or the `event.pageX` and `event.pageY` properties.

Finally, the `Move` function sets the position of the layer to the same position as the mouse pointer. 50 pixels are subtracted from the position to center the graphic at the mouse pointer position, since the graphic is 100 pixels square.

Putting It All Together

To complete this example, you simply need to combine the script functions you have created with a simple HTML document. Listing 22.1 shows the complete example.

LISTING 22.1   Following the Mouse Pointer

```
<html>
<head>
<title>Follow that Mouse!</title>
<script language="JavaScript">
var Netscape=(navigator.appName.indexOf("Netscape") != -1);
function Move(e) {
  if (!document.getElementById) return;
  obj=document.getElementById("mouse");
  if (Netscape)
    event=e;
  if (event.pageX) { // Netscape...
    xpointer=event.pageX;
    ypointer=event.pageY;
  }
  else if (event.x) { // Internet Explorer...
    xpointer=event.x;
```

LISTING 22.1 continued

```
        ypointer=event.y;
    }
    obj.style.left=xpointer - 50;
    obj.style.top=ypointer - 50;
}
function Setup() {
    if (!document.getElementById) return;
    if (Netscape)
        document.captureEvents(Event.MOUSEMOVE);
    document.onmousemove=Move;
}
</script>
</head>
<body onLoad="Setup();">
<h1>Animation in DHTML</h1>
<div ID="mouse" style="position:absolute; left:150; top:150;">
<img src="mouse.gif" width="100" height="100" alt="" border="0">
</div>
</body>
</html>
```

In this listing, the onLoad event handler of the <body> tag calls the Setup function to begin the animation. This function sets up the event handler for mouse movement, and the Move function is called when the mouse moves.

 Since this example uses the W3C DOM for positioning, it requires Netscape 6 or later or Internet Explorer 5.0 or later. However, it could be adapted to work with the 4.0 browsers. See Hour 17, "Dealing with Browser Differences," for techniques you can use.

This example requires a graphic, mouse.gif, which you can download from this book's Web site at http://www.starlingtech.com/dhtml/. To test this example, load it into a browser. The mouse graphic should move continuously as the mouse pointer moves, as if it's stuck to the pointer. Figure 22.1 shows Netscape's display of the example in action.

FIGURE 22.1
*The animation follow-
ing the mouse pointer.*

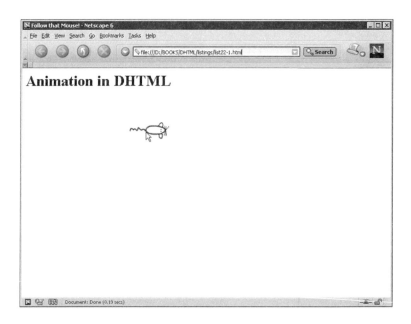

Animation with Multiple Images

While the example you've created is more sophisticated than previous examples, it is
still simplistic: the graphic doesn't change, and it acts like an extension of the mouse
pointer.

In this section, you'll improve the example in two ways: first, you will use four different
graphics to make the mouse change direction as it moves. Second, the mouse will move
at a constant speed and won't immediately catch the mouse pointer.

Creating the Graphics

The new example will use four different graphics, one for each of four directions the
mouse's nose can point. Figure 22.2 shows all four of the graphics you will use in this
example.

These graphics, along with the graphic for the previous example and the
listings for this hour, are available on this book's Web site:
http://www.starlingtech.com/dhtml/.

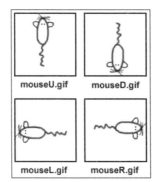

mouseU.gif   mouseD.gif

mouseL.gif   mouseR.gif

Setting Up Positioning Variables

This script will use several global variables to keep track of the animation's status. The following are the declarations for these variables:

```
var x=150,y=150;
var dx=0,dy=1;
var xpointer=0,ypointer=0;
var counter=0;
```

The x and y variables will store the current position of the animated mouse graphic. The dx and dy variables will store the current direction of motion: dx values of –1 or 1 will move left and right, and dy values of –1 or 1 will move up and down.

The xpointer and ypointer variables will store the current position of the mouse pointer. The counter variable will count animation cycles and allow changes of direction.

Setting Up Events

As before, your script will use a Setup function to set up the event handler for mouse movement. The following is the new Setup function:

```
function Setup() {
  if (!document.getElementById) return;
  if (Netscape)
    document.captureEvents(Event.MOUSEMOVE);
  document.onmousemove=SetPointer;
  a1 = new Image();
  a1.src="mouseR.gif";
  a2 = new Image();
  a2.src="mouseL.gif";
  a3 = new Image();
```

```
  a3.src="mouseU.gif";
  a4 = new Image();
  a4.src="mouseD.gif";
  Move();
}
```

This function is different in two ways: first, it assigns the SetPointer function as the event handler rather than the Move function. Second, the statements using the a1 through a4 variables are used to preload the four images used in the animation.

> The statement a1 = new Image(); creates an Image object, and assigning the src property of the object loads the image into the browser's cache. The preloaded images are not displayed until their names are assigned to an image's src property.

The final line of the Setup function calls the Move function to begin the animation. This function will repeat itself to move the graphic repeatedly on a timer.

Tracking the Mouse Pointer

The SetPointer function will be called by the onMouseMove event each time the mouse moves. This function assigns the xpointer and ypointer variables, as the Move function did previously:

```
function SetPointer(e) {
  if (Netscape)
    event=e;
  if (event.pageX) { // Netscape...
    xpointer=event.pageX;
    ypointer=event.pageY;
  }
  else if (event.x) { // Internet Explorer...
    xpointer=event.x;
    ypointer=event.y;
  }
}
```

This version of the script will declare xpointer and ypointer as global variables. They are set by the SetPointer function, and will be read by the Move function.

Creating the Move Function

Rather than executing each time the mouse pointer moves, the Move function will now execute on a timer. Here is the new Move function:

```
function Move() {
  if (!document.getElementById) return;
  obj=document.getElementById("mouse");
  xdist=Math.abs(xpointer-x);
  ydist=Math.abs(ypointer-y);
  ChangeDirection(xdist,ydist);
  if (xdist>2) x += dx*2;
  if (ydist>2) y += dy*2;
  obj.style.left=x - 50;
  obj.style.top=y - 50;
  window.setTimeout("Move();",1);
}
```

This function first checks that the `getElementById` method is supported, and uses this method to find the object for the layer. Next, it calculates the distance from the mouse graphic to the mouse pointer, and stores it in the `xdist` and `ydist` variables.

> The `Math.abs` function returns the *absolute value* of its argument. This is essentially the value with its negative sign removed: `Math.abs(1)` is 1, and `Math.abs(-1)` is also 1.

Next, the `Move` function passes `xdist` and `ydist` to the `ChangeDirection` function. This function will change the animation's direction if needed. Next, the `dx` and `dy` variables are used to change the `x` and `y` position, and the layer is moved to this position. Finally, the `setTimeout` method calls the `Move` function again in one millisecond.

Changing Direction

The `ChangeDirection` function checks the current distance between the graphic and the mouse pointer, and potentially changes the animation's direction to head closer to it. The following is the JavaScript code for this function:

```
function ChangeDirection(xdist,ydist) {
  counter++;
  if (counter<30 || (xdist<2 && ydist<2)) return;
  counter=0;
  if (xdist > ydist)  {
    dx = (xpointer-x<0) ? -1 : 1;
    dy = 0;
  } else if (ydist > xdist) {
    dy = (ypointer-y<0) ? -1 : 1;
    dx = 0;
  }
  if (dx>0) fn="mouseR.gif";
  if (dx<0) fn="mouseL.gif";
```

```
    if (dy>0) fn="mouseD.gif";
    if (dy<0) fn="mouseU.gif";
    document.images["mouseimg"].src=fn;
}
```

This function first increments the counter variable. The if statement exits the function if counter has not yet reached 30. It also exits if the xdist and ydist variables are less than two, meaning the animated mouse has "caught" the mouse pointer.

 The counter variable is used to make sure the graphic (and its direction) doesn't change too rapidly, which would create a flickering effect.

If counter has reached 30, it is reset to zero. Next, dx and dy are set depending on which distance is greater. These values are set to –1 or 1 depending on the direction the graphic needs to move.

The final four if statements set the fn variable depending on the current direction: mouseR.gif for right, mouseL.gif for left, mouseD.gif for down, or mouseU.gif for up. The src property for the image is set to change the image.

Workshop: Completing and Testing the Animation

To complete this example, you need to combine the JavaScript functions you've created into the HTML document. Listing 22.2 shows the complete HTML document.

LISTING 22.2   The Complete Animation Example

```
<html>
<head>
<title>Follow that Mouse!</title>
<script language="JavaScript">
var x=150,y=150;
var dx=0,dy=1;
var xpointer=0,ypointer=0;
var counter=0;
var Netscape=(navigator.appName.indexOf("Netscape") != -1);
function SetPointer(e) {
  if (Netscape)
    event=e;
  if (event.pageX) { // Netscape...
    xpointer=event.pageX;
```

LISTING 22.2   continued

```
      ypointer=event.pageY;
    }
    else if (event.x) { // Internet Explorer...
      xpointer=event.x;
      ypointer=event.y;
    }
  }
  function Move() {
    if (!document.getElementById) return;
    obj=document.getElementById("mouse");
    xdist=Math.abs(xpointer-x);
    ydist=Math.abs(ypointer-y);
    ChangeDirection(xdist,ydist);
    if (xdist>2) x += dx*2;
    if (ydist>2) y += dy*2;
    obj.style.left=x - 50;
    obj.style.top=y - 50;
    window.setTimeout("Move();",1);
  }
  function ChangeDirection(xdist,ydist) {
    counter++;
    if (counter<30 || (xdist<2 && ydist<2)) return;
    counter=0;
    if (xdist > ydist)  {
      dx = (xpointer-x<0) ? -1 : 1;
      dy = 0;
    } else if (ydist > xdist) {
      dy = (ypointer-y<0) ? -1 : 1;
      dx = 0;
    }
    if (dx>0) fn="mouseR.gif";
    if (dx<0) fn="mouseL.gif";
    if (dy>0) fn="mouseD.gif";
    if (dy<0) fn="mouseU.gif";
    document.images["mouseimg"].src=fn;
  }
  function Setup() {
    if (!document.getElementById) return;
    if (Netscape)
      document.captureEvents(Event.MOUSEMOVE);
    document.onmousemove=SetPointer;
    a1 = new Image();
    a1.src="mouseR.gif";
    a2 = new Image();
    a2.src="mouseL.gif";
    a3 = new Image();
    a3.src="mouseU.gif";
    a4 = new Image();
```

LISTING 22.2   continued

```
    a4.src="mouseD.gif";
    Move();
}
</script>
</head>
<body onLoad="Setup();">
<h1>Animation in DHTML</h1>
<div ID="mouse" style="position:absolute; left:150; top:150;">
<img ID="mouseimg" src="mouseR.gif" width="100" height="100" border="0">
</div>
</body>
</html>
```

To test this document, save it and load it into a browser. Now, rather than being stuck to the mouse pointer, the animated mouse will chase the pointer, not stopping until it catches it. Figure 22.3 shows Internet Explorer's display of the animation in action.

FIGURE 22.3

The new animation example in action.

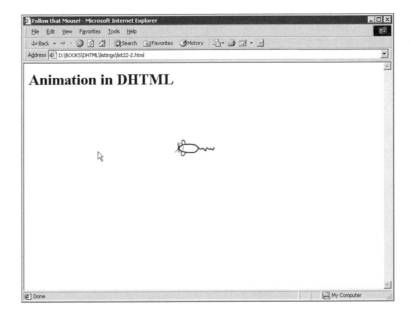

Summary

In this hour, you've created two animation examples, including one that combines dynamic images with DHTML animation to create a complete effect.

22

In the next hour, you'll create another advanced DHTML application: a complete game that uses JavaScript and DHTML to interact with the user.

Q&A

Q. Can I hide the mouse pointer and use a graphic as a custom pointer?

A. Yes, depending on the browser. See Hour 10, "Using Style Sheet Properties," for information.

Q. Why don't these animation examples use a separate JavaScript file for the functions?

A. While separating HTML and JavaScript can often make life easier, these examples use much JavaScript and very little HTML, so there isn't much need for a separate document. Nonetheless, you can use a separate script file if you prefer.

Q. Can I use more than four graphics for different directions of the animation?

A. Yes. If you changed the example to allow diagonal movement, you could add four additional graphics to create a more realistic animation.

Quiz

Test your knowledge of the material covered in this hour by answering the following questions.

Questions

1. Which of the following properties must be set for event capturing in Netscape?

    a. `document.mousemove`

    b. `document.captureEvents`

    c. `document.onmousemove`

2. Which of the following is the correct command to set the `onMouseMove` event handler for the document?

    a. `document.onmousemove=SetPointer;`

    b. `document.onMouseMove=SetPointer;`

    c. `document.mousemove=SetPointer;`

3. Which property should you change to change the image file displayed by an `<img>` tag with the `ID` attribute "mouseimg"?

   a. `document.mouseimg.src`

   b. `document.images.src["mouseimg"]`

   c. `document.images["mouseimg"].src`

Answers

1. b. The `document.captureEvents` property is required for event capturing in Netscape.

2. a. The correct statement is `document.onmousemove=SetPointer;`

3. c. The correct property is `document.images["mouseimg"].src`.

Exercises

If you'd like to experiment further with this hour's examples before moving on, try the following exercises:

- Try changing Listing 22.2 to speed up the mouse graphic's movement.
- Add `if` statements to Listing 22.2 to restrict the animated mouse's movements to a box within the Web page.

HOUR 23

Creating a DHTML Game

You're nearing the end of your 24-hour tour of DHTML. At this point, you should feel comfortable working with DHTML and ready to move on to more complicated tasks.

In this hour, you'll create a version of the word-guessing game Hangman using DHTML. Using dynamic features will allow you to create a friendly, attractive user interface for the game.

This hour covers the following topics:

- Creating the HTML document
- Planning the dynamic features
- Creating graphics for the game
- Adding JavaScript functions
- Creating the word list
- Adding the style sheet
- Completing and testing the game

Creating the HTML Document

The game will use a simple HTML document as its basis. This document will include links to JavaScript files for the DHTML features, along with a link to a style sheet to format the text. Listing 23.1 shows the complete HTML document.

LISTING 23.1   The HTML Document for the Hangman Game

```
<html>
<head>
<title>DHTML Hangman Game</title>
<script language="JavaScript" src="wordlist.js">
</script>
<script language="JavaScript" src="hangman.js">
</script>
<link rel="stylesheet" href="hangman.css">
</head>
<body onLoad="Setup();">
<h1>Hangman Game</h1>
<p>This is a simple Hangman game that uses DHTML and JavaScript.
Click on a blue letter to guess that letter. If your guess is correct, the
letter turns green and you're closer to winning - but if your guess is
wrong, the letter turns red and you're closer to hanging. You're allowed
a total of seven incorrect guesses.</p>
<table>
<tr>
<td rowspan="3">
  <img ID="hangman" src="hangman0.gif" width="80" height="105">
</td>
<td>
  <b ID="status">Guess a Letter Below.</b>
</td>
</tr>
<tr>
<td valign="top">
  <span ID="alphabet"></span>
</td>
</tr>
<tr>
<td align="center" id="theword">
</td>
</tr>
</table>
</body>
</html>
```

The table in the body of the page will provide the game display. Notice that the <span> tag with the ID attribute "alphabet" is empty—this will contain a clickable alphabet used for guessing letters, which will be added using a script. Similarly, the `<td>` tag with the ID attribute "theword" will display the current word as letters are guessed.

Figure 23.1 shows how the initial game display will look. However, keep in mind that the alphabet and word displays will be generated by JavaScript functions, and the fonts will be defined by a style sheet. You'll need to create these before the game will work. In the meantime, save the HTML document.

FIGURE 23.1

The display at the beginning of a game.

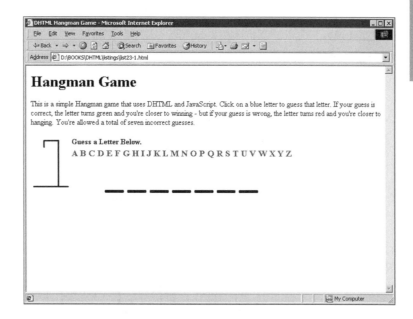

This example's listings are long, and additionally, graphics are required. All of these can be downloaded from this book's Web site, `http://www.starlingtech.com/dhtml/`.

Planning Dynamic Features

While you could create a Hangman game without using DHTML, this one will take full advantage of the W3C DOM's dynamic features:

- The letters of the alphabet that you click to guess letters will change color to indicate whether the guess was correct, and will no longer be clickable links after being guessed once.

- The status line above the alphabet will update with the latest game status. A link will appear there at the end of the game to allow the user to start a new game.
- The large word display will update with letters and blanks as you guess correct letters.

Additionally, the hangman graphic will change with each incorrect guess. However, this feature uses the Level 0 DOM and does not require DHTML.

> Due to the dynamic features used, this example will require Netscape 6 or later or Internet Explorer 5.0 or later.

Creating Graphics

The HTML document includes a single <img> tag to display the hanging man graphic. This graphic will be changed to one of eight images depending on the number of incorrect guesses.

Figure 23.2 shows all eight of the graphics that will be used in this game. You can download them from this book's Web site, http://www.starlingtech.com/dhtml/.

FIGURE 23.2
The graphics for the Hangman game.

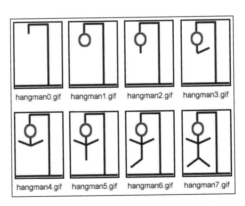

Creating the JavaScript Functions

This example will use more JavaScript functions than previous examples in this book, but they're short and easy to understand. Here is a summary of the functions this game will use:

- The `Setup` function will start the game when the page loads.
- The `DrawAlphabet` function will be called by `Setup`, and will create the clickable letters for guessing.
- The `ChooseWord` function will be called by `Setup`, and will choose a random word for each game.
- The `Guess` function will be called when the user clicks on the alphabet links, and will handle the game play.
- The `AddLetter` function will be called by `Guess`, and will display correct letters as they are guessed.
- The `Hang` function will handle incorrect guesses.
- The `GameOver` function will end the game when the word is guessed completely, or when the maximum number of incorrect guesses is reached.

The following sections describe each of the functions for the Hangman game.

Setting Up Variables

The game will use three global variables to keep track of the status of the game. The following lines of JavaScript define the global variables:

```
var answer="",currentword="";
var gamestatus=0;
```

The `answer` variable will store the correct word, chosen randomly at the beginning of the game. The `currentword` variable will store the current word as letters are guessed, beginning as a series of blanks. The `gamestatus` variable will keep track of the number of incorrect guesses.

 The game will require one more global variable—an array with a large list of words that can be guessed. This will be defined in a separate JavaScript file, which you'll create later this hour.

The `Setup` Function

The `Setup` function will execute when you first load the page, and will set up the variables for the game and call other setup-related functions. The following is the definition for the `Setup` function:

```
function Setup() {
  if (!document.getElementById) return;
  DrawAlphabet();
```

```
ChooseWord();
dispword=document.getElementById("theword");
for (i=0;i<answer.length;i++) {
  currentword += "_";
}
dispword.innerHTML=currentword;
}
```

This function first checks the getElementById method, so the game won't start unless the browser supports the required DOM features. Next, it calls two other setup functions, DrawAlphabet and ChooseWord, which you'll create next.

Next, the Setup function finds the object for the word display and stores it in the dispword variable. The for loop constructs the currentword variable, which contains a string of underscore (_) characters the same length as the answer variable, which has been assigned by the ChooseWord function. Finally, it displays the current word by assigning it to dispword's innerHTML property.

Drawing the Alphabet

The DrawAlphabet function is called by the Setup function when the game begins. This function creates the alphabet of clickable letters that will be used for each guess.

```
function DrawAlphabet() {
  alpha=document.getElementById("alphabet");
  for (i=65;i<91;i++) {
    letter=String.fromCharCode(i);
    node=document.createElement("A");
    node.id=letter;
    quoted="\"" + letter + "\"";
    node.setAttribute("href","javascript:Guess("+quoted+");");
    node.className="letter";
    node.innerHTML=letter;
    alpha.appendChild(node);
  }
}
```

This function first finds the object for the <span> element with the ID attribute "alphabet". The for loop executes the remaining statements once for each letter from A-Z.

> The loop actually sets the variable i to the numbers 65 to 90 in sequence. These are the character codes for the capital letters A through Z. The String.fromCharCode method converts each code to the corresponding letter.

In each iteration of the loop, the `letter` variable stores the current letter. A new `<a>` node is created with the `ID` attribute of the current letter. The `href` attribute is set to link to the `Guess` function. For example, the letter `G` will be linked to this URL:

```
javascript:Guess("G");
```

Last but not least, the `className` of the `<a>` element is set to `"letter"`. This class will be used to format the alphabet with a style sheet. The `innerHTML` property is set to display the letter, and the new node is appended to the alphabet `<span>` element.

Choosing a Word

The `ChooseWord` function is called by the `Setup` function. This function chooses a random word to be guessed in each round of the game.

```
function ChooseWord() {
  num=Math.floor(Math.random()*words.length);
  answer=words[num].toUpperCase();
}
```

This function uses JavaScript's built-in `Math.random` function to choose a random number between zero and the length of the `words` array, and assigns the `answer` variable to the corresponding element of the `words` array. You'll define this array later with a list of potential words.

Handling Guesses

The `Guess` function will handle the actual game play. This function will be called when one of the letters of the alphabet is clicked to make a guess. Its parameter, `letter`, is the letter currently being guessed. The following is the `Guess` function:

```
function Guess(letter) {
  stat=document.getElementById("status");
  alpha=document.getElementById("alphabet");
  displetter=document.getElementById(letter);
  node=document.createElement("span");
  node.innerHTML=letter;
  node.id=letter;
  if (answer.indexOf(letter) != -1) {
    AddLetter(letter);
    stat.innerHTML="Correct!  Guess another letter.";
    node.style.color="green";
    alpha.replaceChild(node,displetter);
    if (currentword==answer) GameOver("You Win! ");
  } else {
    stat.innerHTML="Incorrect!  Guess again!";
    node.style.color="red";
```

```
    alpha.replaceChild(node,displetter);
    Hang();
  }
}
```

This function first finds objects for three parts of the Web page: `stat`, the status line within the table, `alpha`, the alphabet display, and `displetter`, the <a> element for the letter that is being guessed.

First, the `Guess` function creates a new <span> node. This node will replace the <a> node for the letter, so it can't be guessed again. The `innerHTML` and `id` properties are set to the letter.

Next, the `if` statement determines whether the letter appears in the answer, using the `indexOf` method. If the guess was correct, it calls the `AddLetter` function, which adds the guessed letter to `currentword` and displays it.

It then displays a congratulatory message in the status area, sets `node`'s `style.color` property to green, and uses the `replaceChild` method to replace the <a> node with the new <span> node. If `currentword` is now equal to the `answer` variable, it calls the `GameOver` function to end the game.

If the guessed letter was not found in the answer, the `else` clause takes over. This first displays a message in the status area and sets `node`'s color to red. It replaces the <a> node with the <span> node, and calls the `Hang` function. This function will update the game status and the hangman graphic.

Figure 23.3 shows how the game will appear in progress. In the figure, a correct letter has just been guessed.

Displaying Correct Letters

The `AddLetter` function will be called by the `Guess` function. This function updates the `currentword` variable with the guessed letter, and displays it in the game area.

```
function AddLetter(letter) {
  dispword=document.getElementById("theword");
  newword="";
  for (i=0;i<answer.length;i++) {
    if (answer.charAt(i)==letter)  newword += letter;
      else newword += currentword.charAt(i);
  }
  currentword=newword;
  dispword.innerHTML=currentword;
}
```

FIGURE 23.3

The Hangman game in progress, after a correct guess.

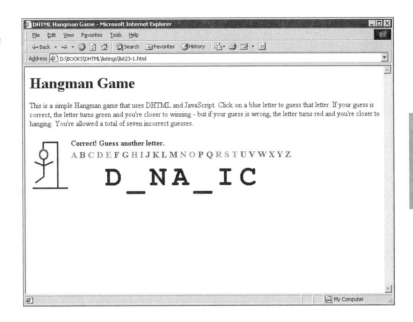

This function first finds the object for the word display area. The `for` loop creates `newword` with the letters and blanks of the current word, combined with the new letter that was guessed. The `currentword` variable is replaced with the value of `newword`, and it is displayed in the word display area.

Updating the Hangman Graphic

The `Hang` function is called each time a letter is guessed incorrectly:

```
function Hang() {
  gamestatus++;
  newsrc="hangman" + gamestatus + ".gif";
  document.images["hangman"].src=newsrc;
  if (gamestatus==7) GameOver("Sorry! ");
}
```

This function increments the `gamestatus` variable, which stores the number of incorrect guesses. It changes the hangman graphic to the corresponding image. Finally it calls the `GameOver` function to end the game if `gamestatus` has reached seven incorrect guesses.

Ending the Game

The `GameOver` function is called by the `Guess` function if the game ends with a successful guess, and by the `Hang` function if the maximum number of incorrect guesses is reached. The following is the `GameOver` function:

```
function GameOver(text) {
  stat=document.getElementById("status");
  alpha=document.getElementById("alphabet");
  dispword=document.getElementById("theword");
  newlink=" <a href='javascript:location.reload();'>Click Here</a>";
  newlink+=" to start a new game.";
  stat.innerHTML="<b ID='gameover'>GAME OVER</b> - " + text + newlink;
  dispword.innerHTML=answer;
  for (i=65;i<91;i++) {
    letter=String.fromCharCode(i);
    oldnode=document.getElementById(letter);
    if (oldnode.nodeName=="A") {
      node=document.createElement("span");
      node.innerHTML=letter;
      node.className="letter";
      alpha.replaceChild(node,oldnode);
    } // end if
  } // end for
}
```

This function first creates a link to the `location.reload` method, which will start a new game, in the `newlink` variable. It stores this link, along with the words GAME OVER and the text sent by the `Guess` or `Hang` functions, in the status area.

Next, it displays the answer in the word display area. This way, if you lose the game, you can see what the correct answer was.

Finally, the `for` loop finds each of the elements within the <span> area for the alphabet. For each letter that is still a link, it replaces it with a new <span> node. This prevents any guessing after the game has ended.

Completing the JavaScript File

Now that you have created the JavaScript functions to handle the game play, you can combine them into a JavaScript file. Listing 23.2 shows the complete JavaScript file.

LISTING 23.2   The Complete Hangman JavaScript File

```
var answer="",currentword="";
var gamestatus=0;
function Setup() {
  if (!document.getElementById) return;
  DrawAlphabet();
  ChooseWord();
  dispword=document.getElementById("theword");
  for (i=0;i<answer.length;i++) {
```

LISTING 23.2   continued

23

```
        currentword += "_";
      }
      dispword.innerHTML=currentword;
  }
  function DrawAlphabet() {
    alpha=document.getElementById("alphabet");
    for (i=65;i<91;i++) {
      letter=String.fromCharCode(i);
      node=document.createElement("A");
      node.id=letter;
      quoted="\"" + letter + "\"";
      node.setAttribute("href","javascript:Guess("+quoted+");");
      node.className="letter";
      node.innerHTML=letter;
      alpha.appendChild(node);
    }
  }
  function ChooseWord() {
    num=Math.floor(Math.random()*words.length);
    answer=words[num].toUpperCase();
  }
  function Guess(letter) {
    stat=document.getElementById("status");
    alpha=document.getElementById("alphabet");
    displetter=document.getElementById(letter);
    node=document.createElement("span");
    node.innerHTML=letter;
    node.id=letter;
    if (answer.indexOf(letter) != -1) {
      AddLetter(letter);
      stat.innerHTML="Correct!  Guess another letter.";
      node.style.color="green";
      alpha.replaceChild(node,displetter);
      if (currentword==answer) GameOver("You Win! ");
    } else {
      stat.innerHTML="Incorrect!  Guess again!";
      node.style.color="red";
      alpha.replaceChild(node,displetter);
      Hang();
    }
  }
  function AddLetter(letter) {
    dispword=document.getElementById("theword");
    newword="";
    for (i=0;i<answer.length;i++) {
      if (answer.charAt(i)==letter)  newword += letter;
```

LISTING 23.2   continued

```
        else newword += currentword.charAt(i);
    }
    currentword=newword;
    dispword.innerHTML=currentword;
}
function Hang() {
    gamestatus++;
    newsrc="hangman" + gamestatus + ".gif";
    document.images["hangman"].src=newsrc;
    if (gamestatus==7) GameOver("Sorry! ");
}
function GameOver(text) {
    stat=document.getElementById("status");
    alpha=document.getElementById("alphabet");
    dispword=document.getElementById("theword");
    newlink=" <a href='javascript:location.reload();'>Click Here</a>";
    newlink+=" to start a new game.";
    stat.innerHTML="<b ID='gameover'>GAME OVER</b> - " + text + newlink;
    dispword.innerHTML=answer;
    for (i=65;i<91;i++) {
        letter=String.fromCharCode(i);
        oldnode=document.getElementById(letter);
        if (oldnode.nodeName=="A") {
            node=document.createElement("span");
            node.innerHTML=letter;
            node.className="letter";
            alpha.replaceChild(node,oldnode);
        } // end if
    } // end for
}
```

To use the JavaScript file, save it as hangman.js in the same directory as the HTML file. You can't test the game yet, though, since you still need to create the word list and the style sheet.

Creating the Word List

The word list for the game will be stored in a separate JavaScript file. Listing 23.3 shows this JavaScript file.

LISTING 23.3   The Word List JavaScript File

```
var words = new Array(
"accept","account","achieve","across","action","actually","addition",
"analysis","animal","announce","another","answer","anyone","anything",
"audience","because","become","before","behind","believe","better",
"central","century","certain","chance","change","charge","choice",
"complete","concern","congress","consider","contain","continue","control",
"defense","demand","describe","design","detail","develop","direct",
"division","doctor","dollar","during","economic","effect","effort","either",
"evidence","example","except","expect","explain","express","extend",
"finger","finish","fiscal","follow","foreign","forget","former","freedom",
"happen","herself","higher","himself","history","hospital","however",
"instance","instead","interact","interest","involve","language","larger",
"maintain","manager","manner","market","marriage","material","matter",
"method","military","million","minute","modern","moment","morning",
"nearly","normal","nothing","number","object","obtain","office","officer",
"period","permit","person","personal","physical","picture","police",
"prevent","private","probably","problem","process","produce","product",
"question","rather","reaction","realize","really","reason","receive",
"religion","remain","remember","remove","report","require","research",
"section","select","series","serious","service","settle","several",
"source","southern","special","specific","spring","square","station",
"suddenly","suffer","suggest","summer","supply","support","suppose",
"toward","trouble","usually","various","volume","weapon","western",
"whether","window","within","without","wonder","worker","writer");
```

This file is essentially a single JavaScript statement, which declares the words array and fills it with about 150 words. To add the word list to the game, save it as wordlist.js in the same folder as the other HTML and JavaScript files.

> This word list is short for the sake of simplicity. You'll find a longer word list on this book's Web site, http://www.starlingtech.com/dhtml/.

Workshop: Adding the Style Sheet

The final step in creating the game is to create the style sheet. The styles not only make the game look good, but also perform some important functions: in particular, they create large letters with space between them in the current word display.

Listing 23.4 shows the complete style sheet.

LISTING 23.4   The Style Sheet for the Game

```
#theword {font-size: 60px;
    font-family: monospace;
    font-weight: bold;
    letter-spacing: 12px;}
#alphabet {font-size: 19px;
    font-weight: bold;
    letter-spacing: 5px;
    text-decoration: none;}
#gameover {color: red; }
A.letter {text-decoration: none;
    color: blue;}
.letter {color: silver;}
```

This style sheet sets styles for three explicit identifiers: #theword, the current word display; #alphabet, the alphabet for guessing letters, and #gameover, the words GAME OVER that will be displayed by the GameOver function.

It also sets styles for the .letter class, which will be assigned to each letter in the alphabet. The text-decoration attribute removes the underlines from the linked letters. Their color is also set, to blue for linked letters and silver for unlinked ones.

To add the style sheet to the game, save it as hangman.css in the same folder as the HTML and JavaScript files.

Testing the Complete Example

You are now ready to test the Hangman game. To make the game work, you'll need to store the HTML file, the JavaScript file for the functions, the JavaScript file for the word list, and the style sheet in the same folder. The eight hangman graphics also need to be in the same folder.

After all of the files are assembled, you can load the HTML document into a browser and try the game. Figure 23.4 shows the game display after a game has been completed (and lost).

FIGURE 23.4

The game display after a game is lost.

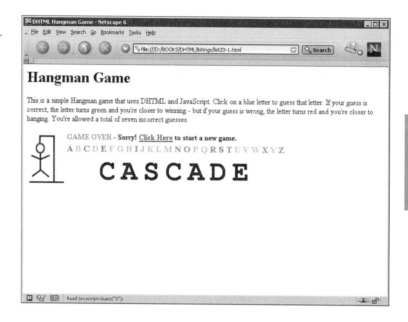

Summary

In this hour, you've created a more complex example that uses DHTML, JavaScript, and CSS styles to create a complete game application. This is just the beginning—you can actually create even more complex applications using DHTML.

In the final hour of this book, you'll explore some tips to use DHTML more effectively, and learn what the future holds for DHTML and the Web.

Q&A

Q. Why doesn't the game check whether a letter has already been guessed?

A. When a letter is guessed, its entry in the alphabet is changed to no longer link to the Guess function, so it's actually impossible to guess the same letter twice. The letter simply won't be clickable the second time.

Q. Is there a limit on the length of words used in this game?

A. No, but the words in the included list range from 6-8 letters to make for a consistent game. Words with fewer letters are harder to guess. You can expand the word list with words of any size.

Q. Why is the `location.reload` method used to start a new game?

A. This method has the same effect as the browser's Reload button. It effectively clears the contents of the alphabet and word displays, allowing them to be re-created by the `Setup` function. This could also be done without reloading, but would require more code.

Quiz

Test your knowledge of the material covered in this hour by answering the following questions.

Questions

1. Which of the following is the correct JavaScript function to return a random number?

    a. `random()`

    b. `Math.random()`

    c. `Math.rand()`

2. Which of the following characters is represented by the character code 65?

    a. `A`

    b. `Z`

    c. `a`

3. Which of the following style sheet selectors refers to a CLASS attribute?

    a. `#alphabet`

    b. `BODY`

    c. `.letter`

Answers

1. b. The `Math.random` function returns a random number.

2. a. The character code 65 represents the capital letter `A`.

3. c. The `.letter` selector refers to a class.

Exercises

If you'd like to experiment further with this hour's example before moving on, try the following exercises:

- Add a feature to the Hangman game to display the number of incorrect guesses left in the status area after each incorrect guess.
- Modify the example so that the words GAME OVER that appear at the end of the game are green in color if the game was won, and red if it was lost.

23

HOUR **24**

DHTML Tips and Tricks

Welcome to the final hour of your 24-hour tour of DHTML! You've now explored the many things that DHTML can do, and created many working examples.

In this hour, you'll create two more simple, but useful, examples. You'll also take a look at what the future holds for DHTML, and learn where to go to continue your DHTML education.

This hour covers the following topics:

- Creating DHTML tool tips
- The future of DHTML
- Learning more about DHTML
- Creating a scrolling text window

Creating Tool Tips

While you've explored much of what DHTML can do, there are still some useful things that can be done, often with a minimum of scripting. One such example is displaying tool tips, or floating text descriptions of links. This is a common use for DHTML.

Creating the HTML Document

This example begins with an HTML document. This will define a bulleted list of links, each with event handlers that will display the tips. Listing 24.1 shows the HTML document.

As usual, you can download this hour's examples from this book's Web site: http://www.starlingtech.com/dhtml/.

LISTING 24.1 The HTML Document for the Tool Tip Example

```html
<html>
<head>
<title>DHTML Tool Tips</title>
<script language="JavaScript" src="tooltip.js">
</script>
</head>
<body style="margin-left:0; margin-top:0;">
<h1>DHTML Tool Tips</h1>
<p>This example displays "tool tips", or pop-up hints,
for each of the links in the bulleted list below. This is a great
way to describe links without taking up space.</p>
<ul>
<li><a ID="thisbook"
  onMouseOver="ShowTip('thisbook');" onMouseOut="HideTip('thisbook');"
  href="http://www.starlingtech.com/dhtml/">This Book</a></li>
<li><a ID="microsoft"
  onMouseOver="ShowTip('microsoft');" onMouseOut="HideTip('microsoft');"
  href="http://www.microsoft.com/">Microsoft</a></li>
<li><a ID="netscape"
  onMouseOver="ShowTip('netscape');" onMouseOut="HideTip('netscape');"
  href="http://www.netscape.com/">Netscape</a></li>
<li><a ID="w3c"
  onMouseOver="ShowTip('w3c');" onMouseOut="HideTip('w3c');"
  href="http://www.w3.org/">The W3C</a></li>
</ul>
<div ID="tip-thisbook" style="position:absolute; visibility:hidden;">
Check out this book's Web site!
</div>
```

LISTING 24.1   continued

```
<div ID="tip-microsoft" style="position:absolute; visibility:hidden;">
Visit Microsoft's Web site
</div>
<div ID="tip-netscape" style="position:absolute; visibility:hidden;">
Visit Netscape's Web site
</div>
<div ID="tip-w3c" style="position:absolute; visibility:hidden;">
Visit the World Wide Web Consortium
</div>
</body>
</html>
```

24

Along with the list of links with `onMouseOver` and `onMouseOut` event handlers, this HTML document includes a `<div>` layer definition for each of the tool tips. These have their `visibility` style property set to `hidden` by default.

To test this document, save it and load it into a browser. The links should be displayed, but the tips won't work until you add the JavaScript functions.

Looking for a challenge? Try creating the JavaScript file for the tips yourself. You should know enough about DHTML by now to do it easily.

Showing Tips

If you look at how tool tips work on other Web pages or in your operating system, you'll notice that they don't display immediately. Instead, they display only when the mouse pointer hovers over an object for a certain time. You can create the same behavior in DHTML.

The `ShowTip` function will be called when the mouse is over one of the links. The following is the JavaScript code for this function:

```
var t=0;
function ShowTip(item) {
  if (!document.getElementById) return;
  thelink=document.getElementById(item);
  thetip=document.getElementById("tip-" + item);
  thetip.style.left=thelink.offsetLeft + thelink.offsetWidth + 10;
  thetip.style.top=thelink.offsetTop;
  t=window.setTimeout("ShowIt(\""+item+"\");",1000);
  thetip.style.backgroundColor="yellow";
}
```

Some versions of Netscape 6 report a slightly different offset than other browsers. This example's HTML document sets the left and top margins to zero to avoid this problem. The only other solution is to check for specific browsers. See Hour 17, "Dealing with Browser Differences," for information about browser sensing.

This function first checks for the needed DOM support, and finds two objects: the link (i.e. `thebook`) and the corresponding tip (i.e. `tip-thebook`). It sets the `style.left` and `style.top` properties for the tip based on the link's `offsetLeft` and `offsetTop` properties, to make it appear near the link.

Next, the function sets a timeout to call the `ShowIt` function in one second. This function will make the tip become visible if the mouse remains over the link. Finally, it sets the tip's background color to yellow.

Notice the variable `t` used with the `setTimeout` method. This was declared as a global variable, and will store an identifier for the timeout. This will be used by the `HideTip` function to prevent the tip from displaying at the wrong time.

The `ShowIt` function will make the tip visible. This function is simple:

```
function ShowIt(item) {
  t=0;
  thetip=document.getElementById("tip-" + item);
  thetip.style.visibility="visible";
}
```

This function first clears the `t` variable that was used for the timeout. Next, it finds the object for the tip, and sets its `visibility` property to show it.

Hiding Tips

The `HideTip` function is called by the `onMouseOut` event when the mouse moves away from a link. Here's the code for this function:

```
function HideTip(item) {
  if (!document.getElementById) return;
  if (t) window.clearTimeout(t);
  thetip=document.getElementById("tip-" + item);
  thetip.style.visibility="hidden";
}
```

This function checks for the required DOM support, and then looks at the variable t. If it is set, the clearTimeout method clears the timeout. This stops the ShowIt function from making the tip visible if the mouse didn't stay over the link for the full one second.

Finally, the HideTip function finds the object for the tip, and sets its visibility property to hide the tip.

Completing the JavaScript File

The HTML document in Listing 24.1 refers to an external JavaScript file, tooltip.js. This file will contain the JavaScript functions you've created. Listing 24.2 shows the complete JavaScript file.

LISTING 24.2　The Complete Tool Tip JavaScript File

```
var t=0;
function ShowTip(item) {
  if (!document.getElementById) return;
  thelink=document.getElementById(item);
  thetip=document.getElementById("tip-" + item);
  thetip.style.left=thelink.offsetLeft + thelink.offsetWidth + 10;
  thetip.style.top=thelink.offsetTop;
  t=window.setTimeout("ShowIt(\""+item+"\");",1000);
  thetip.style.backgroundColor="yellow";
}
function ShowIt(item) {
  t=0;
  thetip=document.getElementById("tip-" + item);
  thetip.style.visibility="visible";
}
function HideTip(item) {
  if (!document.getElementById) return;
  if (t) window.clearTimeout(t);
  thetip=document.getElementById("tip-" + item);
  thetip.style.visibility="hidden";
}
```

24

To use this file, save it as tooltip.js in the same folder as the HTML document. You can then load the HTML document into a browser and verify that the tips work. Figure 24.1 shows the example in action in Netscape 6. In the figure, the mouse cursor is over the first link.

FIGURE **24.1**

The tool tip example in action.

Internet Explorer 4.0 and later support an easier way to create tool tips: set the `title` attribute of a link's <a> tag to a description, and it will be displayed as a tool tip. The DHTML alternative here has the advantage of working in other browsers, and giving you control over color, font size, and other aspects.

Where Do You Go from Here?

Having nearly finished your 24-hour look at DHTML, you might be wondering where to go next. There is much more to learn, and on top of that, DHTML and other Web technologies are constantly changing.

The Future of DHTML

DHTML is a relatively new technology. While the version 4.0 browsers supported basic DHTML, the new W3C DOM has revolutionized cross-browser DHTML, and its potential is only beginning to be realized on the Web.

As more users adopt browsers with W3C DOM support, you can use DHTML more freely without worrying about older browsers, and you can expect DHTML to start popping up all over the Web. Additionally, browsers will continue to improve, and will hopefully support the DOM level 2 and 3 standards completely.

The Future of HTML and JavaScript

HTML itself is changing with the emerging XHTML standard, a version of HTML that fits into the stricter confines of XML (extensible markup language). The W3C has published XHTML 1.1 as a recommendation, and it will soon make its way to browsers.

The JavaScript language is also continuously changing. Netscape is working with ECMA, the international organization that maintains the standard for JavaScript, on a new version currently known as JavaScript 2.0. For more information, see Netscape's Mozilla Web site:

```
http://www.mozilla.org/js/language/js20/index.html
```

Learning More

While you've created a wide range of applications with DHTML in this book, there is much more that could be done. See Appendix A for a list of resources to learn more about DHTML and JavaScript, and you can move on to even more impressive DHTML examples.

24

 If you improve one of the examples in this book or create something new, you can submit it to this book's Web site and share it with other readers.

Workshop: Creating a Scrolling Window

Just to show you that you haven't seen everything DHTML can do, here's one final example. While scrolling messages, such as the one you created in Hour 15, "Creating DHTML Text Effects," are common on the Web, you might have seen a few more complex scrolling windows that scroll a few paragraphs of news or links.

Scrolling windows like this are traditionally created with the Java language, but you can create one easily with DHTML using two layers. One large layer will contain all of the text, and a smaller layer will show a "window" on the larger layer.

Creating the HTML Document

The scrolling window example begins with the HTML document, which defines the layers and the content for the window. Listing 24.3 shows the complete HTML document.

LISTING 24.3   The HTML Document for the Scrolling Window

```html
<html>
<head>
<title>A DHTML Scrolling Window</title>
<script language="JavaScript" src="window.js">
</script>
</head>
<body onLoad="Scroll();">
<h1>Scrolling Window Example</h1>
<p>This example shows a scrolling window created in DHTML. The window
is actually a layer that shows a portion of a larger layer.</p>
<div id="thewindow" style="position:relative;width:180;height:150;
  overflow:hidden; border-width:2px; border-style:solid; border-color:red">
<div id="thetext" style="position:absolute;width:170;left:5;top:100">
<p>This is the first paragraph of the scrolling message. The message
is created with ordinary HTML.</p>
<p>Entries within the scrolling area can use any HTML tags. They can
contain <a href="http://www.starlingtech.com/dhtml/">Links</a>.</p>
<p>There's no limit on the number of paragraphs that you can include
here. They don't even need to be formatted as paragraphs.</p>
<ul><li>For example, you could format items using a bulleted list.</li></ul>
<p>The scrolling ends when the last part of the scrolling text
is on the screen. You've reached the end.</p>
<p><b>[<a href="javascript:pos=100;Scroll();">Start Over</a>]</b></p>
</div>
</div>
</body>
</html>
```

The <div> tags in this document create two nested layers: one, thewindow, will form the
small window for text to display in. The other, thetext, contains the text to scroll.

Since the text doesn't all fit in the small window, you'll only see part of it at a time. The
overflow property on the window layer prevents the rest of the content from showing.
Your script will manipulate the text window's style.top property to move it relative to
the window, creating a scrolling effect.

The text layer is actually ten pixels narrower than the window layer. This,
along with the left property, creates a small margin of white space on
either side of the window, preventing any of the text from being
obstructed.

The actual text to scroll is placed within the inner <div> element. You can use any HTML here, although it should be able to wrap to the small window.

To use this document, save it as an HTML file. It won't scroll until you add the JavaScript functions in the next section.

Creating the JavaScript Function

This example's JavaScript function is simple, but it's confined to a separate JavaScript file for clarity. Listing 24.4 shows the complete JavaScript file.

LISTING 24.4   The JavaScript File for the Scrolling Window

```
var pos=100;
function Scroll() {
  if (!document.getElementById) return;
  obj=document.getElementById("thetext");
  pos -=1;
  if (pos < 0-obj.offsetHeight+130) return;
  obj.style.top=pos;
  window.setTimeout("Scroll();",30);
}
```

The first line declares the global variable pos, which will store the text layer's current position. The Scroll function, called by the onLoad event handler of the <body> tag, handles the actual scrolling.

The scrolling stops at the end of the text. The last line of the text includes a javascript: link that resets the pos variable and restarts the Scroll function.

This function finds the object for the text layer. It then subtracts one from the pos variable. The if statement checks whether the layer has moved to the point where the last part of the text is shown through the window, and stops the scrolling.

The Scroll function next sets the style.top property for the text layer to move it to the new position. Last of all, it uses the setTimeout method to repeat itself in 30 milliseconds.

The window should scroll at about the right speed for reading. You can vary the speed by changing the timeout value.

To use this document, save it as window.js in the same folder as the HTML document. You can then load the HTML document into a browser. Figure 24.2 shows Internet Explorer's display of this example after the scrolling text has reached its final position.

FIGURE **24.2**

The scrolling window example, as displayed by Internet Explorer.

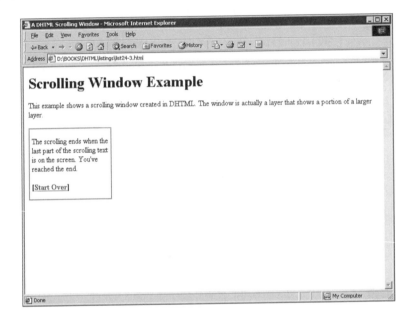

Summary

In this hour, you've completed your exploration of DHTML by creating two final examples. You've also taken a quick look at what the future holds for DHTML, and where you can go to further your DHTML education.

Time's up! You've reached the end of your 24-hour DHTML course. I hope you've enjoyed learning how JavaScript, HTML, CSS, and the DOM work together to make DHTML a powerful tool for the Web. Be sure to look at the list of resources in Appendix A to find out how you can learn more.

Q&A

Q. Can the tool tip example be modified to work in the 4.0 browsers?

A. Yes, since it uses layers. See Hour 17, "Dealing with Browser Differences," for a review of cross-browser layers.

Q. Doesn't the scrolling window example set the layer's position to negative numbers? Why doesn't this create an error?

A. Yes, it does—but browsers allow this. This simply positions the layer off the top of the screen.

Q. In Netscape, why does a scroll bar appear on the right side of the page during the scrolling?

A. This happens when the hidden text layer is longer than the current browser window would hold—even though the bottom part of it is invisible. This problem doesn't occur in Internet Explorer.

Quiz

Test your knowledge of the material covered in this hour by answering the following questions.

24

Questions

1. Suppose you have set a timeout using the statement t=window.setTimeout
   (statements);. Which of the following is the correct way to prevent the timeout's statements from executing?

   a. `window.setTimeout(0);`

   b. `window.clearTimeout(t);`

   c. `window.stopTimeout(t);`

2. Which of the following properties prevents the scrolling window text from showing below the window?

   a. `overflow: hidden`

   b. `border-style: solid`

   c. `position: relative`

3. Which of the following is the latest version of HTML?

   a. HTML 4.1

   b. DHTML 4.0

   c. XHTML 1.1

Answers

1. b. The `window.clearTimeout` method can stop the statements in the `window.setTimeout` method from executing.

2. a. The `overflow: hidden` property prevents the scrolling text from showing outside the window.

3. c. XHTML 1.1 is the latest version of HTML. DHTML (choice B) isn't actually a version of HTML.

Exercises

If you'd like to gain more experience with DHTML, try the following exercises:

- In Hour 22, "Creating Complex Animations," you created an animated mouse that follows the mouse cursor. Use the techniques you learned in that example to make the tooltips in Listing 24.1 display at the mouse cursor's location instead of at a fixed location.

- Visit this book's Web site at `http://www.starlingtech.com/dhtml/`. Check for updates to the book, and look for more examples from the author and other readers.

PART VII

Appendixes

Hour

APPENDIX **A**

Other JavaScript and DHTML Resources

While you've learned quite a bit about DHTML in 24 hours, there's more to learn if you're willing. The resources listed in this appendix will help you learn more about DHTML and JavaScript, and serve as references while you develop applications of your own.

JavaScript Web Sites

The following Web sites will help you learn more about JavaScript:

- JavaScript Developer Central, part of Netscape's DevEdge site, includes links to a wide variety of JavaScript resources.

  `http://developer.netscape.com/tech/javascript/index.html`

- Netscape's JavaScript Reference is the definitive JavaScript reference. This site also has a complete list of objects and properties for the Level 0 DOM.

  `http://developer.netscape.com/docs/manuals/js/client/jsref/index.htm`

- Website Abstraction has a number of sample scripts and JavaScript tutorials, and some DHTML information too.

  `http://wsabstract.com/`

- The JavaScript FAQ, from Internet Related Technologies, includes sample scripts and answers to many JavaScript questions.

  `http://developer.irt.org/script/script.htm`

- The JavaScript Workshop, maintained by the author of this book, has many JavaScript links and examples.

  `http://www.jsworkshop.com/`

Dynamic HTML Web Sites

You'll find the following resources useful for learning more about DHTML and CSS:

- The Web Design Group has several useful references about HTML and CSS.

  `http://www.htmlhelp.com/`

- WebReference.com's DHTML Lab has many DHTML tutorials and examples, both for the new DOM and for 4.0 browsers.

  `http://www.webreference.com/dhtml/`

Other Sites

The following sites might also be of interest:

- The W3C (World Wide Web Consortium) is the definitive source for information about the HTML and CSS standards.

  `http://www.w3.org/`

- HTMLcenter has reviews, news, and tutorials about HTML, CSS, JavaScript, and other Web technologies.

  `http://www.htmlcenter.com/`

- Internet Related Technologies' DOM cross-reference describes the objects of the W3C DOM and their support in current browsers.

  `http://www.irt.org/xref/dom_objects.htm`

Other Books

If you would like to learn more about JavaScript and HTML, you might find these other books useful:

- *Sams Teach Yourself JavaScript in 24 Hours, Second Edition*, by Michael Moncur. ISBN 0-672-32025-8.

- *JavaScript Developer's Dictionary*, by Alexander J. Vincent and John Krutsch. ISBN 0-672-32201-3.

- *Sams Teach Yourself Web Publishing with HTML and XHTML in 21 Days, Third Edition*, by Laura Lemay. ISBN 0-672-32077-0.

Development Tools

The following tools might make your life easier as you develop DHTML Web pages:

- HomeSite, from Allaire and Macromedia, is a full-featured HTML editor for Windows. It is similar to a text editor, but includes features to automatically add HTML tags, and to easily create complicated HTML elements such as tables. Syntax coloring helps you create valid HTML, JavaScript, and CSS. I use it to create and maintain all of my sites.

  `http://www.allaire.com/`

- TextPad, from Helios Software Solutions, is a Windows text editor intended as a replacement for the basic Notepad accessory. It's a fast, useful editor, and also includes a number of features for working with HTML, Java, and other languages. TextPad is shareware, and a fully-working version can be downloaded from this site.

  `http://www.textpad.com/`

- BBEdit, from Bare Bones Software, is a popular HTML and text editor for Macintosh systems.

  `http://www.bbedit.com/`

- SlickEdit, from MicroEdge, is a sophisticated programmer's editor for Windows and UNIX platforms.

  `http://www.slickedit.com/`

A

Debugging Tools and Resources

You might find the following software tools and sites useful when debugging JavaScript and DHTML applications:

- CSE HTML Validator, from AI Internet Solutions, is an excellent stand-alone utility for Windows that checks HTML documents against your choice of HTML versions. It can also be integrated with HomeSite, TextPad, and several other HTML and text editors.

    http://www.ht1mlvalidator.com/

- The W3C's HTML Validation Service is a Web-based HTML validator. Just enter your URL, and it will be immediately checked for HTML compliance.

    http://validator.w3.org/

- Netscape's JavaScript debugger allows you to set breakpoints, display variable values, and perform other debugging tasks. It works with Netscape 4.x.

    http://developer.netscape.com/software/jsdebug.html

- Netscape's Mozilla team is working on a debugger for Netscape 5 and 6. Find out more here:

    http://www.mozilla.org/projects/venkman/

- Microsoft Script Debugger works with JavaScript and VBScript in Internet Explorer.

    http://msdn.microsoft.com/library/en-us/sdbug/Html/sdbug_1.asp

- WebReview.com has an excellent tutorial that covers the basics of JavaScript debugging.

    http://www.webreview.com/2000/10_06/webauthors/10_06_00_1.shtml

CGI Resources

Sometimes JavaScript and DHTML can't do everything you need. The following Web sites have information about CGI and server-side programming languages:

- The CGI Resource Index has links to thousands of CGI scripts. You can copy some of these to your own server, while others are remotely hosted services.

    http://cgi.resourceindex.com/

- Perl is the original language for CGI programming, and still among the most popular. Find out more about this language at Perl.com.

    http://www.perl.com/

- PHP is a newer open-source language that works on Web servers, and its simplicity makes it a perfect choice for those experienced with JavaScript. Full documentation is available at the official PHP site.

  `http://www.php.net/`

- The PHP Resource Index has links to many freely available PHP programs.

  `http://php.resourceindex.com/`

In addition, you might find the following books useful:

- *Sams Teach Yourself CGI in 24 Hours*, by Rafe Colburn, ISBN 0-672-31880-6
- *Sams Teach Yourself PHP4 in 24 Hours*, by Matt Zandstra, ISBN 0-672-31804-0
- *Sams Teach Yourself Perl in 24 Hours*, by Clinton Pierce, ISBN 0-672-31773-7

A

Appendix B

Glossary

Anchor   In HTML, a named location within a document, specified using the <a> tag. Anchors can also act as links.

Argument   A parameter that is passed to a function when it is called. Arguments are specified within parentheses in the function call.

Array   A set of variables that can be referred to with the same name and a number, called an index. Arrays can also use alphanumeric keys.

Attribute   A property value that can be defined within an HTML tag. Attributes specify style, alignment, and other aspects of the element defined by the tag.

Boolean   A type of variable that can store only two values: true and false.

Browser sensing   A scripting technique that detects the specific browser in use by clients to provide compatibility for multiple browsers.

Cascading Style Sheets (CSS)   The W3C's standard for applying styles to HTML documents. CSS can control fonts, colors, margins, borders, and positioning.

Child node   In the DOM, a node that is contained by the current node.

Class   An attribute that can be assigned to one or more HTML tags within a document. CSS rules can be made to affect all elements within a class.

Concatenate   The act of combining two strings into a single, longer string.

Conditional   A JavaScript statement that performs an action if a particular condition is true, usually using the `if` statement.

Deprecated   A term the W3C applies to HTML tags or other items that are no longer recommended for use, and might not be supported in the future. For example, the `<font>` tag is deprecated in HTML 4.0, since style sheets can provide the same capability.

Document Object Model (DOM)   The set of objects that JavaScript can use to refer to the browser window and portions of the HTML document. The W3C (World-wide Web Consortium) DOM is a standardized version supported by the latest browsers, and allows access to every object within a Web page.

Dynamic HTML (DHTML)   The combination of HTML, JavaScript, CSS, and the DOM, which allows dynamic Web pages to be created. DHTML is not a W3C standard or a version of HTML.

Dynamic fonts   Fonts that are embedded with a Web page and downloaded for use. Dynamic fonts are part of the W3C's CSS Level 2 recommendation.

Element   A single member of an array, referred to with an index. In the DOM, an element is a single node defined by an HTML tag.

External style sheet   A style sheet that is stored in an external file, typically with the `.css` extension, and referenced in a `<link>` tag within an HTML document.

Event   A condition, often the result of a user's action, that can be acted upon by a script.

Event handler   A JavaScript statement or function that will be executed when an event occurs.

Event capturing   A browser feature that allows you to enable events that are not detected by default, such as mouse movement.

Expression   A combination of variables, constants, and operators that can be evaluated to a single value.

Feature sensing   A scripting technique that detects whether a feature, such as a DOM method, is supported before using it to avoid browser incompatibilities.

Function   A group of JavaScript statements that can be referred to using a function name and arguments.

Global variable   A variable that is available to all JavaScript code in a Web page. It is declared (first used) outside any function.

Hypertext Markup Language (HTML)   The language used to create Web pages. HTML is standardized by the W3C.

Italic   A version of a font that has been designed with slanted characters.

Inline style   One or more styles defined using the `style` attribute of an HTML tag.

JavaScript   A scripting language for Web documents, loosely based on Java's syntax, developed by Netscape. JavaScript is now supported by the most popular browsers.

Kerning   In typography, the spacing between adjacent characters in a font.

Layer   An area of a Web page that can be positioned and can overlap other sections in defined ways. Layers are also known as positionable elements.

Leading   In typography, the distance between corresponding points in adjacent lines of text.

Local variable   A variable that is available to only one function. It is declared (first used) within the function.

Loop   A set of JavaScript statements that are executed a number of times, or until a certain condition is met.

Method   A specialized type of function that can be stored in an object, and acts on the object's properties.

Monospace   A type of font in which all characters have the same width. This contrasts with proportional fonts, in which letters have varying width.

Node   In the DOM, an individual container or element within a Web document. Each HTML tag defines a node.

Object   A type of variable that can store multiple values, called properties, and functions, called methods.

Oblique   A slanted version of a font that has been created by computer processing of the original font, rather than designing an italic font.

Operator   A character used to manipulate variables or constants used in an expression.

Parameter   A variable sent to a function when it is called, also known as an argument.

Parent node   In the DOM, the node that contains the current node.

Positionable element   See *layer*.

B

Property   A variable that is stored as part of an object. Each object can have any number of properties. DOM objects and CSS styles have a wide variety of properties you can manipulate.

Pseudo-class   In CSS, a special selector that can set the appearance of certain elements in certain states. Pseudo-classes are available for links in visited, unvisited, active, or hovering states.

Rule   In CSS, an individual element of a style block that specifies the style for an HTML tag, class, or identifier.

Scope   The part of a JavaScript program that a variable was declared in and is available to.

Selection list   An HTML form element that usually displays as a drop-down list of choices. Selection lists are defined with the <select> tag.

Selector   In a CSS rule, the first portion of the rule that specifies the HTML tag, class, or identifier that the rule will affect.

Serif   In typography, a perpendicular stroke at the end of lines within a character. Fonts are generally categorized into serif and sans-serif (without serifs) types.

Sibling node   In the DOM, a node that has the same parent node as the current node.

Statement   A single line of a script or program.

String   A group of text characters that can be stored in a variable.

Tag   In HTML, an individual element within a Web document. HTML tags are contained within angle brackets, as in <body> and <p>.

Text node   In the DOM, a node that stores a text value rather than an HTML element. Nodes that contain text, such as paragraphs, have a text node as a child node.

Variable   A container, referred to with a name, that can store a number, a string, or an object.

World Wide Web Consortium (W3C)   An international organization that develops and maintains the standards for HTML, CSS, and other key Web technologies.

XHTML (Extensible Hypertext Markup Language)   A new version of HTML developed by the W3C. XHTML is similar to HTML, but conforms to the XML specification.

XML (Extensible Markup Language)   A generic language developed by the W3C (World-wide Web Consortium) that allows the creation of standardized HTML-like languages, using a DTD (Document Type Definition) to specify tags and attributes.

APPENDIX C

Browser Compatibility Chart

The charts in this appendix list the W3C DOM properties and methods, and indicate whether they are supported by Netscape (6.0 or later) or Internet Explorer (5.0 or later).

This information should only be used as a rough guideline, because browsers are continually changing.

TABLE C.1 Document Properties and Methods

Name	Internet Explorer support	Netscape support
createAttribute	Windows version 6 only	Yes
createElement	Yes	Yes
createTextNode	Yes	Yes
getElementById	Yes	Yes
getElementsByTagName	Yes	Yes
documentElement	Yes	Yes
implementation	Macintosh only	Yes

TABLE C.2 Object Properties and Methods

Name	Internet Explorer support	Netscape support
appendChild	Yes	Yes
appendData	Macintosh only	Yes
applyElement	Yes	No
attributes	Yes	No
childNodes	Yes	Yes
ClassName	Yes	Yes
clearAttributes	Yes	No
CloneNode	Yes	Yes
Contains	Yes	No
Data	Yes	Yes
deleteData	Macintosh only	Yes
firstChild	Yes	Yes
getAttribute	Yes	Yes
getAttributeNode	Macintosh only	Yes
getElementsByTagName	Yes	Yes
hasAttributes	No	Yes
hasChildNodes	Yes	Yes

TABLE C.2 continued

Name	Internet Explorer support	Netscape support
Id	Yes	Yes
InnerHTML	Yes	Yes
insertBefore	Yes	Yes
LastChild	Yes	Yes
Name	Yes	Yes
nextSibling	Yes	Yes
NodeName	Yes	Yes
NodeType	Yes	Yes
NodeValue	Yes	Yes
parentNode	Yes	Yes
previousSibling	Yes	Yes
removeChild	Yes	Yes
replaceChild	Yes	Yes
replaceNode	Windows only	Yes
setAttribute	Yes	Yes
Specified	Yes	Yes
TagName	Yes	Yes

C

APPENDIX D

DOM Quick Reference

This appendix presents a quick overview of the DOM objects available, including the basic Level 0 DOM and the W3C Level 1 DOM.

DOM Level 0

The Level 0 DOM includes objects that represent the browser window, the current document, and its contents. The following is a basic summary of Level 0 DOM objects.

For detailed information about the properties and methods of each of the objects in the Level 0 DOM, consult Netscape's JavaScript Reference: `http://developer.netscape.com/docs/manuals/js/client/jsref/index.htm`

Window

The window object represents the current browser window. If multiple windows are open or frames are used, there might be more than one window object. These are given aliases to distinguish them:

- self represents the current window, as does window. This is the window containing the current JavaScript document.
- top is the window currently on top (active) on the screen.
- parent is the window that contains the current frame.
- The frames array contains the window object for each frame in a framed document.

The window object has three child objects:

- location stores the location (URL) of the document displayed in the window.
- document stores information about the current Web page.
- The history object contains a list of sites visited before or after the current site in the window.

Location

The location object contains information about the current URL being displayed by the window. It has a set of properties to hold the different components of the URL:

- location.hash is the name of an anchor within the document, if specified.
- location.host is a combination of the host name and port.
- location.hostname specifies the host name.
- location.href is the entire URL.
- location.pathname is the directory to find the document on the host, and the name of the file.
- location.port specifies the communication port.
- location.protocol is the protocol (or *method*) of the URL.

- `location.query` specifies a query string.
- `location.target` specifies the TARGET attribute of the link that was used to reach the current location.

History

The `history` object holds information about the URLs that have been visited before and after the current one in the window, and includes methods to go to previous or next locations:

- `history.back` goes back to the previous location.
- `history.forward` goes forward to the next location.
- `history.go` goes to a specified offset in the history list.

Document

The `document` object represents the current document in the window. It includes the following child objects:

- `document.forms` is a collection with an element for each form in the document.
- `document.links` is a collection containing elements for each of the links in the document.
- `document.anchors` is a collection with elements for each of the anchors in the document.
- `document.images` contains an element for each of the images in the current document.
- `document.applets` is a collection with references to each embedded Java applet in the document.

Navigator

The `navigator` object includes information about the current browser version:

- `appCodeName` is the browser's code name, usually "Mozilla."
- `appName` is the browser's full name.
- `appVersion` is the version number of the browser. (Example: "4.0(Win95;I)".)
- `userAgent` is the user-agent header, which is sent to the host when requesting a Web page. It includes the entire version information, such as "Mozilla/4.5(Win95;I)."

D

- `plugIns` is a collection which contains information about each currently-available plug-in. (Netscape only)
- `mimeTypes` is a collection containing an element for each of the available MIME types. (Netscape only)

DOM Level 1

The Level 1 DOM is the first cross-browser DOM standardized by the W3C. Its objects are stored under the `document` object of the Level 0 DOM.

Basic Node Properties

Each object has certain common properties:

- `nodeName` is the name of the node (not the ID). The name is the tag name for HTML tag nodes, `#document` for the document node, and `#text` for text nodes.
- `nodeType` is a number describing the node's type: `1` for HTML tags, `3` for text nodes, and `9` for the document.
- `nodeValue` is the text contained within a text node.
- `innerHTML` is the HTML contents of a container node. You used this property in the previous hour to change the text within a node.
- `id` is the value of the `ID` attribute for the node.
- `classname` is the value of the `class` attribute for the node.

Relationship Properties

The following properties describe an object's relationship with others in the hierarchy:

- `firstChild` is the first child node for the current node.
- `lastChild` is the last child object for the current node.
- `childNodes` is an array of all of the child nodes under a node.
- `previousSibling` is the sibling before the current node
- `nextSibling` is the sibling after the current node.
- `parentNode` is the object that contains the current node.

Offset Properties

While not part of the W3C DOM, both Netscape and Internet Explorer support the following properties that provide information about a node's position:

- `offsetLeft` is the distance from the left-hand side of the browser window or containing object to the left edge of the node object.
- `offsetTop` is the distance from the top of the browser window or containing object to the top of the node object.
- `offsetHeight` is the height of the node object.
- `offsetWidth` is the width of the node object.

Style Properties

The `style` child object under each DOM object includes its style sheet properties. These are based on attributes of a `style` attribute, `<style>` tag, or external style sheet. See Part III, "Working with Style Sheets," for details on these properties.

Node Methods

The following methods are available for all DOM nodes:

- `appendChild(node)` adds a new child node to the node after all of its existing children.
- `insertBefore(node,oldnode)` inserts a new node before the specified existing child node.
- `replaceChild(node,oldnode)` replaces the specified old child node with a new node.
- `removeChild(node)` removes an existing child node.
- `hasChildNodes()` returns a Boolean value of `true` if the node has one or more children, or `false` if it has none.
- `cloneNode()` returns a copy of the current node.
- `getAttribute(attribute_name)` gets the value of the attribute you specify and stores it in a variable.
- `setAttribute(attribute_name, value)` sets the value of an attribute.
- `removeAttribute(attribute_name)` removes the attribute you specify.
- `hasAttributes()` simply returns `true` if the node has attributes, and `false` if it has none.

D

Document Object Methods and Properties

The following are methods and properties of the document object:

- document.getElementById(*ID*) returns the element with the specified ID attribute.
- document.getElementsByTagName(*tag*) returns an array of the elements with the specified tag name. You can use the asterisk (*) as a wildcard to return an array containing all of the nodes in the document.
- document.createElement(*tag*) creates a new element with the specified tag name.
- document.createTextNode(*text*) creates a new text node containing the specified text.
- document.documentElement is an object that represents the document itself, and can be used to find information about the document.

INDEX

SYMBOLS

< > (angle brackets), 91
* (asterisk wildcard), 66
@font-face selector, 264
{ } (braces), 38
[ ] (brackets), 149
, (comma), 41
" " (double quotation marks), 36, 102, 146, 159
/ (forward slash), 18
// (double forward slashes), 35
> (greater-than) symbol, 35, 227
(hash symbol), 204
- (hyphen), 77
< (less than symbol), 227
- (minus sign) icon, 188-193
( ) (parentheses), 39-41
% (percent sign) units, 120
. (period), 119

+ (plus sign) icon, 188-193, 218, 221-222
' ' (single quotation marks), 102
_ (underscore), 222
= (equal sign) (assignment operator), 39
= assignment operator, 273
== (double-equal sign) (equality operator), 39
== equality operator, 273
<!-- and --> comment tag, 118, 293
>-- tag, 35
<!-- tag, 35
<<< icon (MoveLeft function), 223
>>> icon (MoveRight function), 223-224
<<< or >>> icon (ShowHide function), 222-223

A

<a> tag, 22, 135, 146, 189-190, 321-322
a1 = new Image(), 308
absolute value (position property), 75
action attribute, 252
adding
  elements to forms, 249
  HTML documents, 96-98
  items to dynamic order forms, 253
  JavaScript files, 296
  scrolling messages, 296
AddItems function, 249-253
AddLetter function, 319, 322-323
AddNode function, 97
addresses (ship-to), 253